NATIONAL ACCLAIM FOR STEPHEN AMBROSE'S EPIC ACCOUNT OF THE MEN OF EASY COMPANY

BAND OF BROTHERS

"Although no book can wholly convey the experience of combat, *BAND OF BROTHERS* gives a taste of it, not blinking either at the most dreadful moments or at the extraordinary abilities some soldiers reveal under pressure and the collapse of others. Addicts of military history will relish its finely detailed account of the World War II service of E Company."

—*San Francisco Chronicle*

"This is more than military history the way it should be written: it is military history the way it can be written. *BAND OF BROTHERS* is an absorbing, compelling, and even stunning book. . . . This may be as close as any reader will wish to come to war without actually taking part in it."

—*Richmond Times-Dispatch*

"Within the ranks of the military, a rifle company is unique. Its prolonged exposure to the horrors of face-to-face combat forges bonds that are virtually unbreakable. As Mr. Ambrose makes clear in the 18 chapters chronicling Easy Company's terrible journey, the result of their shared experience creates 'a closeness unknown to all outsiders. Their trust in, and knowledge of, each other is total.' "

—*The New York Times Book Review*

BY STEPHEN E. AMBROSE

The Wild Blue

Nothing Like It in the World:
The Men Who Built the Transcontinental Railroad, 1863–1869

The Victors: Brothers, Fathers, Heroes, Sons, Pals

Americans at War

Citizen Soldiers: The U.S. Army from the Normandy Beaches to
the Bulge to the Surrender of Germany, June 7, 1944–May 7, 1945

Undaunted Courage: Meriwether Lewis, Thomas Jefferson,
and the Opening of the American West

D-Day, June 6, 1944: The Climactic Battle of World War II

Band of Brothers: E Company, 506th Regiment, 101st Airborne
from Normandy to Hitler's Eagle's Nest

Nixon: Ruin and Recovery, 1973–1990

Eisenhower: Soldier and President

Nixon: The Triumph of a Politician, 1962–1972

Nixon: The Education of a Politician, 1913–1962

Pegasus Bridge: June 6, 1944

Eisenhower: The President

Eisenhower: Soldier, General of the Army, President-Elect,
1890–1952

The Supreme Commander: The War Years of
General Dwight D. Eisenhower

Duty, Honor, Country: A History of West Point

Eisenhower and Berlin, 1945

Crazy Horse and Custer: The Parallel Lives
of Two American Warriors

Rise to Globalism: American Foreign Policy, 1938–1992

Ike's Spies: Eisenhower and the Espionage Establishment

Halleck: Lincoln's Chief of Staff

Upton and the Army

Stephen E. Ambrose

BAND OF BROTHERS

*E Company, 506th Regiment,
101st Airborne from Normandy
to Hitler's Eagle's Nest*

POCKET STAR BOOKS

NEW YORK   LONDON   TORONTO   SYDNEY   SINGAPORE

A Pocket Star Book published by
POCKET BOOKS, a division of Simon & Schuster, Inc.
1230 Avenue of the Americas, New York, NY 10020

ISBN: 0-7434-6411-7

First Pocket Books printing September 2002

10 9 8 7 6 5 4 3 2 1

POCKET STAR BOOKS and colophon are registered trademarks
of Simon & Schuster, Inc.

For information regarding special discounts for bulk
purchases, please contact Simon & Schuster Special Sales at
1-800-456-6798 or business@simonandschuster.com

Cover photo by Walter Gordon

Printed in the U.S.A.

To all those members of the Parachute Infantry,
United States Army, 1941–1945,
who wear the Purple Heart not as a decoration
but as a badge of office.

"From this day to the ending of the World,
. . . we in it shall be remembered
. . . we band of brothers."

HENRY V
William Shakespeare

CONTENTS

FOREWORD

TOM HANKS AND STEVEN SPIELBERG came to New Orleans in June 2000 to spend a few days participating in the Grand Opening of the National D-Day Museum. They got a lot of attention from visitors, members of the board, reporters, TV cameras—the works. There were thousands of World War II veterans at the various events—most of all in a two-mile-long parade where they rode in army trucks, waving to the hundreds of thousands of people lining the streets, many holding signs that said, simply, "Thank you," others holding up the front page of the New Orleans *Times-Picayune* from V-E Day or V-J Day. It was the biggest military parade—bands, marching units, reenactors, fly-overs, and, of course, veterans—since World War II. When a group of Rangers marched by, Tom leaped out of the reviewing stand to shake their hands and ask for autographs. He asked if he could have his picture taken with them. Steven also went up to veterans to ask for autographs and photographs. The stars had become the fans.

Tom and Steven began work on a series for Home Box Office based on this book. What impressed me was how careful they were to be accurate. They sent me scripts for each of the episodes. They paid attention to my comments and suggestions—although I

must say that in no way am I a scriptwriter. I know
how to write books, not how to make a series or a
movie. They also sent scripts to the leading personali-
ties in the story. And they interviewed the men of
Easy Company to get new information from them.
Even more, the actors began calling the men they were
portraying. How did you feel, they would ask, after
this or that happened? Did you smile? Were you
elated? Were you depressed? And more. Tom even persuaded Dick Winters to fly to England to be present at
the filming.

I've already told, in the Acknowledgments of this
book, how I came to write about Easy Company. Tom
and Steven read the book and decided to make a series
out of it, but things weren't quite that simple. First of
all, there are hundreds, indeed thousands, of books on
World War II. What they liked about *Band of Brothers*
was its scope—almost the whole of the campaign in
Northwest Europe—but even more, the concentration
on one outstanding light infantry company and the per-
sonalities and actions of the men. It is that personaliza-
tion that they, I, and many readers are drawn to. The
war was so big, with so many characters and outstanding—and not so outstanding—generals and statesmen
that people grow weary of reading about Dwight
Eisenhower and the Supreme Command, or Franklin
Roosevelt and his high command, or the strategy of the
war. What they seek is the experience of the individual
solider or sailor or airman. They want to know, What
did he do? How could he have done that? They read for
entertainment, of course, and enlightenment, but also,
and perhaps most of all, for inspiration.

Tom and Steven, like many others, are fascinated
by World War II. They are aware of how much all of us

owe the men who fought it. They have put in a good part of their careers honoring the veterans. That is what stands out.

I share their feelings and am delighted to participate with them in bringing the action to life through the individual stories.

1

"We Wanted Those Wings"

———

CAMP TOCCOA

July–December 1942

THE MEN OF EASY COMPANY, 506th Parachute Infantry Regiment, 101st Airborne Division, U.S. Army, came from different backgrounds, different parts of the country. They were farmers and coal miners, mountain men and sons of the Deep South. Some were desperately poor, others from the middle class. One came from Harvard, one from Yale, a couple from UCLA. Only one was from the Old Army, only a few came from the National Guard or Reserves. They were citizen soldiers.

They came together in the summer of 1942, by which time the Europeans had been at war for three years. By the late spring of 1944, they had become an elite company of airborne light infantry. Early on the morning of D-Day, in its first combat action, Easy captured and put out of action a German battery of four 105 mm cannon that were looking down on Utah

Beach. The company led the way into Carentan, fought in Holland, held the perimeter at Bastogne, led the counteroffensive in the Battle of the Bulge, fought in the Rhineland campaign, and took Hitler's Eagle's Nest at Berchtesgaden. It had taken almost 150 percent casualties. At the peak of its effectiveness, in Holland in October 1944 and in the Ardennes in January 1945, it was as good a rifle company as there was in the world.

The job completed, the company disbanded, the men went home.

• • •

Each of the 140 men and seven officers who formed the original company followed a different route to its birthplace, Camp Toccoa, Georgia, but they had some things in common. They were young, born since the Great War. They were white, because the U.S. Army in World War II was segregated. With three exceptions, they were unmarried. Most had been hunters and athletes in high school.

They were special in their values. They put a premium on physical well-being, hierarchical authority, and being part of an elite unit. They were idealists, eager to merge themselves into a group fighting for a cause, actively seeking an outfit with which they could identify, join, be a part of, relate to as a family.

They volunteered for the paratroopers, they said, for the thrill, the honor, and the $50 (for enlisted men) or $100 (for officers) monthly bonus paratroopers received. But they really volunteered to jump out of airplanes for two profound, personal reasons. First, in Robert Rader's words, "The desire to be better than the other guy took hold." Each man in his own way had gone through what Richard Winters experienced: a realization that doing his best was a better way of getting through the Army than hanging around with the sad excuses for soldiers they met in the recruiting depots or basic training. They wanted to make their Army time positive, a learning and maturing and challenging experience.

Second, they knew they were going into combat, and they did not want to go in with poorly trained, poorly conditioned, poorly motivated draftees on either side of them. As to choosing between being a paratrooper spearheading the offensive and an ordinary infantryman who could not trust the guy next to him, they decided the greater risk was with the infantry. When the shooting started, they wanted to look up to the guy beside them, not down.

They had been kicked around by the Depression, had the scars to show for it. They had grown up, many of them, without enough to eat, with holes in the soles of their shoes, with ragged sweaters and no car and often not a radio. Their educations had been cut short, either by the Depression or by the war.

"Yet, with this background, I had and still have a great love for my country," Harry Welsh declared forty-eight years later. Whatever their legitimate complaints about how life had treated them, they had not soured on it or on their country.

They came out of the Depression with many other positive features. They were self-reliant, accustomed to hard work and to taking orders. Through sports or hunting or both, they had gained a sense of self-worth and self-confidence.

They knew they were going into great danger. They knew they would be doing more than their part. They resented having to sacrifice years of their youth to a war they never made. They wanted to throw baseballs, not grenades, shoot a .22 rifle, not an M-1. But having been caught up in the war, they decided to be as positive as possible in their Army careers.

Not that they knew much about airborne, except that it was new and all-volunteer. They had been told that the physical training was tougher than anything they had ever seen, or that any other unit in the Army would undergo, but these young lions were eager for that. They expected that, when they were finished with their training, they would be bigger, stronger, tougher than when they started, and they would have gone through the training with the guys who would be fighting beside them.

"The Depression was over," Carwood Lipton recalled of that summer of 1942, "and I was beginning a new life that would change me profoundly." It would all of them.

• • •

First Lt. Herbert Sobel of Chicago was the initial member of E Company, and its C.O. His executive officer (X.O.) was 2d Lt. Clarence Hester, from northern California. Sobel was Jewish, urban, with a commission from the National Guard. Hester had started as a private, then earned his commission from Officer Candidate's School (OCS). Most of the platoon and assistant platoon leaders were newly commissioned graduates of OCS, including 2d Lts. Dick Winters from Pennsylvania, Walter Moore from California's racetracks, and Lewis Nixon from New York City and Yale. S. L. Matheson was an ROTC graduate from UCLA. At twenty-eight years of age, Sobel was the old man in the group; the others were twenty-four or younger.

The company, along with Dog, Fox, and Battalion HQ Companies, made up the 2d Battalion of the 506th PIR. The battalion commander was Maj. Robert Strayer, a thirty-year-old reserve officer. The regimental commander was Col. Robert Sink, a 1927 West Point graduate. The 506th was an experimental outfit, the first parachute infantry regiment in which the men would take their basic training and their jump training together, as a unit. It would be a year before it was attached to the 101st Airborne, the Screaming Eagles. The officers were as new to this paratrooping business as the men; they were teachers who sometimes were not much more than one day ahead of the class.

The original N.C.O.s were Old Army. "We looked up to them," Pvt. Walter Gordon of Mississippi remembered, "as almost like gods because they had their wings, they were qualified jumpers. But, hell, if they knew how to do an about-face, they were ahead of us, we were raw recruits. Later, looking back, we regarded them with scorn. They couldn't measure up to our own people who moved up to corporals and sergeants."

The first privates in Easy were Frank Perconte, Herman Hansen, Wayne Sisk, and Carwood Lipton. Within a few days of its formation, Easy had a full complement of 132 men and eight officers. It was divided into three platoons and a headquarters section. There were three twelve-man rifle squads plus a six-man mortar team squad to a platoon. A light infantry outfit, Easy had one machine-gun to each of the rifle squads, and a 60 mm mortar in each mortar team.

Few of the original members of Easy made it through Toccoa. "Officers would come and go,"

Winters remarked. "You would take one look at them and know they wouldn't make it. Some of those guys were just a bowl of butter. They were so awkward they didn't know how to fall." This was typical of the men trying for the 506th PIR; it took 500 officer volunteers to produce the 148 who made it through Toccoa, and 5,300 enlisted volunteers to get 1,800 graduates.

• • •

As the statistics show, Toccoa was a challenge. Colonel Sink's task was to put the men through basic training, harden them, teach them the rudiments of infantry tactics, prepare them for jump school, and build a regiment that he would lead into combat. "We were sorting men," Lieutenant Hester recalled, "sorting the fat to the thin and sorting out the no guts."

Pvt. Ed Tipper said of his first day in Easy, "I looked up at nearby Mount Currahee and told someone, 'I'll bet that when we finish the training program here, the last thing they'll make us do will be to climb to the top of that mountain.' [Currahee was more a hill than a mountain, but it rose 1,000 feet above the parade ground and dominated the landscape.] A few minutes later, someone blew a whistle. We fell in, were ordered to change to boots and athletic trunks, did so, fell in again—and then ran most of the three miles to the top and back down again." They lost some men that first day. Within a week, they were running—or at least double-timing—all the way up and back.

At the end of the second week, Tipper went on, "We were told, 'Relax. No runs today.' We were taken to the mess hall for a tremendous meal of spaghetti at lunchtime. When we came out of the mess hall, a whistle blew, and we were told, 'The orders are changed. We run.' We went to the top of Currahee and back with a couple of ambulances following, and men vomiting spaghetti everywhere along the way. Those who dropped out and accepted the medics' invitation to ride back in the ambulances found themselves shipped out that same day."

The men were told that Currahee was an Indian word that meant "We stand alone," which was the way these paratroopers expected to fight. It became the battle cry of the 506th.

The officers and men ran up and down Currahee three or four times a week. They got so they could do the six-plus-mile round-trip in fifty minutes. In addition, they went through a grueling obstacle course daily, and did push-ups and pull-ups, deep-knee bends and other calisthenics.

When the men were not exercising, they were learning the basics of soldiering. They began with close order drill, then started making night marches with full field equipment. The first night march was eleven miles; on each march that followed a mile or two was added on. These marches were made without a break, without a cigarette, without water. "We were miserable, exhausted, and thought that if we did not get a drink of water we were certain to collapse," Pvt. Burton "Pat" Christenson recalled. At the end of a march Sobel would check each man's canteen to see that it was still full.

Those who made it got through because of an intense private determination and because of their desire for public recognition that they were special. Like all elite units around the world, the Airborne had its unique badges and symbols. Once through jump school, they would receive silver wings to wear on the left pocket of their jackets, a patch for their left shoulder, a patch for their hats, and the right to wear paratrooper boots and "blouse" their trousers (tuck the trousers into their boots). Gordon said that "it doesn't make much sense now [1990], but at the time we were all ready to trade our lives in order to wear these accoutrements of the Airborne."

The only rest came when they got lectures, on weapons, map and compass reading, infantry tactics, codes, signaling, field telephones, radio equipment, switchboard and wire stringing, demolitions. For unarmed combat and bayonet drills, it was back to using those trembling muscles.

When they were issued their rifles, they were told to treat the weapon as they would treat a wife, gently. It was theirs to have and to hold, to sleep with in the field, to know intimately. They got to where they could take it apart and put it back together blindfolded.

To prepare the men for jump school, Toccoa had a mock-up tower some 35 feet high. A man was strapped into a parachute harness that was connected to 15-foot risers, which in turn were attached to a pulley that rode a cable. Jumping from the tower in the harness, sliding down the cable to the landing, gave the feeling of a real parachute jump and landing.

All these activities were accompanied by shouting in unison, chanting, singing together, or bitching. The language was foul. These nineteen- and twenty-year-old enlisted men, free from the restraints of home and culture, thrown together into an all-male society, coming from all over America, used words as one form of bonding. The one most commonly used, by far, was the *f*-word. It substituted for adjectives, nouns, and verbs. It was used, for example, to describe the cooks: "those f——ers," or "f——ing cooks"; what they did: "f——ed it up again"; and what they produced. David Kenyon Webster, a Harvard English major, confessed that he found it difficult to adjust to the "vile, monotonous, and unimaginative language." The language made these boys turning into men feel tough and, more important, insiders, members of a group. Even Webster got used to it, although never to like it.

The men were learning to do more than swear, more than how to fire a rifle, more than that the limits of their physical endurance were much greater than they had ever imagined. They were learning instant, unquestioning obedience. Minor infractions were punished on the spot, usually by requiring the man to do twenty push-ups. More serious infractions cost a man his weekend pass, or several hours marching in full field pack on the parade ground. The Army had a saying, Gordon related: "We can't make you do anything, but we can make you wish you had." Brought together by their misery, held together by their cadence counts, singing, and common experiences, they were becoming a family.

The company learned to act as a unit. Within days of the formation of Easy, the 140 men could make a one-quarter or one-half turn, or an about-face, as if one. Or set off at double-time, or on a full run. Or drop to the ground to do push-ups. Or shout "Yes, Sir!" or "No, Sir!" in unison.

All this was part of the initiation rites common to all armies. So was learning to drink. Beer, almost exclusively, at the post PX, there being no nearby towns. Lots of beer. They sang soldiers' songs. Toward the end of the evening, invariably someone would insult someone else with a slurring reference to his mother, his sweetheart, his home town, or his region. Then they would fight, as soldier boys do, inflicting bloody noses and blackened eyes, before staggering back to their barracks, yelling war chants, supporting each other, becoming comrades.

The result of these shared experiences was a closeness unknown to all outsiders. Comrades are closer than friends, closer than brothers. Their relationship is different from that of lovers. Their trust in, and knowledge of, each other is total. They got to know each other's life stories, what they did before they came into the Army, where and why they volunteered, what they liked to eat and drink, what their capabilities were. On a night march they would hear a cough and know who it was; on a night maneuver they would see someone sneaking through the woods and know who it was from his silhouette.

Their identification worked downward, from the Army to the Airborne to the 506th to 2d Battalion to Easy Company to platoon to squad. Pvt. Kurt Gabel of the 513th PIR described his experience in words that any member of E Company could have used: "The three of us, Jake, Joe, and I, became . . . an entity. There were many entities in our close-knit organizations. Groups of threes and fours, usually from the same squads or sections, core elements within the families that were the small units, were readily recognized as entities. . . . This sharing . . . evolved never to be relinquished, never to be repeated. Often three such entities would make up a squad, with incredible results in combat. They would literally insist on going hungry for one another, freezing for one another, dying for one another. And the squad would try to protect them or bail them out without the slightest regard to consequences, cussing them all the way for making it necessary. Such a rifle squad, machine gun section, scout-observer section, pathfinder section was a mystical concoction."[1]

Philosopher J. Glenn Gray, in his classic work *The Warriors*, got it exactly right: "Organization for a common and concrete goal in peacetime organizations does not evoke anything like the degree of comradeship commonly known in war. . . . At its height, this sense of comradeship is an ecstasy. . . . Men are true comrades only when each is ready to give up his life for the other, without reflection and without thought of personal loss."[2]

The comradeship formed in training and reinforced in combat lasted a lifetime. Forty-nine years after Toccoa, Pvt. Don Malarkey of Oregon wrote of the summer of 1942, "So this was the beginning of the most momentous experience of my life, as a member of E Company. There is not a day that has passed since that I do not thank Adolf Hitler for allowing me to be associated with the most talented and inspiring group of men that I have ever known." Every member of Easy interviewed by this author for this book said something similar.

•   •   •

---

[1] Kurt Gabel, *The Making of a Paratrooper: Airborne Training and Combat in World War II* (Lawrence, Kan.: University of Kansas, 1990), 142.

[2] J. Glenn Gray, *The Warriors: Reflections on Men in Battle* (New York: Harper & Row, 1959), 43, 45, 46.

The N.C.O.s came up from the ranks, gradually replacing the Old Army cadre types who quit as the training grew more intense. Within a year, all thirteen sergeants in Easy were from the original group of privates, including 1st Sgt. William Evans, S. Sgts. James Diel, Salty Harris, and Myron Ranney, and Sgts. Leo Boyle, Bill Guarnere, Carwood Lipton, John Martin, Robert Rader, and Amos Taylor. "These were men," as one private said, "who were leaders that we respected and would follow anywhere."

The officers were also special and, except for Company Commander Sobel, universally respected. "We couldn't believe that people like Winters, Matheson, Nixon, and the others existed," Private Rader remembered. "These were first-class people, and to think these men would care and share their time and efforts with us seemed a miracle. They taught us to trust." Winters, Rader went on, "turned our lives around. He was openly friendly, genuinely interested in us and our physical training. He was almost shy—he wouldn't say 'shit' if he stepped in it." Gordon said that if a man called out, "Hey, Lieutenant, you got a date tonight?" Winters would turn beet red.

Matheson, who was soon moved up to battalion staff as adjutant and who eventually became a Regular Army major general, was the most military minded of the young officers. Hester was "fatherly," Nixon flamboyant. Winters was none of these, nor was he humorous or obstinate. "Nor at any time did Dick Winters pretend to be God, nor at any time did he act other than a man!", according to Rader. He was an officer who got the men to perform because he expected nothing but the best, and "you liked him so much you just hated to let him down." He was, and is, all but worshiped by the men of E Company.

• • •

Second Lieutenant Winters had one major, continuing problem, 1st Lieutenant (soon promoted to captain) Sobel.

The C.O. was fairly tall, slim in build, with a full head of black hair. His eyes were slits, his nose large and hooked. His face was long and his chin receded. He had been a clothing salesman and knew nothing of the out-of-doors. He was ungainly, uncoordinated, in no way an athlete. Every man in the company was in better physical condition. His mannerisms were "funny," he "talked different." He exuded arrogance.

Sobel was a petty tyrant put into a position in which he had absolute power. If he did not like a man, for whatever reason, he would flunk him out for the least infraction, real or imagined.

There was a cruelty to the man. On Saturday morning inspections, he would go down the line, stop in front of a man who had displeased him in some way, and mark him down for "dirty ears." After denying three or four men their weekend passes on those grounds, he would shift to "dirty stacking swivels" and keep another half-dozen or so in barracks for that reason. When someone was late returning on Sunday night, the next evening, after a full day's training, Sobel would order him to dig a 6 x 6 x 6-foot pit with his entrenching tools. When the pit was finished, Sobel would tell him to "fill it up."

Sobel was determined that his company would be the best in the regiment. His method of insuring this result was to demand more of Easy's men. They drilled longer, ran faster, trained harder.

Running up Currahee, Sobel was at the head of the company, head bobbing, arms flapping, looking back over his shoulder to see if anyone was dropping out. With his big flat feet, he ran like a duck in distress. He would shout, "The Japs are going to get you!" or "Hi-ho Silver!"

"I remember many times finishing a long run," Tipper said. "Everyone at the point of exhaustion and waiting in formation for the command, 'Fall out!' Sobel would be running back and forth in front of his men shouting, 'Stand still, STAND STILL!' He would not dismiss us until he was satisfied that we had the discipline to impersonate statues at his command. Impossible, of course. But we did what he wanted when he wanted. We wanted those wings."

Gordon developed a lifelong hatred of Sobel. "Until I landed in France in the very early hours of D-Day," Gordon said in 1990, "my war was with this man." Along with other enlisted, Gordon swore that Sobel would not survive five minutes in combat, not when his men had live ammunition. If the enemy did not get him, there were a dozen and more men in Easy who swore that they would. Behind his back the men cursed him, "f——ing Jew" being the most common epithet.

Sobel was as hard on his officers as on the enlisted men. Their physical training was the same, but when the men heard the final "fall out" of the day, they were free to go to their bunks, while the officers had to study the field manuals, then take a test on the assignment Sobel had given them. When he held officers' meetings, Winters recalled, "He was very domineering. There was no give-and-take. His tone of voice was high-pitched, rasplike. He shouted instead of speaking in a normal way. It would just irritate you." The officers' nickname for their captain was "The Black Swan."

Sobel had no friends. Officers would avoid him in the officers' club. None went on a pass with him, none sought out his company. No one in Easy knew anything about his previous life and no one cared. He did have his favorites, of whom No. 1 was company 1st Sgt. William Evans. Together, Sobel and Evans played men off against one another, granting a privilege here, denying one there.

Anyone who has ever been in the Army knows the type. Sobel was the classic chickenshit. He generated maximum anxiety over matters of minimum significance. Paul Fussell, in his book *Wartime*, has the best definition: "Chickenshit refers to behavior that makes military life worse than it need be: petty harassment of the weak by the strong; open scrimmage for power and authority and prestige; sadism thinly disguised as necessary discipline; a constant 'paying off of old scores'; and insistence on the letter rather than the spirit of ordinances. Chickenshit is so called—instead of horse- or bull- or elephant shit—because it is small-minded and ignoble and takes the trivial seriously."[3]

* * *

Sobel had the authority over the men. Lieutenant Winters had their respect. The two men were bound to clash. No one ever said so directly, and not everyone in

---

[3]Paul Fussell, *Wartime: Understanding and Behavior in the Second World War* (New York: Oxford University Press, 1989), 80.

Easy recognized what was happening, and Winters did not want it that way, but they were in competition to be the leader.

Sobel's resentment of Winters began during the first week at Toccoa. Winters was leading the company in calisthenics. He was up on a stand, demonstrating, "helping the fellows get through the exercise. These boys, they were sharp. And I had their complete attention." Colonel Sink walked past. He stopped to watch. When Winters finished, Sink walked up to him. "Lieutenant," he asked, "how many times has this company had calisthenics?"

"Three times, sir," Winters replied.

"Thank you very much," Sink said. A few days later, without consulting Sobel, he promoted Winters to 1st lieutenant. For Sobel, Winters was a marked man from that day. The C.O. gave the platoon leader every dirty job that he could find, such as latrine inspection or serving as mess officer.

Paul Fussell wrote, "Chickenshit can be recognized instantly because it never has anything to do with winning the war."[4] Winters disagreed. He believed that at least some of what Sobel was doing—if not the way he was doing it—was necessary. If Easy ran farther and faster than the other companies, if it stayed on the parade ground longer, if its bayonet drills were punctuated by "The Japs are going to get you!" and other exhortations, why, then, it would be a better company than the others.

What Winters objected to, beyond the pettiness and arbitrary methods, was Sobel's lack of judgment. The man had neither common sense nor military experi-

---

[4]*Ibid.*

ence. He could not read a map. On field exercises, he would turn to his X.O. and ask, "Hester, where are we?" Hester would try to locate the position for him without embarrassing him, "but all the men knew what was going on."

Sobel made up his mind without reflection and without consultation, and his snap decisions were usually wrong. One night at Toccoa the company was out in the woods on an exercise. It was supposed to be on the defensive, stay in position and be quiet and let the enemy come into the killing zone. "No problem," as Winters recalled, "just an easy job. Just spread the men out, get them in position, 'everyone be quiet.' We're waiting, waiting, waiting. Suddenly a breeze starts to pick up into the woods, and the leaves start to rustle, and Sobel jumps up. 'Here they come! Here they come!' God Almighty! If we were in combat, the whole damn company would be wiped out. And I thought, 'I can't go into combat with this man! He has no damn sense at all!'"

Winters recognized that Sobel was "a disciplinarian and he was producing a hell of a company. Anytime you saw Easy, by God, the men were sharp. Anything we did, we were out in front." Private Rader said of Sobel, "He stripped away your civilian way of doing things and your dignity, but you became one of the best soldiers in the Army." In Winters's opinion the trouble was Sobel could not see "the unrest and the contempt that was breeding in the troops. You lead by fear or you lead by example. We were being led by fear."

I asked every member of Easy that I interviewed for this book if the extraordinary closeness, the outstanding unit cohesion, the remarkable staying power of the identification with Easy came about because of or in spite of Sobel. Those who did not reply "Both," said it was because of Sobel. Rod Strohl looked me in the eye and said flatly, "Herbert Sobel made E Company." Others said something similar. But they nearly all hated him.

That feeling helped bring the company together. "No doubt about it," Winters said. "It was a feeling everybody shared. Junior officers, noncoms, enlisted men, we all felt exactly the same way." But, he added, "It brought us together. We had to survive Sobel."

They hated him so much that even when he should have earned their respect, he failed. While at Toccoa everyone, enlisted and officer, had to pass a qualifying physical test. By then they were in such good shape that no one was really worried about it. Almost all of them could do thirty-five or forty push-ups, for example, and the requirement was only thirty. But there was great excitement, Tipper said, because "we knew Sobel could barely do twenty push-ups. He always stopped at that point when leading the company in calisthenics. If this test were fair, Sobel would fail and wash out.

"Sobel's test was public and fair. I was part of a not-so-casual audience perhaps fifty feet away. At twenty push-ups he was noticeably bushed, but kept going. At twenty-four or twenty-five his arms were trembling, and he was turning red, but slowly continuing. How he managed to complete the thirty push-ups I don't know, but he did. We were silent, shook our heads, but did not smile. Sobel did not lack determination. We comforted ourselves with the idea that he was still a joke, no matter what."

The paratroopers were volunteers. Any man or officer was free at any time to take a walk. Many did. Sobel did not. He could have walked away from the challenge of being an Airborne officer and walked into a staff job with a supply company, but his determination to make it was as great as that of any member of the company.

• • •

Pushing Easy harder than Dog and Fox was difficult, because 2d Battalion commander Major Strayer was almost as fanatic as Sobel. On Thanksgiving Day, Sink let his regiment feast and relax, but Major Strayer decided it was time for a two-day field exercise for the 2d Battalion. It included long marches, an attack against a defended position, a gas alarm in the middle of the night, and an introduction to K rations (tins containing a sort of stew, crackers, candy, and powdered fruit juice).

Strayer made that Thanksgiving even more memorable by laying on the Hawg Innards Problem. He stretched wires across a field, at about 18 inches off the ground. Machine-gunners fired over the top of the wire. Beneath it, Strayer spread the ground with the intestines of freshly slaughtered hogs—hearts, lungs, guts, livers, the works. The men crawled through the vile mess. Lipton recalled that "the army distinction between 'creep' and 'crawl' is that a baby creeps, and a snake crawls. We crawled." No one ever forgot the experience.

• • •

By the end of November, basic training had been completed. Every man in the company had mastered his own specialty, be it mortars, machine-guns, rifles, communications, field dressings, and the rest. Each man was capable of handling any job in the platoon, at least in a rudimentary fashion. Each private knew the duties of a corporal and sergeant and was prepared to take over if necessary. Each one who made it through Toccoa had been harassed almost to the point of rebellion. "We all thought," Christenson said, "after this, I can take anything they can throw at me."

• • •

A day or so before leaving Toccoa, Colonel Sink read an article in the *Reader's Digest* that said a Japanese Army battalion had set a world record for marching endurance by covering 100 miles down the Malayan Peninsula in seventy-two hours. "My men can do better than that," Sink declared. As Strayer's 2d Battalion had trained the hardest, Sink picked it to prove his point. The 1st Battalion took the train to Fort Benning, the 3d took the train to Atlanta, but the 2d marched.

At 0700, December 1, Dog, Easy, Fox, and Battalion HQ Companies set out, each man wearing all his gear and carrying his weapon. That was bad enough for the riflemen, terrible for those like Malarkey in the mortar squad or Gordon, who carried a machine-gun. The route Strayer chose was 118 miles long, 100 miles of that on back-country, unpaved roads. The weather was miserable, with freezing rain, some snow, and thus slippery, muddy roads. As Webster recalled it, "The first day we sloshed and fell in the red mud and cursed and damned and counted the minutes before the next break." They marched through the day, through twilight, into the dark. The rain and snow stopped. A cold, biting wind came up.

By 2300 hours the battalion had covered 40 miles. Strayer picked the campsite, a bare, windswept hill devoid of trees or bushes or windbreaks of any kind. The temperature dipped into the low twenties. The men were issued bread smeared with butter and jam, as they couldn't get the field stoves started. When they woke at 0600, everything was covered with a thick layer of frost. Boots and socks were frozen solid. The officers and men had to take the shoestrings out of the boots to get them onto their swollen feet. Rifles, mortars, and machine-guns were frozen to the ground. The shelter halves cracked like peanut brittle.

The second day it took some miles for stiff, aching muscles to warm up, but the third day was the worst. With 80 miles covered, there were still 38 to go, the last 20 or so on the highway leading into Atlanta. Marching in mud had been bad, but the cement was much worse on the feet. The battalion camped that night on the grounds of Oglethorpe University, on the outskirts of Atlanta.

Malarkey and his buddy Warren "Skip" Muck put up their pup tent and lay down to rest. Word came that chow was ready. Malarkey could not stand up. He crawled on his hands and knees to the chow line. His platoon leader, Winters, took one look and told him to ride in an ambulance the next morning to the final destination, Five Points in downtown Atlanta.

Malarkey decided he could make it. So did nearly all the others. By this time the march had generated publicity throughout Georgia, on the radio and in the newspapers. Cheering crowds lined the route of march. Strayer had arranged for a band. It met them a mile from Five Points. Malarkey, who had struggled along in terrible pain, had "a strange thing happen to me when that band began to play. I straightened up, the pain disappeared, and I finished the march as if we were passing in review at Toccoa."

They had covered 118 miles in 75 hours. Actual marching time was 33 hours, 30 minutes, or about 4 miles an hour. Of the 586 men and officers in the battalion, only 12 failed to complete the march, although some had to be supported by comrades the last day. Colonel Sink was appropriately proud. "Not a man fell out," he told the press, "but when they fell, they fell face forward." Lieutenant Moore's 3d platoon of Easy was the only one in the battalion in which every man walked every step of the way on his own. As a reward, it led the parade through Atlanta.

2

"Stand Up and Hook Up"

BENNING, MACKALL, BRAGG, SHANKS

December 1942–September 1943

ENNING WAS, if possible, even more miserable than Toccoa, especially its infamous Frying Pan area, where the jump training went on. This was the regimental bivouac area, consisting of scrubby little wooden huts set on barren, sandy soil. But Benning was a welcome relief to the men of E Company in the sense that they were getting realistic training for becoming paratroopers rather than spending most of their waking hours doing physical exercises.

Parachute school was supposed to begin with physical training (A stage), followed by B, C, and D stages, each lasting a week, but the 506th skipped A stage. This happened because the 1st Battalion arrived ahead of the others, went into A stage, and embarrassed the jump school sergeants who were assigned to lead the calisthenics and runs. The Toccoa graduates would laugh at the sergeants. On the runs they would begin running backward, challenge the sergeants to a race, ask them—after a couple of hours of exercises that left the sergeants panting—when they were going to get past the warm-up and into the real thing. After two days of such abuse, the sergeants told the C.O. that the 506th was in much better physical condition than they were, so all the companies of the 506th started in immediately on B stage.

For a week, the company double-timed each morning to the packing sheds, where the men learned how to fold and pack their parachutes. They ran back to the Frying Pan for lunch, then spent the afternoon leaping into sawdust piles from mock doors on dummy fuselages raised 4 feet off the ground, handling parachutes on a suspended harness, or jumping off 30-foot towers in parachute harnesses suspended from a steel cable.

The following week, in C stage, the men made free and controlled jumps from the 250-foot towers. One tower had seats, shock absorbers, and chute guide wires; the others had four chutes that released when they reached the suspension arm. From these, each man made several daylight jumps and one at night.

C stage also featured a wind machine, which blew a gale along the ground, moving both chute and jumper to teach the men how to control and collapse their canopies after landing.

After a week at the towers, the enlisted men were ready for D stage, the real thing, the five jumps from a C-47 that would earn those who completed the process their parachutists' wings. The men packed their chutes the night before, checked them, then packed them again, checked them again, until past

2300. Reveille was at 0530. They marched to the hangers at Lawson Field, singing and shouting in anticipation. They put on their chutes, then sat on rows of benches waiting to be summoned to the C-47s. There was joshing, joke telling, lots of smoking, nervous laughter, frequent trips to the latrine, and repeated checking of the chute and the reserve chute worn on the chest.

They loaded up, twenty-four to a plane. With only one or two exceptions, it was the first plane ride for the men. When the C-47 reached 1,500 feet, it circled. The red light went on; the jumpmaster, a sergeant instructor, called out, "Stand up and hook up." Each man hooked the line attached to the backpack cover of his main chute to the anchor line running down the middle of the top of the fuselage.

"Sound off for equipment check!" shouted the jumpmaster.

"Number twelve O.K.!" "Number eleven O.K.!" and so on down the line.

"Close up and stand in the door!"

The first man stepped up to the open door. All the men had been ordered to look out at the horizon, not straight down, for obvious psychological reasons. They had also been taught to place their hands on the outer edge of the door, never on the inside. With the hands on the outside, there was nothing to hold a man in the plane, and the slightest nudge, even just the sense of the next man pressing forward, would be enough to get him out of the plane. If he tried to steady himself by putting his hands on the inside, as Gordon said, "twelve men behind couldn't push that fellow out of there if he didn't want to go. That's the power of fear." When a jumpmaster saw a man put his hands on the inside, he would pull him back and let the others go out.

Most of the men, according to Gordon, "were so psyched up and in the swim of this thing that we would almost have gone out without a parachute. It was almost that bad." Overall, 94 percent of the men of the 506th qualified, which set a record that still stands.

On the first jump, the men went one at a time. As soon as he was in the door, the jumpmaster tapped him on the leg. Out he went.

"I shuffled up to the door and leaped into a vast, breathtaking void," Webster remembered. "My heart popped into my mouth, my mind went blank." The static line attached to the hook on the anchor line in the plane pulled the back cover off his main chute; a break cord, tied to the apex of the chute, pulled the canopy out of the pack and then parted. The prop blast inflated the chute, and he felt the terrific opening shock.

"From then on the jump was fun. I drifted down, oscillating, or, as civilians would say, swinging to and fro, and joyously looking around. The sky was filled with high-spirited troopers shouting back and forth."

•   •   •

Standing in that open door was an obvious moment of truth. Men who had been outstanding in training, men who later won medals for bravery in combat as ordinary infantry, would freeze. Sometimes they were given a second chance, either on that flight after the others had jumped, or the next day. Usually, however, if a man froze once, he would never jump.

Two members of E Company froze. They refused to jump. One of them, Pvt. Joe Ramirez, was pushed to the back of the plane, but after everyone jumped out, he told the jumpmaster that he wanted to jump. The plane circled the field. On the second pass, he jumped. As Pvt. Rod Strohl put it, "That took more guts than for a guy to go out the first time."

• • •

Easy made its second jump that afternoon, with the men again going out one at a time. The next jump was a mass affair, the jumpmaster shouting "Go! Go! Go!" as the twelve men in the stick moved into the doorway. The sticks cleared the plane in six seconds, to the astonishment of the jumpmaster. Carson wrote in his diary, "I think I am getting jump crazy because when I am on the ground I think of the thrill of jumping and I want to jump some more. When I feel that opening jerk, I shout with all my might."

The fourth jump came on Christmas Eve. On Christmas Day, the company got the day off and a nice turkey feast. It was the first Christmas away from home for virtually every man in the company. Carson wrote, "It don't seem like Christmas, no snow, no tree, no presents, no mom and dad."

On December 26, the last jump, each man got a certificate declaring that he was "entitled to be rated from this date as a qualified Parachutist." Then the proudest moment of all, the one toward which they had been working for six months, the pinning on of the silver wings. From that moment, never to be forgotten, each member of Easy, every member of the 506th, was forever special.

• • •

Colonel Sink held a regimental parade, then gathered the men around him. Standing on a platform, he read out an order of the day (the men later got printed copies). "You are a member of one of the finest regiments in the United States Army," Sink declared, "and consequently in the world." He said he was sending them home on a ten-day furlough, and reminded them that there were "certain things that are expected of you—not only while on furlough, but also a creed by which you are expected to govern your life." They should walk with pride and military bearing, take care of their personal appearance, and "Remember our battlecry and motto, 'Currahee,' and its meaning: 'Standing Alone.' *We Stand Alone Together.*"

He ordered the men to "Stay out of jail," and dismissed them. Wearing their wings, their boots polished, the trousers bloused into the boots, off they went. When they got home, they were objects of wonder to their parents and friends, obviously because of their physical fitness, but even more because of the self-confidence they had acquired in the past half year. They had been through a training course that three out of five volunteers could not complete; they had survived Sobel's wrath and harassment; they had jumped out of an airplane in flight. They were elite.

Not so elite, however, that they were free to ignore Army rules and regulations. Colonel Sink had warned them to get back to Benning when the furlough was up, but what with the inadequacies of the air, rail, and bus transportation systems in America in January 1943, an alarming number of the 506th were late reporting back for duty.

Colonel Sink held a regimental parade. The men turned out in their class A, or dress, uniforms. They were marched down a sandy street to an empty lot behind the cooks' hutments. Sink called them to attention, then gave the command "At ease." They watched and listened in silence as a lieutenant read a list of names, one from each company, from among the men who had reported in last.

"Private John Doe, E Company," the lieutenant called out. A drummer, standing beside the lieutenant, beat a soft, mournful roll. Two sergeants, bearing submachine-guns, moved to Private Doe. He stepped from the ranks. His face was pale. The sergeants, one on each side, escorted him forward. The drum continued to roll. They stopped in front of the lieutenant. He read out the orders. Private Doe was being drummed out of the paratroopers, condemned to the infantry.

The lieutenant ripped the 506th patch from the private's arm, the wings from his chest, the parachute patch from his hat, and threw them all on the ground. It was so humiliating that the officers and men were cursing under their breath. Webster wrote his mother, "One thing stirred us all up to a fighting madness; some cheap lieutenant without any sense of decency or good taste stood beside the drummer, snapping pictures of all the fellows who came up. Bad enough to be humiliated before your friends, but to be photographed in your disgrace—that lieutenant ought to be shot."

There was more. A jeep drove up and dumped out Private Doe's barracks bags. He had to take off his boots, put on regular shoes, wear his pants down like a regular infantryman ("straight legs," as the paratroopers called them). He picked up his bags and, followed by the submachine-gunners, marched sadly away, the drum continuing to roll, a picture of bleak loneliness. This was repeated nine times.

After that, the 506th had little problem with men returning late from a furlough.

•   •   •

In late January, Easy and the rest of the 506th moved across the Chattahoochee River to the Alabama side of Fort Benning. It was like going from prison to freedom. The barracks were comfortable and the food good. There was a fine PX and a movie theater. The training concentrated on squad problems, especially house-to-house fighting, which was fun, with lots of explosions, firing blanks at one another, tossing smoke grenades. The men made their sixth jump, the first with rifles.

Carson's diary entries capture the flavor of those winter days. February 8: "Last night we were in a hell raising mood, so we tore the barracks apart in a pillow fight. After three hours of fighting we finally decided that we were tired and went to bed."

February 11: "[Cpl. Joe] Toye, [Sgt. George] Luz, and I to Columbus. Called up the girls and had a party, fun and more fun. Sometime during the party I ran into Betty the Key to Columbus. We finally had to get home, and got here 4:45 A.M." February 12: "Back to Chickasaw Gardens in Columbus and another lovely evening. Betty and I hit it off swell. Really had fun. Got home at 4:45 A.M. and went on duty at 5:30 with one eye open."

•   •   •

In March, it was "pack 'em up, we're moving out." Camp Mackall, North Carolina, was a marvel of wartime construction. On November 7, 1942, it consisted of 62,000 acres of wilderness. Four months later it had 65 miles of paved roads, a 1,200-bed hospital, five movie theaters, six huge beer gardens, a complete all-weather airfield with three 5,000-foot runways, and 1,750 buildings. The barracks were heated; the cots had mattresses. It was named for Pvt. John T. Mackall of the 82d Airborne Division, the first American paratrooper to be killed in combat in World War II. He died on November 8, the day construction began, in North Africa. Camp Mackall was home to the Airborne Command.

Training intensified and became more sophisticated. The jumps now included not only rifles, but other small arms. The bazooka had to be jumped in one piece, the light machine-guns also (although the tripod could be separated and carried by a second man). Two men split the 60 mm mortar and its base plate. Food, ammunition, maps, hand grenades, high explosives, and more were attached to the paratroopers. Some men were jumping with 100 extra pounds.

After the jumps, there were two- and three-day exercises in the woods, with the main focus on quick troop movements and operating behind enemy lines as large forces. At dusk, platoon leaders were shown their location on maps, then told to be at such-and-so by morning.

Captain Sobel made Pvt. Robert "Popeye" Wynn his runner. He sent Wynn out to locate his platoons. Wynn managed to get "lost," and spent the night catching up on his sleep. In the morning, Sobel demanded to know why Wynn got lost.

"Because I can't see in the dark," Wynn replied.

"You had better learn to see in the dark," Sobel rejoined, and sent Wynn back to his squad, replacing him with Ed Tipper as runner. "With my help," Tipper recounted, "Sobel was able to mislay his maps, compass, and other items when he most needed them. He was getting similar 'assistance' from others and was disoriented and lost even more than usual. We were all hoping that he'd screw up so badly that he'd be replaced and we wouldn't have to go into combat under his command."

"Your rifle is your right arm!" Sobel would tell his men. "It should be in your possession every moment." On one night exercise he decided to teach his men a lesson. He and Sergeant Evans went sneaking through the company position to steal rifles from sleeping men. The mission was successful; by daylight Sobel and Evans had nearly fifty rifles. With great fanfare, Evans called the company together and Sobel began to tell the men what miserable soldiers they were.

As he was yelling, the C.O. of Fox Company, accompanied by some forty-five of his men, came up. To Sobel's great embarrassment, it turned out that he and Evans had been lost, strayed into Fox Company's bivouac area, and stolen their rifles.

A couple of weeks later, Sobel hurt his feet on a jump. He and Sergeant Evans returned to barracks while the company stayed in the field. The captain and the first sergeant conducted a private inspection. They searched through all the footlockers, clothing, and personal possessions of the men of E Company. They went through pockets, broke open boxes, rifled letters from girlfriends and family, and confiscated all items they considered contraband. "I don't know what the hell they were looking for," Gordon Carson commented. "Those were the days before drugs."

Sobel posted a list identifying the contraband, the offender, and the punishment. The men returned from the field exercise, exhausted and filthy, to find that everything they thought of as personal property was in disarray, underwear, socks, toothpaste and toothbrushes, all piled up on top of the bunks. Many items were missing.

Nearly every soldier had something confiscated. Generally it was unauthorized ammunition, nonregulation clothing, or pornography. Cans of fruit cocktail and sliced peaches, stolen from the kitchen, were gone, along with expensive shirts, none of it ever returned. One soldier had been collecting prophylactic kits. A few condoms were evidently acceptable, but 200 constituted contraband; they were posted on Sobel's list of confiscated items.

"That marked a turning point for me," Tipper recalled. "Before Sobel's raid I had disliked him but had not really hated the man. Afterward I decided Sobel was my personal enemy and I did not owe him loyalty or anything else. Everyone was incensed."

There was talk about who was going to shoot Sobel when the company got into combat. Tipper thought it was just talk, but "on the other hand I was aware of a couple of guys in Company E who said little but who in my judgment were fully capable of killing Sobel if they got the chance."

On the next field exercise, E Company was told that a number of its men would be designated as simulated casualties so the medics could practice bandaging wounds, improvising casts and splints, evacuating men on litters and so forth. Sobel was told that he was a simulated casualty. The medics put him under a real anesthetic, pulled down his pants, and made a real incision simulating an appendectomy. They sewed up the incision and bound it up with bandages and surgical tape, then disappeared.

Sobel was furious, naturally enough, but he got nowhere in pressing for an investigation. Not a man in E Company could be found who could identify the guilty medics.

•   •   •

How fit the men of Easy were was determined at Mackall when the Department of the Army had Strayer's 2d Battalion—already famous for the march to Atlanta—take a standard physical fitness test. The battalion scored 97 percent. As this was the highest score ever recorded for a battalion in the Army, a Colonel Jablonski from Washington thought Strayer had rigged the score. Winters recalled, "They had us run it a second time, officers, men, service personnel, cooks, everybody—and we scored 98 percent."

•   •   •

Promotions were coming Easy's way. All three staff sergeants, James Diel, Salty Harris, and Mike Ranney, were original members of the company who had started out as privates. So too with the sergeants, Leo Boyle, Bill Guarnere, Carwood Lipton, John Martin, Elmer Murray, Bob Rader, Bob Smith, Buck Taylor, and Murray Roberts. Carson made corporal. Lieutenant Matheson moved up to regimental staff, while Lieutenants Nixon, Hester, and George Lavenson moved on to the battalion staff. (Through to the end of the war, every vacancy on the 2d Battalion staff was filled with an officer from Easy. Companies D, F, and HQ did not send a single officer up to battalion. Winters commented, "This is why communications between battalion, regiment HQ, and Company E were always excellent. It is also why

Company E always seemed to be called upon for key assignments.")

In early May, Winters's 1st platoon got a new second lieutenant, Harry Welsh. He was a reluctant officer. In April 1942, he had volunteered for the paratroopers and been assigned to the 504th PIR of the 82d Airborne. After jump school, he made sergeant. Three times. He kept getting busted back to private for fighting. But he was a tough little Irishman with obvious leadership potential. His company commander noticed and recommended Welsh for OCS.

Welsh was assigned to Easy Company, 2d Battalion, 506th PIR. He had wanted to return to the 504th, but Army doctrine was to send OCS graduates to new units, because it feared that if they went back to their old outfit, they would be too familiar with their enlisted friends. Sobel put Welsh in Winters's platoon. They immediately became the closest of friends. The relationship was based on mutual respect brought about by an identical view of leadership. "Officers go first," as Welsh put it.

• • •

At the end of May, the men of Easy packed up their barracks bags and joined the other companies of the 506th for a stop-and-go train ride to Sturgis, Kentucky. At the depot Red Cross girls had coffee and doughnuts for them, the last bit of comfort they would know for a month. They marched out into the countryside and pitched pup tents, dug straddle trenches for latrines, and ate the Army's favorite meal for troops in the field, creamed chipped beef on toast, universally known as SOS, or Shit on a Shingle.

This was not combat, but it was as close as the

Army could make it. The maneuvers held in Kentucky, Tennessee, and Indiana from June 5 to July 15, 1943, combined paratroopers and gliderborne troops in the largest airborne exercise to date.

On June 10, the 506th PIR officially joined the 101st Airborne Division, thus making that date the greatest day the 101st ever had. Adding the 506th noticeably raised the morale of the 101st, at least according to the men of E Company.

The maneuvers, pitting the Red Army against the Blue Army, ranged over a wide area of backwoods hills and mountains. Easy made three jumps. Christenson remembered one of them vividly. It was hot, stifling inside the C-47, and the heated air rising in currents from the hills cause the plane to bob and weave. Cpl. Denver "Bull" Randleman, at the back of the stick and thus farthest from the open door, began vomiting into his helmet. The man in front of him took one look and lost his lunch. The process worked right up the line. Not everyone managed to vomit into his helmet; the floor was awash in vomit, the plane stank. Christenson, at the front, was hanging on, but barely. "My stomach was on the verge of rebellion. . . . 'Why don't they turn on the green light? There it is!' From behind, shouts of 'Go!' 'Go! Goddamn it, Go!' Out I went into the clean fresh air. I felt as if someone had passed a magic wand over my head and said, 'Christenson, you feel great.' And I did."

The maneuvers featured extended night marches, wading through streams, climbing the far bank, making 3 feet only to slide back 2, stumbling over rocks, stumps, and roots, cutting a swath through matted underbrush and occasionally enjoying fried chicken prepared by Tennessee hill people. The men were tired, filthy, itching all over.

In late July, the maneuvers completed, the 2d Battalion of the 506th received a commendation from Maj. Gen. William C. Lee, commander of the 101st, for "splendid aggressive action, sound tactical doctrine, and obviously well trained individuals." General Lee expressed his confidence that "future tests will reveal further indications of excellent training and leadership."

Easy moved from Sturgis to Camp Beckinridge, Kentucky, where there were barracks, hot showers, and other luxuries. But the camp was overflowing, and once again it was the little pup tents for sleeping quarters, the ground for a mattress. It did not last long, as most of the men got ten-day furloughs, and shortly after they reported back, the entire division took trains to Fort Bragg, North Carolina.

It was immediately obvious that Bragg was a staging area, as the division prepared to ship overseas. The food was better; there were beds in barracks with hot showers and other improvements. But the real giveaway was a total reoutfitting. The men got new clothes, new weapons, new gear. They spent their days on the firing range, sighting in the rifles and machineguns.

Where were they going, east or west, the European, Mediterranean, or the Pacific theater? No one knew, rumors flew from platoon to platoon, bets were made.

On weekends, the men went into Fayetteville to "prime the Pump," at the Town Pump, one of the local bars. Brawls were frequent. Most were started by the paratroopers, who would pitch into the regular soldiers stationed at Bragg. They also goaded the glider troops who were part of the 101st.

The glider troops were regular soldiers assigned to

the glider regiment. Although they were airborne, they were not volunteers and were treated by the Army as second-class men. They did not receive the $50 per month bonus, they had no special badges, they did not wear boots and bloused trousers. Some of them made up posters showing photographs of crashed and burned gliders, with a caption that read: "Join the glider troops! No flight pay. No jump pay. But never a dull moment!"

A few members of Easy went down to the airfield at Bragg to take a ride on a glider. The experience of landing in one of those plywood crates convinced them jumping with a chute was a better way to land. When General Lee made a glider flight, the landing fractured several of his ribs. "Next time I'll take a parachute," he remarked. "We told you so!" the glider troops shouted. (In July 1944, the glidermen finally got the hazardous duty bonus of $50 per month and a special insignia.)

• • •

In mid-August, the division assembled in regimental formation. A band played "Over There" and the Red Cross girls cried as the men marched to the twenty trains waiting to take them off to war. Once aboard and somewhat settled down, the betting began over which way the trains would head, north toward New York and then Europe or the Mediterranean, or west toward California and then the Pacific.

The trains headed north, toward Camp Shanks, 30 miles up the Hudson River from New York City. Promises were made about passes into the city, promises that were not kept. Instead it was more inspections, followed by inoculations. "Shot followed shot," Christenson remembered, "until our arms hung from our bodies like limp ropes." Officers and non-coms got to know the *Preparation for Overseas Movement* manual by heart.

Sobel wrote up a form letter to send to the mothers of his troopers. "Dear Madam," it began. "Soon your son, Pfc. Paul C. Rogers [each name was typed in] will drop from the sky to engage and defeat the enemy. He will have the best of weapons, and equipment, and have had months of hard, and strenuous training to prepare him for success on the battlefield.

"Your frequent letters of love, and encouragement will arm him with a fighting heart. With that, he cannot fail, but will win glory for himself, make you proud of him, and his country ever grateful for his service in its hour of need." He signed each letter with a flourish, "Herbert M. Sobel, Capt., Commanding."

• • •

The enlisted men got hold of some whiskey. They were accustomed to beer, so the whiskey hit them hard. Christenson got so drunk he was "making out with the toilet," a condition common to young men who have just been introduced to whiskey. Corporal Randleman found him and gently carried him to bed. The next morning, the air filled with the moans and groans of the hungover men, the company marched down to the docks. A ferry carried the men to a pier, where hot coffee and doughnuts from the Red Cross girls helped revive the near-dead.

There was a great deal of cursing, partly because the men had hoped to march through New York City on their way to war and did not, also because they were not allowed to wear their jump boots. The reason: enemy spies might see them and would know that an airborne division was shipping out. They had to take the patch of the 101st, the Screaming Eagle, off their shoulders.

Winters remembered only one case of Gangplank Fever. A medical officer was "just smart enough to know what to take to be assigned to sick call and miss the voyage." All the others lined up in single file to walk up the gangplank, lugging their barracks bags and weapons. As they stepped onto the liner converted into a troop transport and called out their names, a checker marked them present. It took almost a full day to get the 5,000 men aboard a transport built to carry 1,000 passengers. Finally tugs towed the ship from her berth, and she started steaming out to sea. The men of Easy Company lined the rails to see the Statue of Liberty slip astern. For nearly every one of them, it was his first trip outside the United States. A certain homesickness set in, coupled with a realization, as the regimental scrapbook *Currahee* put it, of "how wonderful the last year had been."

3

"Duties of the Latrine Orderly"

ALDBOURNE

September 1943–March 1944

THE *Samaria* was an old India mail liner and
passenger ship converted to a troop transport.
Originally built for 1,000 passengers, she carried 5,000 men from the 506th. The overcrowding
created really dreadful conditions. Fresh water was
severely rationed; the men could drink only at stipu-
lated fifteen-minute intervals for a grand total of an
hour and a half a day. The showers ran salt water, cold.
The men had to wear their life jackets at all times,
and their cartridge belts with canteens attached, which
meant they were constantly bumping into one another.
They slept in their clothes. One bunk was assigned to
two men, which meant they alternated, sleeping every
other night on the deck or in a hallway or wherever
space to lie down could be found. The stench was
simply awful.

There were two meals a day. Christenson described his first breakfast: "I didn't think we would ever stop going down stairs to the mess hall on the lowest deck, stairs that were slippery with grease and when we finally reached the bottom, the stench was almost overpowering. They fed us from large pots, containing boiled fish and tomatoes. The cooks wore stained white clothing, stains on stains showing they hadn't changed for days." The men ate the slop because they were hungry; to Webster, the mess hall had "the air of a floating madhouse."

At least the meals were a break from the routine, which consisted of walking the decks, leaning on the rail watching the convoy, or gambling. The gambling was continuous: poker, blackjack, and craps. Large amounts of money changed hands. Carson won $125 one night, lost it all the next day. Men tried to read, but they had precious few books. Captain Sobel tried to lead the men in calisthenics, but the space was insufficient and it became another Sobel joke.

On September 15, the *Samaria* docked in Liverpool. The next day a train took the men south. Trucks picked them up at the station at Ogbourne St. George and carried them on to their new home. They marched the last mile and a half, after dark, with only flashlights to show the way; the wartime blackout impressed upon the men that they were in a combat zone. They got to their barracks, which were Nissen huts heated by twin pot-bellied stoves, were given mattress covers and shown the straw they could stuff into them, along with heavy wool blankets that itched, and went to bed.

Webster wrote that when he woke the next morning, "I thought I'd passed out on a Hollywood movie set. All around the area were fairybook cottages with thatched roofs and rose vines on their sides. Vast horses shaking long manes stomped down narrow winding cobblestone lanes. A soft village green set off a weathered old grey eleventh century Norman church whose clock chimed the hours just like Big Ben, and five ancient public houses, their signboards swinging in the breeze, bade us welcome to the land of mild and bitter beer." They were in Aldbourne, in Wiltshire, near Hungerford, not far from Swindon, 80 miles due west of London. It would be home for Company E for almost nine months, by far the longest period it stayed in one place.

Aldbourne was vastly different from Toccoa, Benning, or Bragg. There the men of Easy had been in self-contained, isolated posts, completely military. In Aldbourne, they were in the midst of a small English village, where the people were conservative, set in their ways, apprehensive about all these young Yanks in their midst. The danger of friction was great, but the Army put together an excellent orientation program that worked well. Beginning that first morning and continuing most of the week, the men were briefed in detail on English customs, manners, habits. Well-disciplined as they were, the men quickly caught on to the basic idea that they should save their hell-raising for Swindon, Birmingham, or London; in Aldbourne, they were to drink their beer quietly in the pubs, in the British manner.

They also learned to eat what the British were eating: powdered milk, powdered eggs, dehydrated apricots, dehydrated potatoes, horse meat, Brussels sprouts, turnips, and cabbage. The PX goods were rationed: seven packs of cigarettes per week, plus three candy bars, one pack of gum, one cake of soap, one box of matches, one package of razor blades.

Sobel didn't change. At the end of the first week, the men got passes to go to Swindon for a Saturday night dance. Sobel put out a regulation: no man would take his blouse off while dancing. Pvt. Thomas Burgess, a farm boy from central Illinois, got to sweating while dancing in a wool shirt with a wool blouse over it, so he took off the blouse.

Monday morning, Sobel called Burgess into his office. "Burgess, I understand you were in town Saturday night with your blouse off at a dance."

"That's right, Captain Sobel," Burgess replied, "but I checked Army regulations and it's very plainly written that you can take your blouse off if you've got a wool shirt on and you are moving about or dancing or whatever."

Sobel looked him up and down. "I'll tell you what I'm going to do, Burgess. You're gonna wear your blouse over your fatigues all week, you're gonna sleep with it on every night."

Burgess wore his blouse during the day, but he figured Sobel would not be checking on him at night, so he hung it on the edge of the bed. The following Saturday he went to Sobel's office to get a pass to go to the dance. Sobel looked him over. "Burgess," he said, "that blouse don't look to me like you slept in it all night." No pass.

• • •

They were in England to prepare for the invasion of Europe, not to dance, and the training schedule was intense. Malarkey thought he was back in Toccoa. Six days a week, eight to ten hours a day, they were in the field. They made 15-, 18-, 21-, and 25-mile hikes, went on night operations, spent an hour daily in close combat exercises, did some street fighting, and got training in map reading, first aid, chemical warfare, and the use and characteristics of German weapons. They made a 25-mile hike with full field equipment in twenty-four hours, then a few days later a 25-mile hike with combat pack in twelve hours. There were specialized courses on booby traps, removal of mines, communications, and the like.

Once a week or so they went out on a two- or three-day exercise. The problems were designed not only to give them a working knowledge of the mechanics of combat but to teach the most basic thing an infantryman has to know: how to love the ground, how to use it to advantage, how the terrain dictates tactics, above all how to live on it and in it for days at a time without impairment of physical efficiency. Their officers stressed the importance of such things, that it would make the difference between life and death, that the men must do it instinctively right the first time, as there would not be a second.

So the men of Easy got to know the English countryside. They attacked towns, hills, and woods. They dug countless foxholes, and slept in them, learning how to do it despite rain and cold and hunger.

In early December, back in the field again, the company dug in around a high, barren, windswept hill. The platoon leaders told them to dig their foxholes deep, difficult in the rocky soil. Soon an armored combat team of Sherman tanks attacked. "They roared up the hill at us like primeval monsters," Webster wrote in his diary, "stopped, turned, and passed broadside. One charged at me. My hole wasn't deep enough for a single tread to pass safely over me, so I yelled frantically, 'Straddle me! Straddle me,' which he did." Carson's entry read: "It was the first time a tank ran over me in a foxhole, scary."

There was a lot of night work, Gordon recalled. "We would cut across country and crawl over fences and through gaps and go through woods and wade creeks." In the process, the members of the squads and platoons, already familiar with each other, grew intimate. "I could see a silhouette at night," Gordon said, "and tell you who it was. I could tell you by the way he wore his hat, how the helmet sat on his head, how he slung his rifle." Most of what they learned in the training proved to be valuable in combat, but it was that intimacy, that total trust, that comradeship that developed on those long, cold, wet English nights that proved to be invaluable.

They were jumping on a regular basis, in full gear, learning how to use their risers to guide themselves to open, plowed fields rather than come down on a hedgerow, road, telephone pole, stone wall, or woods. In the C-47s in the cold, damp English air, their feet were numb by the time the green light went on, so that when they hit the ground the feet stung and burned from the shock. A major purpose of the jumps was to learn to assemble quickly after landing, not so easy to do for the 2d platoon of Easy on the first jump, as the platoon came down twenty-five miles from the drop zone (DZ).

• • •

There was tension. Members of the 82d Airborne, stationed nearby, would tell the troopers from the 101st what combat in North Africa, Sicily, and Italy had been like. The officers especially felt the pressure of combat coming on, none more so than Sobel. "It showed up in his disposition," Winters said. "He was becoming more sour and sadistic. It was reaching the point that it was unbearable."

Sgt. Earl Hale recalled that "There was a lottery going on about whoever gets Sobel." Sobel had picked up an Air Force sheepskin jacket, of which he was proud and which he wore in the field, making him highly conspicuous. Tipper remembered that when the company was going through a combat range with live ammunition fired at pop-up targets, "Sobel experienced some near misses. More than one shot was aimed from the rear and side to crack by close to Sobel's head. He'd flop down, kind of bounce around and shout something, and jump up again. There was much laughing and gesturing from the men. I can't believe that Sobel thought what was happening was accidental, but maybe he did. Anyway, he kept jumping up and down and running around as if everything were normal."

The men continued to play tricks on Sobel. Pvt. George Luz could imitate voices. One night E Company was leading the battalion on a cross-country march. The barbed-wire fences kept slowing the progress. Sobel was in front.

"Captain Sobel," a voice called out, "what's the holdup?"

"The barbed wire," Sobel replied, thinking he was addressing Maj. Oliver Horton, the battalion executive officer.

"Cut those fences," Luz called out, continuing to imitate Horton's voice. "Yes, sir!" Sobel replied, and he ordered wire cutters to the front.

The next morning a contingent of Wiltshire farmers confronted Colonel Strayer. They complained mightily about the cut fences. Their cows were wandering all over the landscape. Strayer called in Sobel. "Why did you cut those fences?"

"I was ordered to cut them, sir!"

"By whom?"

"Major Horton."

"Can't be. Horton's on leave in London." Sobel caught hell, but he was never able to learn who had fooled him and was therefore unable to retaliate.

It was his jumping around, his "Hi-ho, Silver!" nonsense, his bull-in-the-china-shop approach to tactical problems, that bothered the officers, N.C.O.s, and enlisted men of the company more than his chickenshit. Dissatisfaction grew daily, especially with the N.C.O.s. Sgts. Myron "Mike" Ranney, a twenty-one-year-old from North Dakota, of 1st platoon, and "Salty" Harris of 3d platoon, led the mumble-mumble of the potential disaster of Sobel leading the company into combat. The N.C.O.s were fully aware that they were confronted by a delicate and extremely dangerous situation. To act would open them to charges of insubordination or mutiny in time of war; to fail to act could get the whole company killed.

Ranney, Harris, and the other N.C.O.s hoped that the platoon leaders would bring the problem to Colonel Sink, or that Sink would become aware of the situation on his own and that Sink would then quietly remove Sobel. But that seemed naive. How could young officers whose responsibility was to back up their C.O. go to the colonel to complain about the C.O.? And what would they complain about? Company E continued to lead the way in the regiment, in the field, in barracks, in athletic contests. How could the N.C.O.s expect Colonel Sink to do other than support his company commander in the face of dissension and pressure from a group of sergeants and corporals? These guys were getting ready to go into combat against the most-feared army in the world, not to play a game or have a debate.

So the mumble-mumble continued, and Sobel and 1st Sergeant Evans remained isolated, but still very much in command.

•   •   •

Weekend passes and the excellent British rail service gave the men a break from the tension. England in the late fall and early winter of 1943 was a wonderland for the boys from the States. Most of the British boys their age were off in Italy or in training camps far from their homes, so there were lonely, bored, unattached young women everywhere. The American soldiers were well-paid, much better than the British, and the paratroopers had that extra $50 per month. Beer was cheap and plentiful, once out of Aldbourne all restraints were removed, they were getting ready to kill or be killed, they were for the most part twenty or twenty-one years old.

Webster described the result in an October 23 diary entry: "Although I do not enjoy the army, most of the men in this outfit find it a vacation. Boys who had been working steadily at home enter the army and are relieved of all responsibilities. It is unanimously agreed that they never pitched such glorious drunks back home."

The excitement of the time, the kaleidoscope of impressions that were continually thrust upon them, the desperate need to escape the rigors of training, the thought of upcoming combat and Sobel's chickenshit, combined to make this an unforgettable time and impel most of the men to make the most of it. "London to me was a magic carpet," Carson wrote. "Walk down any of its streets and every uniform of the Free World was to be seen. Their youth and vigor vibrated in every park and pub. To Piccadilly, Hyde Park, Leicester Square, Trafalgar Square, Victoria they came. The uniforms of the Canadians, South Africans, Australians, New Zealanders, the Free French, Polish, Belgium, Holland, and of course the English and Americans were everywhere.

"Those days were not lost on me because even at twenty years of age, I knew I was seeing and being a part of something that was never to be again. Wartime London was its own world."

There was an excess of drinking, whoring, fighting. Older British observers complained, "The trouble with you Yanks is that you are overpaid, oversexed, and over here." (To which the Yanks would reply, "The trouble with you Limeys is that you are underpaid, undersexed, and under Eisenhower.")

•   •   •

E Company was adding officers, with the aim of having two lieutenants per platoon, in expectation of casualties when combat began. One newcomer was 2d Lt. Lynn "Buck" Compton. Born on the last day of 1921 in Los Angeles, he was an all-American catcher on the UCLA baseball team and played football for UCLA in the January 1, 1943, Rose Bowl game. Upon graduation from OCS he went to Fort Benning. After completing jump school, he joined E Company in Aldbourne in December. "I remember feeling rather envious of those who had been at Toccoa," he wrote years later, "and felt sort of 'out of it' as a new member of the company."

Compton quickly learned that Lieutenant Nixon,

now battalion S-2, resented "jocks." Nixon put Compton in charge of physical training for the battalion, which in practice meant Compton had to lead the battalion on long runs, the only officer who had to do so. Whether as a result of this experience, or because of his athletic background, or because he liked to gamble, Compton was close to the N.C.O.s and some of the enlisted men. Too close, some of the other officers felt. He got caught playing craps with some of the men and drew a reprimand from the X.O., Lieutenant Winters.

•   •   •

At 1100 hours on October 30, Lieutenant Colonel Strayer was scheduled to inspect E Company. Sobel gave Lieutenant Winters orders to inspect the latrine at 1000 hours. A few minutes later, at about 0930 hours, Lieutenant Colonel Strayer told Winters to censor the enlisted men's mail. That was a job that could not be done at headquarters, so Winters hopped on his bicycle and rode to his quarters, a small room in a private home in Aldbourne. Promptly at 1000 hours he returned, parked his bicycle outside the barracks, and entered to inspect the latrine. To his surprise, Sobel was there, making his own inspection.

Sobel walked past Winters, head down, giving no indication that he saw the X.O. Behind him walked a most unhappy Pvt. Joachim Melo, carrying a mop, soaking wet, dirty, badly needing a shave, hair uncombed. Sobel left without saying a word. Winters inspected the latrine and found that Melo had done a good job.

At 1045 hours Winters walked into the orderly room to get ready for the company formation. With a hint of a smirk on his face, 1st Sergeant Evans handed him a typed document. It read:

Company E, 506th PIR, 30 Oct. '43
Subject: Punishment under 104th A[rticle of]
W[ar]
To: 1st Lt. R. D. Winters

1. You will indicate by indorsement [*sic*] below
whether you desire punishment under 104th AW
or trial by Courts Martial for failure to inspect the
latrine at 0945 this date as instructed by me.

[Signed, with a grand flourish]
Herbert M. Sobel, Capt., Commanding.

Winters confronted Sobel. "Captain," he said after
saluting and asking permission to speak, "my orders
were to inspect the latrine at 1000 hours."

"I changed that time to 0945."

"No one told me."

"I telephoned, and I sent a runner." Winters bit his
tongue. There was no telephone in his room, and no
runner had come.

It was time for inspection. Strayer went down the
ranks and through the barracks. Everything, including
the latrine, was satisfactory. Winters, meanwhile,
made up his mind on how to respond to Sobel. On the
bottom of the typed sheet, he wrote by hand:

Subject: Punishment under 104 A.W. or Trial by
Courts Martial.
To: Capt. H. M. Sobel

1. I request trial by Courts Martial for failure
to inspect the latrine at 0945 this date.

Lt. R. D. Winters, XO, Co. E

Sobel replied the following day:

1. You will be denied a 48 hour pass until after December 15, 1943.

2. In accordance with the procedure outlined in the Courts-Martial Manual you will iniutate [initiate; Sergeant Evans evidently had trouble either typing or spelling] your own letter of appeal with your reasons for objection and also a request for trial by courts-martial.

Winters simmered for three days. So far as he could make out, Sobel was saying, "Look, don't be silly, take the punishment and forget the courts-martial." Sobel knew that the "punishment" was a matter of indifference to Winters, as Winters spent his weekends on the post, reading or playing sports. But Winters had had enough. He wanted to force the moment to a crisis. The competition he had never wanted, between himself and Sobel for leadership of E Company, had to be settled. The company was not big enough for both of them.

On November 4, Winters appealed his punishment under the 104th Article of War. Sobel made an "indorsement" [Evans's spelling] the next day:

1. Punishment for the above offense given by the undersigned will not be lifted by him.

2. When given another task to perform by a ranking officer to myself [Strayer's order to censor the mail] you should have delegated your task to another officer to inspect the latrine and not let it go until such time that there was little time for corrective measures to be taken before the arrival of the General Officer about ten minutes later.

He signed with his usual flourish.

Winters's request for a court-martial, meanwhile, was posing a problem that was not as funny as it sounded for the 2d Battalion staff. The officers got out the court-martial manual and studied it intensively to try to figure out some way to get out from under this embarrassment. They finally did, and Strayer set aside the punishment and declared the case closed—no court-martial.

Sobel was not finished. The next day, November 12, Evans handed Winters another typed order:

Subject: Failure to Instruct Latrine Orderly
To: 1st Lt. R. D. Winters
  1. You will reply by indorsement hereon your reason for failure to instruct Pvt. J. Melo in his duties as latrine orderly.
  2. You will further reply why he was permitted to be on duty at 1030 Oct. 30 in need of a shave.

"I give up," Winters decided. "Go ahead and shoot me." In that mood he replied, by endorsement:

  1. Reason for failure to instruct Pvt. J. Melo in his duties as latrine orderly: No excuse.
  2. Reason why he was permitted to be on duty at 1030 hr in need of a shave: No excuse.

The next day Strayer decided, for the good of E Company (where, naturally, the long-anticipated showdown between Sobel and Winters was the talk of the barracks), to transfer Winters out of Easy. Strayer made him battalion mess officer.

That was an insult to Winters, in his view: "You only give a job like that to a guy that can't do anything right."

•   •   •

With Winters gone, Sobel still in charge, and combat coming, the N.C.O.s were in an uproar. Sergeants Ranney and Harris called a meeting. With the exception of Evans and one or two others, all the N.C.O.s in E Company attended. Ranney and Harris proposed that they present Colonel Sink with an ultimatum: either Sobel be replaced, or they would turn in their stripes. They stressed that they would have to act together, with no dissenters and no identifiable leader.

This radical proposal elicited much comment, many questions, great concern, but in the end the group decision was that going into combat under Sobel's command was unthinkable. The only way they could let Strayer and Sink know how strongly they felt was to turn in their stripes. Each noncom thereupon wrote out his own resignation: Lipton's went as follows: "I hereby turn in my stripes. I no longer want to be a non-commissioned officer in Company E." Lipton was C.Q. (charge of quarters, the sergeant who slept in the orderly room to be available to handle any problems that came up during the night, to wake the men in the morning, etc.) that night. He gathered up the resignations and put the stack in Sobel's "in" basket.

The N.C.O.s then thought further about what they were doing and decided to consult with Winters. He was invited to the orderly room, where on arrival Ranney told him what the group had done.

"Don't," said Winters. "Don't even think about it. This is mutiny."

The N.C.O.s protested. As the discussion continued, Sobel walked in. Everyone was speechless. Sobel did not say a word, he just walked over to his desk and picked up a book. As he turned to leave, Ranney said in a normal voice, "Now, Lieutenant Winters, what are we going to do about improving our athletic program?" Sobel gave no hint of concern, he just walked out.

Winters felt that Sobel had to have known what was going on. "Hell, there was no secret about it." Ranney had invited Evans to the meeting; it was all but certain Evans had told Sobel.

Indeed, by this time the whole battalion was talking about Sobel's battles, first with Winters, now with his N.C.O.s. Sink would have had to have been deaf, dumb, and blind not to have been aware. He should also have been grateful that Winters had talked the N.C.O.s out of presenting him with an ultimatum. A few days later, Sink came down to Company E, called all the noncoms together, and as Lipton recalled, "Gave us hell. He told us we disgraced our company and that he could put every one of us in the guardhouse for years. As we were preparing for combat, he said that it could be called mutiny in the face of the enemy for which we could be shot."

Fortunately for Sink, the 101st Airborne had just established a Parachute Jumping School at the nearby village of Chilton Foliat, in order to qualify as paratroopers, doctors, chaplains, communications men, forward artillery observers, and others who would be jumping on D-Day. Who better than Sobel to run a training camp?

Sink sent Sobel to Chilton Foliat and brought 1st Lt. Patrick Sweeney from Able Company to be X.O. of

Easy. He made 1st Lt. Thomas Meehan of Baker the C.O. of Easy. And he brought Winters back, as leader of the 1st platoon. Sergeant Ranney was busted to private, and Harris was transferred. The Sobel era of Easy Company had come to an end.

* * *

Meehan was Sobel's opposite. Slender, fairly tall, willowy, he had common sense and competence. He was strict but fair. He had good voice command. "Under Meehan," Winters said, "we became a normal company."

* * *

Training intensified. On December 13, the company made a night jump and lost its first man, Pvt. Rudolph Dittrich of 1st platoon, due to parachute failure. Platoons and squads were being sent out on three-day problems, with different men being put in command as lieutenants and sergeants were declared out of action. "Imagine me platoon leader," Carson wrote in his diary on December 12. "No, it can't be." But it was. They were learning to be resourceful, which included learning to live off the land. This included "fishing" by tossing hand grenades into the streams and improving their diet by finding deer on the country estates that were willing to walk into a bullet in the head.

Christmas was a day off, with all the turkey a man could eat. New Year's Eve was quiet. "We just waited up for the New Year," Carson wrote. "I wonder what it shall bring, wonder how many of us will see 1945."

On January 18, Gen. Bernard Law Montgomery, commander of the 21st Army Group to which the 101st was attached, came to Chilton Foliat for an inspection. He reviewed the regiment, then told the men to break ranks and rally 'round his jeep. Climbing onto the "bonnet," he told them how good they were. "After seeing the 506th," he said, "I pity the Germans."

• • •

As the days slowly began to lengthen, meaning decent fighting weather was approaching, tension increased. Inevitably the young men thought of death. Few made their thoughts articulate, but Webster dealt with his directly. He wrote his mother, instructing her to "stop worrying about me. I joined the parachutists to fight. I intend to fight. If necessary, I shall die fighting, but don't worry about this because no war can be won without young men dying. Those things which are precious are saved only by sacrifice."

• • •

In February, training became more big unit–oriented as the 101st, and indeed the entire invasion force of more than seven divisions, began rehearsals for the attack on Normandy.

On March 23, the 2d and 3d Battalions of the 506th made a combined jump, by far the largest of the war to date for the regiment. The occasion was an inspection visit by Prime Minister Winston Churchill, Supreme Allied Commander Dwight D. Eisenhower, U.S. First Army commander Omar Bradley, Gen. Maxwell Taylor, commander of the 101st (General Lee had a heart attack in February and was forced to return to the States), and numerous other big shots.

The jump was a huge success. The C-47s came roaring through the sky in a perfect V of Vs. Churchill and the generals were watching from a specially constructed grandstand. The troopers began leaping out of their planes, stick after stick, more than 1,000 men and parachutes filling the sky in a seemingly unending deluge. The instant they hit the ground the troopers were twisting out of their chutes and heading for the assembly area on a dead run, putting their weapons together without slackening speed. The visitors were amazed at the rapidity of the movement; as the regimental scrapbook put it, "the Boys from Currahee" had made a grand impression.

Later, the regiment assembled in front of the reviewing stand. Taylor invited Churchill and Eisenhower to inspect the ranks. They did, stopping occasionally to ask a question or two of one of the men.

Eisenhower stopped in front of Malarkey. "Soldier, where are you from?" (Eisenhower talked to thousands of enlisted men on such inspections before D-Day; invariably his first question was "Where are you from?")

"Astoria, Oregon," Malarkey answered.

"What did you do before the war?" Malarkey said he was a student at the University of Oregon. Ike wanted to know who won last fall's Oregon–Oregon State football game, and whether Malarkey intended to return to college after the war. Then he turned to Churchill and suggested that the Prime Minister might have a question.

"Well, son, how do you like England?" Malarkey assured him that he liked it very much, as he had always enjoyed English literature and history. Churchill promised to get him back to the States as soon as possible. "It was," said Malarkey, "a very memorable occasion."

Even larger maneuvers were held immediately after the Churchill jump, with the purpose of dovetailing the paratroopers, gliderborne units, and ground forces with the air forces and naval elements. Exercises were held throughout southwest England, with mass air drops and amphibious operations.

On one maneuver, Guarnere told Pvts. Warren Muck and Malarkey to drop a mortar shell on a 6-foot-square white target situated on a dune about 600 yards to their front. Malarkey fired once, too long. A second time, too short.

At that moment, some staff officers came up, accompanied by General Taylor. One of the staff officers told Guarnere to have his mortar squad fire at the target as a demonstration for the general.

Guarnere told Malarkey and Muck to fire three rounds. In rapid succession, they dropped three rounds down the barrel. *Boom,* the first hit the target dead center. *Boom, boom,* the other two came down on top of the destroyed target.

"Sergeant, is your squad always that accurate?" Taylor asked.

"Yes, sir," Guarnere replied, "my boys never miss."

The 101st took trains back to barracks in Wiltshire and Berkshire. General Taylor and his staff were well aware that there were many kinks to work out. The Boys from Currahee had learned their lessons about small unit tactics well; now it was up to the generals to fit them properly into the larger whole.

4

"Look Out, Hitler! Here We Come!"

SLAPTON SANDS, UPPOTTERY

April 1–June 5, 1944

THE 101ST AIRBORNE, the 82d Airborne, and the 4th Infantry Division made up the VII Corps. The VII Corps and V Corps (1st Infantry and 29th Infantry Divisions) made up the U.S. First Army, Gen. Omar Bradley commanding. Eisenhower had given Bradley the task of establishing a beachhead on each side of the mouth of the Douve River, where the French coast makes a right angle; running to the east is the Calvados coast, running to the north is the base of the Cotentin Peninsula. The V Corps was to take the Calvados coast (code name for the target area, "Omaha Beach"), while the VII Corps was to take the base of the Cotentin (code name, "Utah Beach"). The VII Corps at Utah would be on the extreme right flank of the invasion area, which stretched from the mouth of the Orne River on the left (east) some 65 to 70 kilometers to the Cotentin.

Eisenhower needed to provide sufficient width to the invasion to bring in enough infantry divisions in the first wave to overpower the enemy, dug in behind Hitler's "Atlantic Wall."[1] In one way, Utah was the easiest of the five assault beaches. At the British and Canadian beaches ("Sword," "Juno," and "Gold," east of Omaha) the numerous vacation homes, small shops, and hotels and casinos that lined the coast provided the Germans with excellent protection for machine-gun nests, while at Omaha a bluff rising from the beach to a height of 200–300 feet gave the German defenders, dug into a trench system on a World War I scale, the ability to shoot down on troops coming out of the landing craft. But Utah had neither bluff nor houses. There were some fixed defenses, made of reinforced concrete, containing artillery and machineguns. The biggest was at La Madeleine, in the middle of Utah (the fortification took its name from a nearby religious shrine that dated back to Viking days). But the gradual slope and low sand dunes at Utah meant that getting across and beyond the beach was not going to be as difficult as at Omaha.

The problem at Utah was what lay inland. Behind the sand dunes was low ground, used by the Norman farmers for grazing cattle. Four narrow, unimproved roads ran inland from the beach; these roads were raised a meter or so above the ground. Field Marshal Erwin Rommel, the German commander, had flooded

---

[1]"Hitler made only one big mistake when he built his Atlantic Wall," the paratroopers liked to say. "He forgot to put a roof on it."

the fields, with the idea of forcing any troops and armor coming inland to use the roads ("causeways," Eisenhower's planners called them). Rommel had most of his artillery in camouflaged positions or reinforced casements and bunkers back from the flooded area, where it could bombard the roads; Rommel had his infantry prepared to take up defensive positions along the western end of the roads, where it could repel any troops moving up them.

The task Eisenhower gave the 101st was to seize these causeway exits. The method to be used was a night drop. The aim was to disrupt the Germans, create surprise and havoc, and get control of those exits and destroy the big guns before the Germans could react.

It would be an intricate, tricky, and risky operation. To have any chance of success, it would be necessary to practice. For the practice to be realistic, it would be necessary to find a piece of the English coastline similar to Utah Beach.

Slapton Sands, in Devonshire, in southwestern England, was similar to Utah. A long narrow stretch of beach was separated from dry ground by a shallow lake and adjoining swamp. Two bridges crossed from the shoreline to high ground. And so it was that the VII Corps carried out its rehearsals for the part it was to play on D-Day at Slapton Sands.

At the end of April, the entire VII Corps participated in Exercise Tiger. Easy Company rode in trucks to a resort hotel on the seashore at Torquay, where it spent a comfortable night. The next day, April 26, it was back into the trucks for a ride to an area back from Slapton Sands from which all civilians had been evacuated. The company slept in the field until midnight, when trucks brought the men forward to a simulated drop zone. After assembly, the company marched overland through a mist to an elevated point a mile back from the beach and set up a defensive position, guarding the bridge.

At dawn, Webster wrote, "We could see a vast fleet of amphibious craft moving slowly in to land. I've never seen so many ships together at one time; an invasion fleet is the most impressive sight in the world." What he had not seen was the disaster of the previous evening. German torpedo boats had slipped in among the LSTs and other big assault craft carrying the 4th Infantry. The Germans sank two LSTs and damaged others; more than 900 men drowned. The incident was covered up by the Allies for fear that it would hurt morale among the troops scheduled to go to France in LSTs (it remained covered up for more than forty years, evidently out of embarrassment).

Webster, watching the men of the 4th Infantry come up from the beach and pass through E Company's positions, noted that they were "sweating, cursing, panting." He also recorded that the officers informed the men that "we cannot write about our Torquay excursion." In the afternoon, the company made a 25-mile march, then bivouacked in a woods for the night. In the morning of April 28, it rode in trucks back to Aldbourne.

•   •   •

That weekend Malarkey, Chuck Grant, Skip Muck, and Joe Toye got passes to London, with Muck's best friend from Tonawanda, New York, Fritz Niland of the 501st PIR. There they met Niland's brother Bob, who was a squad leader in the 82d Airborne and who had seen action in North Africa and Sicily. They spent the evening in a pub listening to Bob Niland talk about combat. He made a remark that Malarkey never forgot: "If you want to be a hero, the Germans will make one out of you real quick—dead!" On the train going back to Aldbourne, Malarkey told Muck that it sounded to him like Bob Niland had lost his effectiveness.

• • •

Back in Aldbourne in the first week of May, E Company went through more problems, attacking gun positions, bridges, causeways, and other objectives, once attacking after a real jump, other times simulating the air flight and "jumping" out of trucks.

From May 9 to 12, the 101st held its dress rehearsal for D-Day, code name "Operation Eagle." The entire division participated. Easy used the same airfield it would use on D-Day, Uppottery. Personnel and equipment were loaded onto the same aircraft the company would use on the real thing; the takeoff, drop, and assembly followed the plan as close to the letter as possible, including spending the same amount of time in flight.[2]

Climbing aboard the C-47s was difficult, because of all the gear each man carried. Individuals were overloaded, following the age-old tendency of soldiers going into combat to attempt to be ready for every conceivable emergency. The vest and long drawers issued each man were impregnated, to ward off a pos-

---

[2]Leonard Rapport and Arthur Northwood, Jr., *Rendezvous with Destiny: A History of the 101st Airborne Division* (Fort Campbell, Ky.: 101st Airborne Division Association, 1948), 68–69.

sible chemical attack; it made them cumbersome, they stank, they itched, they kept in body heat and caused torrents of sweat. The combat jacket and trousers were also treated. The men carried a pocket knife in the lapel of their blouses, to be used to cut themselves out of their harness if they landed in a tree. In their baggy trousers' pockets they had a spoon, razor, socks, cleaning patches, flashlight, maps, three-day supply of K-rations, an emergency ration package (four chocolate bars, a pack of Charms, powdered coffee, sugar, and matches), ammunition, a compass, two fragmentation grenades, an antitank mine, a smoke grenade, a Gammon bomb (a two-pound plastic explosive for use against tanks), and cigarettes, two cartons per man. The soldier topped his uniform with a webbing belt and braces, a .45 pistol (standard for noncoms and officers; privates had to get their own, and most did), water canteen, shovel, first aid kit, and bayonet. Over this went his parachute harness, his main parachute in its backpack, and reserve parachute hooked on in front. A gas mask was strapped to his left leg and a jump-knife/bayonet to his right. Across his chest the soldier slung his musette bag with his spare underwear and ammunition, and in some cases TNT sticks, along with his broken-down rifle or machine-gun or mortar diagonally up-and-down across his front under his reserve chute pack, leaving both hands free to handle the risers. Over everything he wore his Mae West life jacket. Finally, he put on his helmet.

Some men added a third knife. Others found a place for extra ammunition. Gordon, carrying his machine-gun, figured he weighed twice his normal weight. Nearly every man had to be helped into the C-47.

Once aboard, the men were so wedged in they could not move.

General Taylor had moved heaven and earth to get enough C-47s for Operation Eagle. The planes were in constant demand for logistical support throughout ETO, and Troop Carrier Command came last on the list. It was cheated on equipment. The fuel tanks did not have armor protection from flak.

Easy got its briefing for Eagle on May 10–11. The objective was a gun battery covering the beach. At dusk on May 11, Easy took off. The planes made "legs" over England, flying for about two and a half hours. Shortly after midnight, the company jumped. For Easy, the exercise went smoothly; for other companies, there were troubles. Second Battalion headquarters company was with a group that ran into a German air raid over London. Flak was coming up; the formation broke up; the pilots could not locate the DZ. Eight of the nine planes carrying Company H of the 502d dropped their men on the village of Ramsbury, nine miles from the DZ. Twenty-eight planes returned to their airfields with the paratroopers still aboard. Others jumped willy-nilly, leading to many accidents. Nearly 500 men suffered broken bones, sprains, or other injuries.

The only consolation the airborne commanders could find in this mess was that by tradition a bad dress rehearsal leads to a great opening night.

• • •

On the last day of May, the company marched down to trucks lined up on the Hungerford Road. Half the people of Aldbourne, and nearly all the unmarried girls, were there to wave good-bye. There were many tears.

The baggage left behind gave some hope that the boys would be back.

Training had come to an end. There had been twenty-two months of it, more or less continuous. The men were as hardened physically as it was possible for human beings to be. Not even professional boxers or football players were in better shape. They were disciplined, prepared to carry out orders instantly and unquestioningly. They were experts in the use of their own weapon, knowledgeable in the use of other weapons, familiar with and capable of operating German weapons. They could operate radios, knew a variety of hand signals, could recognize various smoke signals. They were skilled in tactics, whether the problem was attacking a battery or a blockhouse or a trench system or a hill defended by machine-guns. Each man knew the duties and responsibilities of a squad or platoon leader and was prepared to assume those duties if necessary. They knew how to blow bridges, how to render artillery pieces inoperative. They could set up a defensive position in an instant. They could live in the field, sleep in a foxhole, march all day and through the night. They knew and trusted each other. Within Easy Company they had made the best friends they had ever had, or would ever have. They were prepared to die for each other; more important, they were prepared to kill for each other.

They were ready. But, of course, going into combat for the first time is an ultimate experience for which one can never be fully ready. It is anticipated for years in advance; it is a test that produces anxiety, eagerness, tension, fear of failure, anticipation. There is a mystery about the thing, heightened by the fact that those who have done it cannot put into words what it is like, how it feels, except that getting shot at and shooting to kill produce extraordinary emotional reactions. No matter how hard you train, nor however realistic the training, no one can ever be fully prepared for the intensity of the real thing.

And so the men of Easy Company left Aldbourne full of self-confidence and full of trepidation.

•   •   •

Easy's marshaling area in southwestern England, about 10 miles from the coast, was an open field beside the airstrip at Uppottery. The company lived in pyramidal tents. "Our standard of living went up considerably," Webster wrote. "We stuffed ourselves at the hospitable mess hall [a wall tent] ('Want some more, boys? Just help yourselves—take all you want.') on such luxuries as fried chicken, fruit cocktail, white bread with lots of butter. The realization that we were being fattened for the slaughter didn't stop us from going back for seconds."

Troops wearing German uniforms and carrying German weapons roamed constantly through the marshaling area, to familiarize the men with what the enemy looked like and what weapons they carried.

On June 2, the company officers got their briefings from former E Company officers, 1st Lieutenant Nixon (now 2d Battalion S-2) and Captain Hester (S-3). On sand tables that showed terrain features, houses, roads, dunes, and the rest, and on maps, Nixon and Hester explained that Easy would be dropping near Ste. Marie-du-Mont, about 10 kilometers south of Ste. Mère-Eglise, with the objective of killing the German garrison in the village and seizing the exit at causeway No. 2, the road coming up from the coast just north of the village of Pouppeville. The 3d platoon was given the task of blowing up a communications line leading inland from La Madeleine.

The detailed information given out by Nixon and Hester, and by other intelligence officers briefing other companies, was truly amazing. They passed around aerial photographs of the DZ that showed not only roads, buildings, and the like, but even foxholes. One member of the 506th recalled that his company was told that the German commandant at its objective, St. Côme-du-Mont, owned a white horse and was going with a French schoolteacher who lived on a side street just two buildings away from a German gun emplacement that was zeroed in on causeway No. 1. He took his dog for a walk every evening at 2000.[3]

Each officer had to learn the company mission by heart, know his own and every other platoon's mission to the most minute detail, and be able to draw a map of the whole area by memory. One point was made very clear, that the Germans relied less on their fixed coastal defenses than on their ability to counterattack. Mobile reserve units would start hitting the 4th Infantry wherever its units threatened to make it across the causeways. The briefers therefore impressed strongly on the officers that, regardless of where their platoons were or how many of their men they had managed to collect, if they spotted German units moving toward the causeways, they should fire upon them with everything they had. Even a five-minute delay thus imposed on the Germans could mean the difference between success and failure at Utah Beach. The importance of each mission was likewise emphasized, most effectively. Winters said, "I had the feeling that we were going in there and win the whole damn thing ourselves. It was our baby."

On June 3, Winters and the other platoon leaders walked their men through the briefing tent, showing them the sand tables and maps, telling them what they had learned.

•   •   •

Sergeant Guarnere needed to use the latrine. He grabbed a jacket and strolled over to the facility. Sitting down, he put his hand in a pocket and pulled out a letter. It was addressed to Sergeant Martin—Guarnere had taken Martin's jacket by mistake—but Guarnere read it anyway. Martin's wife was the author; they had been married in Georgia in 1942, and Mrs. Martin knew most of the members of the company. She wrote, "Don't tell Bill [Guarnere], but his brother was killed in Cas[s]ino, Italy."

"You can't imagine the *anger* I felt," Guarnere said later. "I swore that when I got to Normandy, there ain't no German going to be alive. I was like a maniac. When they sent me into France, they turned a killer loose, a wild man."

•   •   •

On June 4, Easy was issued its ammunition, $10 worth of new French francs just printed in Washington, an escape kit containing a silk map of France, a tiny brass compass, and a hacksaw. The men were given an American flag to sew on the right sleeves of their jump jackets. Officers removed their insignia from their uniforms and painted vertical stripes on the back of their helmets; N.C.O.s had horizontal stripes. Everyone was given the verbal challenge, "Flash," the password, "Thunder," and the response, "Welcome." They were also given small metal dime-store crickets, for alternative identification: one squeeze *(click-clack)* to be answered by two *(click-clack . . . click-clack)*.

The men spent the day cleaning weapons, sharpening knives, adjusting the parachutes, checking equipment over and over, chain-smoking cigarettes. Many of the men shaved their heads, or got Mohawk haircuts (bald on each side, with a one- or two-inch strip of short hair running from the forehead to the back of the neck). Pvts. Forrest Guth and Joseph Liebgott did the cutting, at 15¢ per man.

Colonel Sink came round, saw the haircutting going on, smiled, and said, "I forgot to tell you, some weeks ago we were officially notified that the Germans are telling French civilians that the Allied invasion forces would be led by American paratroopers, all of them convicted felons and psychopaths, easily recognized by the fact that they shave their heads or nearly so."

• • •

First Lt. Raymond Schmitz decided to ease the tension with some physical activity. He challenged Winters to a boxing match. "Come on, Winters, let's go out there behind the tents and box."

"No, go away."

Schmitz kept after him. Finally he said, "O.K., let's wrestle."

"Dammit, enough, you've been egging me long enough, let's go."

Winters had been a wrestler in college. He took

Schmitz down immediately, but he threw him too hard. Schmitz suffered two cracked vertebrae, went to the hospital, and did not get to go to Normandy. His assistant leader of the 3d platoon, 2d Lt. Robert Mathews, took his place, with Sergeant Lipton as his second in command. The rest of that day and night on up to the time the men strapped on their parachutes, Winters had a constant line of troopers asking him, with smiles on their faces, to break their arms or crack their vertebrae.

General Taylor circulated among the men. He told them, "Give me three days and nights of hard fighting, then you will be relieved." That sounded good. Three days and three nights, Winters thought to himself. I can take that. Taylor also said that when the C-47s crossed the coastline of France, he wanted every man to stand up; if a trooper got hit by flak, he wanted him to be standing and take it like a man. There was a point to the order that went beyond bravado; if a plane got hit the men hooked up and ready to jump would stand some chance of getting out. Taylor told Malarkey's platoon to fight with knives until daylight, "and don't take any prisoners."

That night, June 4, the company got an outstanding meal. Steak, green peas, mashed potatoes, white bread, ice cream, coffee, in unlimited quantities. It was their first ice cream since arriving in England nine months earlier. Sergeant Martin remembered being told, "When you get ice cream for supper, you know that's the night." But a terrific wind was blowing, and just as the men were preparing to march to their C-47s, they were told to stand down. Eisenhower had postponed the invasion because of the adverse weather.

Easy went to a wall tent to see a movie. Gordon

remembered that it was *Mr. Lucky*, starring Cary Grant and Laraine Day. Sergeants Lipton and Elmer Murray (the company operations sergeant) skipped the movie. They spent the evening discussing different combat situations that might occur and how they would handle them.

• • •

By the afternoon of June 5, the wind had died down, the sky cleared a bit. Someone found cans of black and green paint. Men began to daub their faces in imitation of the Sioux at the Little Bighorn, drawing streaks of paint down their noses and foreheads. Others took charcoal and blackened their faces.

At 2030 hours the men lined up by the planeload, eighteen to a group, and marched off to the hangars. "Nobody sang, nobody cheered," Webster wrote. "It was like a death march." Winters remembered going past some British antiaircraft units stationed at the field, "and that was the first time I'd ever seen any real emotion from a Limey, they actually had tears in their eyes."

At the hangars, each jumpmaster was given two packs of papers, containing an order of the day from Eisenhower and a message from Colonel Sink, to pass around to the men. "Tonight is the night of nights," said Sink's. "May God be with each of you fine soldiers." Eisenhower's began, "Soldiers, Sailors and Airmen of the Allied Expeditionary Force! You are about to embark upon the Great Crusade, toward which we have striven these many months. The eyes of the world are upon you. . . . Good Luck! And let us all beseech the blessing of Almighty God upon this great and noble undertaking."

In addition to the exhortations, the jumpmasters passed around airsickness pills. Who thought of the pills is a mystery; why they were passed around an even greater mystery, as airsickness had seldom been a problem.

Something else was new. The British airborne had come up with the idea of "leg bags." These bags contained extra ammunition, radios, machine-gun tripods, medical gear, high explosives, and other equipment. They were to be attached to individual paratroopers by a quick release mechanism and fastened to his parachute harness by a coiled 20-foot rope. When the chute opened, the trooper was supposed to hold the weight of the leg pack, pull its release to separate it from his leg, and let it down to the end of the rope. It would hit the ground before he did. In theory, the trooper would land on top of the bundle and not have to waste any time looking for his equipment. It seemed sensible, but no one in the American airborne had ever jumped with a leg bag. The Yanks liked the idea of the thing, and stuffed everything they could into those leg bags—mines, ammunition, broken-down Tommy guns, and more.

The men threw their kits, parachutes, and leg bags into the waiting trucks, climbed in themselves, and were driven out to the waiting planes.

"With that done," Winters wrote in his diary, "we went to work harnessing up. It's here that a good jumpmaster can do the most for his men. Getting all that equipment on, tied down, make it comfortable and safe, then a parachute over the top, calls for a lot of ingenuity and sales talk to satisfy the men that all's well."

Dressed for battle, they sat under the wings of the

planes, waiting. The nervousness increased. "This is the jump where your problems begin *after* you land," they told one another. It was the "$10,000 jump" (the men had $10,000 G.I. life insurance). Men struggled to their feet to go to the edge of the runway to relieve themselves, got back, sat down, and two minutes later repeated the process. Joe Toye recalled Lieutenant Meehan coming over to his plane to tell the men, "No prisoners. We are not taking any prisoners."

At 2200, mount up. The jumpmasters pushed their men up the steps, each of them carrying at least 100 pounds, many 150 pounds. One 101st trooper spoke for all 13,400 men in the two airborne divisions when he got to the door of his C-47, turned to the east, and called, "Look out, Hitler! Here we come!"

Sitting in his plane, company commander Thomas Meehan scribbled a short note to his wife. "Dearest Anne: In a few hours I'm going to take the best company of men in the world into France. We'll give the bastards hell. Strangely I'm not particularly scared but in my heart is a terrific longing to hold you in my arms.

"I love you Sweetheart—forever. Your Tom."

Meehan handed the note through the open door to a friend on the plane's crew and told him to get it to Anne.

On May 26, Meehan had written Anne a much longer letter in which he described why he, and all his men, were sitting in the planes, waiting to go into France to liberate it and conquer Nazi Germany. Among other things, he wrote, "We're fortunate in being Americans. At least we don't step on the underdog. I wonder if that's because there are no 'Americans'—only a stew of immigrants—or if it's because the earth from which we exist has been so kind to us and our fore-fathers; or if it's because the 'American' is the off-spring of the logical European who hated oppression and loved freedom beyond life? Those great mountains and the tall timber; the cool deep lakes and broad rivers; the green valleys and white farmhouses; the air, the sea and wind; the plains and great cities; the smell of living—all must be the cause of it. And yet, with all that, we can't get away from the rest. For every one of our millions who has that treasure in his hand there's another million crying for that victory of life. And for each of us who wants to live in happiness and give happiness, there's another different sort of person wanting to take it away . . .

"Those people always manage to have their say, and Mars is always close at hand. We know how to win wars. We must learn now to win peace . . . If I ever have a son, I don't want him to go through this again, but I want him powerful enough that no one will be fool enough to touch him. He and America should be strong as hell and kind as Christ."

At 2310 the C-47s began roaring down the runway. When they reached 1,000 feet, they began to circle, getting into a V of Vs formation, three planes to each V. As they straightened out for France, most of the men found it difficult to stay awake. This was the effect of those pills. Through that night, and into the next day, paratroopers had trouble staying awake. Joe Toye did fall asleep on his flight: "I was never so calm in all my life," he recalled. "Jesus, I was more excited on practice jumps."

On Winters's plane, Pvt. Joe Hogan tried to get a song going, but it was soon lost in the roar of the motors. On Gordon's plane, as on most, men were lost in their own thoughts or prayers. Pvt. Wayne Sisk of West Virginia broke the mood by calling out, "Does anybody here want to buy a good watch?" That brought a roar of laughter and a lessening of the tension.

Winters prayed the whole way over, prayed to live through it, prayed that he wouldn't fail. "Every man, I think, had in his mind, 'How will I react under fire?'"

•   •   •

With Lieutenant Schmitz in hospital, Sergeant Lipton was jumpmaster on his plane. The pilot gave the paratroopers a choice; they could ride with the door off, giving them fresh air and a chance to get out if the plane was hit, or ride with the door in place, which would allow them to smoke. They chose to take it off, which allowed Lipton to lie on the floor with his head partly out the door. Most of the men were asleep, or nearly so, a consequence of the airsickness pills.

As the C-47 crossed the Channel, Lipton saw a sight no one had ever seen before, nor would anyone ever see again, a sight that every man who was in the air that night never forgot: the invasion fleet, 6,000 vessels strong, heading toward Normandy.

Gordon Carson was with Lieutenant Welsh. As the plane crossed the Channel, Welsh told the men near the front, "Look down." They did, "and all you could see was wakes. No one ever saw so many ships and boats before." Carson commented, "You had to be a little bit awed that you were part of a thing that was so much greater than you."

•   •   •

At 0100, June 6, the planes passed between the islands of Guernsey and Jersey. In his plane, the pilot called back to Winters, "Twenty minutes out." The crew chief removed the door of the plane, giving Winters, standing No. 1, a rush of fresh air and a view of the coast. "Stand up and hook up," he called out. The red light went on.

At 0110, the planes passed over the coast and into a cloud bank. This caused the formation to break up. The lead V plowed straight ahead, but the Vs to each side veered off, the one to the right breaking away in that direction, the one on the left over the opposite way. This was the natural, inevitable reaction of the pilots, who feared midair collisions. When they broke out of the cloud bank, which was only a mile or two across, every pilot was on his own. Only the lead pilots had the device that would lead them to the Pathfinders' Eureka signals;[4] with the formation gone, none of the others knew when or where to turn on the green light. They could only guess.

Lost, bewildered, frightened, the pilots immediately had another worry. Antiaircraft fire began coming up at them, blue, green, and red tracers indicating its path. It was light stuff, 20 and 40 mm. When it hit the planes, it made a sound like rocks being shaken in a tin can. On Harry Welsh's plane, some ack-ack came through exactly where he had been sitting a minute before.

The pilots were supposed to slow down before turning on the green light, but as Gordon put it, "here they were thrust into the very jaws of this violence and they had never had one minute of combat experi-

---

[4]Pathfinders were specially trained volunteers who dropped in an hour ahead of the main body of troops to set up a radio beacon on the DZ to guide the lead plane. Easy's Pathfinders were Cpl. Richard Wright and Pvt. Carl Fenstermaker.

ence, so they were absolutely terrified. And rather than throttle down, they were kind of like a fellow thinking with his feet, they thought with that throttle. And they said, 'My God, common sense will tell me the quicker I get out of here, the better chance I have of surviving, and that's unfortunate for the boys back there, but be that as it may, I'm getting out of here.'"

So they increased speed, up to 150 miles per hour in many cases, and although they did not have the slightest idea where they were, except that it was somewhere over Normandy, they hit the green light.

Men began shouting, "Let's go, let's go." They wanted out of those planes; never had they thought they would be so eager to jump. Lipton's plane was "bouncing and weaving, and the men were yelling, 'Let's get out of here!'" They were only 600 feet up, the 40 mm antiaircraft tracers coming closer and closer. "About the time the tracers were popping right past the tail of the plane," Lipton remembered, "the green light went on." He leaped out. Pvt. James Alley was No. 2, Pvt. Paul Rogers No. 3. Alley had been told to throw his leg bag out the door and follow it into the night. He did as told and ended up flat on the floor with his head and half his body out of the plane, his bag dangling in the air, about to pull him in half. Rogers, who was "strong as a bull," threw him out the door and jumped right behind.

Leo Boyle was the last man in the stick on his plane. There was this "tremendous turbulence" as the green light went on and the men began leaping out into the night. The plane lurched. Boyle was thrown violently down to the floor. The plane was flying at a tilt. Boyle had to reach up for the bottom of the door, pull himself to it, and roll out of the C-47 into the night.

Tracers were everywhere. The lead plane in stick 66, flown by Lt. Harold Cappelluto, was hit with bullets going through it and out the top, throwing sparks. The plane maintained course and speed for a moment or two, then did a slow wingover to the right. Pilot Frank DeFlita, just behind, remembered that "Cappelluto's landing lights came on, and it appeared they were going to make it, when the plane hit a hedgerow and exploded." It was the plane carrying Lieutenant Meehan, 1st Sergeant Evans, and the rest of the company headquarters section, including Sergeant Murray, who had held that long talk with Lipton about how to handle different combat situations. He never got to experience any of the possibilities he and Lipton had tried to visualize.

Easy Company had not put one man into combat yet, and it had already lost platoon leader Schmitz, company commander Meehan, and its first sergeant.

• • •

Pvt. Rod Strohl was one of those so overloaded that he could not put on his reserve chute. "I remember thinking, well, hell, if you need it, and it doesn't open, it's going to be over in a hurry, and if you don't need it, you don't need it." His plane got hit and started going down. As his stick went out, "the pilot and copilot came out with us."

• • •

George Luz was on Welsh's plane. He had barely made it, as in addition to all the regular gear he was carrying a radio and batteries, and had been unable to get into the plane until a bunch of Air Corps guys pushed him in. Once inside, he had turned to Welsh to say, "Lieutenant, you got me fifth man in the stick, and I'll never make it to the door." So Welsh had told him to change places with Pvt. Roy Cobb. When the flak started ("You could walk on it," Luz remembered; Carson said, "We wanted to get out of there so damn bad it was unbelievable") Cobb called out, "I'm hit!"

"Can you stand up?" Welsh shouted.

"I can't."

"Unhook him," Welsh ordered. Mike Ranney unhooked Cobb from the static line. (Private Rader recalled, "Cobb was some pissed. To have trained so hard for two years and not get to make the big jump was hell.") Just then the red light went on, flashed a second, and was hit by flak. "I had no way of telling anything," Welsh recalled, "so I said 'Go' and jumped." Luz kicked his leg bag containing the radio and other equipment out the door and leaped into the night.

Thus did 13,400 of America's finest youth, who had been training for this moment for two years, hurl themselves against Hitler's Fortress Europe.

5

"Follow Me"

NORMANDY

June 6, 1944

THEY JUMPED MUCH TOO LOW from planes that were flying much too fast. They were carrying far too much equipment and using an untested technique that turned out to be a major mistake. As they left the plane, the leg bags tore loose and hurtled to the ground, in nearly every case never to be seen again. Simultaneously, the prop blast tossed them this way and that. With all the extra weight and all the extra speed, when the chutes opened, the shock was more than they had ever experienced. Jumping at 500 feet, and even less, they hit the ground within seconds of the opening of the chute, so they hit hard. The men were black and blue for a week or more afterward as a result.

In a diary entry written a few days later, Lieutenant Winters tried to re-create his thoughts in those few seconds he was in the air: "We're doing 150 MPH.

O.K., let's go. G-D, there goes my leg pack and every bit of equipment I have. Watch it, boy! Watch it! J-C, they're trying to pick me up with those machine-guns. Slip, slip, try and keep close to that leg pack. There it lands beside the hedge. G-D that machine-gun. There's a road, trees—hope I don't him them. Thump, well that wasn't too bad, now let's get out of this chute."

Burt Christenson jumped right behind Winters. "I don't think I did anything I had been trained to do, but suddenly I got a tremendous shock when my parachute opened." His leg bag broke loose and "it was history." He could hear a bell ringing in Ste. Mère-Eglise, and see a fire burning in town. Machine-gun bullets "are gaining on me. I climb high into my risers. Christ, I'm headed for that line of trees. I'm descending too rapidly." As he passed over the trees, he pulled his legs up to avoid hitting them. "A moment of terror seized me. 70 ft. below and 20 ft. to my left, a German quad-mounted 20 mm antiaircraft gun is firing on the C-47s passing overhead." Lucky enough for Christenson, the Germans' line of fire was such that their backs were to him, and the noise was such that they never heard him hit, although he was only 40 yards or so away.

Christenson cut himself out of his chute, pulled his six-shot revolver, and crouched at the base of an apple tree. He stayed still, moving only his eyes.

"Suddenly I caught movement ten yards away, a silhouette of a helmeted man approaching on all fours. I reached for my cricket and clicked it once, *click-clack*. There was no response. The figure began to move toward me again."

Christenson pointed his revolver at the man's chest and *click-clacked* again. The man raised his hands. "For Christ sake, don't shoot." It was Pvt. Woodrow

Robbins, Christenson's assistant gunner on the machine-gun.

"You dumb shit, what the hell's wrong with you? Why didn't you use your cricket?" Christenson demanded in a fierce whisper.

"I lost the clicker part of the cricket."

Slowly the adrenaline drained from Christenson's brain, and the two men began backing away from the German position. They ran into Bill Randleman, who had a dead German at his feet. Randleman related that the moment he had gotten free of his chute he had fixed his bayonet. Suddenly a German came charging, his bayonet fixed. Randleman knocked the weapon aside, then impaled the German on his bayonet. "That Kraut picked the wrong guy to play bayonets with," Christenson remarked.

• • • •

Lieutenant Welsh's plane was at 250 feet, "at the most," when he jumped. As he emerged from the C-47, another plane crashed immediately beneath him. He claimed that the blast from the explosion threw him up and to the side "and that saved my life." His chute opened just in time to check his descent just enough to make the "thump" when he landed painful but not fatal.

Most of the men of Easy had a similar experience. Few of them were in the air long enough to orient themselves with any precision, although they could tell from the direction the planes were flying which was the way to the coast.

They landed to hell and gone. The tight pattern within the DZ near Ste. Marie-du-Mont that they had hoped for, indeed had counted on for quick assembly of the company, was so badly screwed up by the evasive action the pilots had taken when they hit the cloud bank that E Company men were scattered from Carentan to Ravenoville, a distance of 20 kilometers. The Pathfinders, Richard Wright and Carl Fenstermaker, came down in the Channel after their plane was hit (they were picked up by H.M.S. *Tartar*, transferred to Air Sea Rescue, and taken to England).

Pvt. Tom Burgess came down near Ste. Mère-Eglise. Like most of the paratroopers that night, he did not know where he was. Low-flying planes roared overhead, tracers chasing after them, the sky full of descending Americans, indistinct and unidentifiable figures dashing or creeping through the fields, machineguns *pop-pop-popping* all around. After cutting himself out of his chute with his pocketknife, he used his cricket to identify himself to a lieutenant he did not know. Together they started working their way toward the beach, hugging the ubiquitous hedgerows. Other troopers joined them, some from the 82d (also badly scattered in the jump), some from different regiments of the 101st. They had occasional, brief firefights with German patrols.

The lieutenant made Burgess the lead scout. At first light, he came to a corner of the hedgerow he was following. A German soldier hiding in the junction of hedgerows rose up. Burgess didn't see him. The German fired, downward. The bullet hit Burgess's cheekbone, went through the right cheek, fractured it, tore away the hinge of the jaw, and came out the back of his neck. Blood squirted out his cheek, from the back of his neck, and from his ear. He nearly choked to death.

"I wanted to live," Burgess recalled forty-five years

later. "They had hammered into us that the main thing if you get hit is don't get excited, the worst thing you can do is go nuts." So he did his best to stay calm. The guys with him patched him up as best they could, got bandages over the wounds, and helped him into a nearby barn, where he collapsed into the hay. He passed out.

At midnight, a French farmer "came out to the barn and sat there and held my hand. He even kissed my hand." He brought a bottle of wine. On the morning of June 7, the farmer fetched two medics and lent them a horse-drawn cart, which they used to take Burgess down to the beach. He was evacuated to England, then back to the States. He arrived in Boston on New Year's Eve, 1944. He was on a strictly liquid diet until March 1945, when he took his first bite of solid food since his last meal at Uppottery, June 5, 1944.

•   •   •

Private Gordon hit hard. He had no idea where he was, but he had a definite idea of what he was determined to do first—assemble his machine-gun. He tucked himself into a hedgerow and did the job. As he finished, "I noticed this figure coming, and I realized it was John Eubanks from the way he walked." Shortly thereafter Forrest Guth joined them. Another figure loomed in the dark. "Challenge him," Gordon said to Eubanks. Before Eubanks could do so, the man called out, "Flash." Eubanks forgot the countersign ("Thunder") and forgot that the clicker was an alternative identification option, and instead said, "Lightning." The man lobbed a grenade in on the three E Company men. They scattered, it went off, fortunately no one was hurt, the soldier disappeared, which was probably good for the group, as he was clearly much too nervous to trust.

Gordon, Eubanks, and Guth started moving down a hedgerow toward the beach. They saw an American paratrooper run through the field, crouch, and jump into a drainage ditch (there was a three-quarters moon that night, and few clouds over the land, so visibility was fair). Gordon told the others to stay still, he would check it out. He crept to the ditch, where "I encountered these two eyeballs looking up at me and the muzzle of a pistol right in my face."

"Gordon, is that you?" It was Sgt. Floyd Talbert. Now there were four. Together they continued creeping, crawling, moving toward the beach. A half-hour or so before first light, Guth heard what he was certain was the howling and whining of a convoy of 2½ ton G.I. trucks going past. How could that be? The seaborne invasion hadn't even started, much less put truck convoys ashore. Some tremendous bursts coming from inland answered the question: the noise Guth heard came from the shells passing overhead, shells from the 16-inch naval guns on the battleships offshore.

The E Company foursome joined up with a group from the 502d that had just captured a German strong point in a large farm complex that dominated the crossroads north of the beach at Ravenoville. They spent the day defending the fortress from counterattacks. In the morning of D-Day plus one, they set out southward in search of their company.

•   •   •

Jim Alley crashed into a wall behind a house, one of those French walls with broken glass imbedded in the top. He was cut and bleeding in several places. He backed into the corner of a garden and was in the process of cutting himself out of the harness when someone grabbed his arm. It was a young woman, standing in the bushes.

"Me American," Alley whispered. "Go vay, go vay." She went back into her house.

Alley found his leg pack, got his gear together (thirteen rounds of 60 mm mortar ammunition, four land mines, ammunition for his M-1, hand grenades, food, the base plate for the mortar, and other stuff), climbed to the top of the wall, and drew machine-gun fire. It was about a foot low. He got covered with plaster before he could fall back into the garden.

He lay down to think about what to do. He ate one of his Hershey bars and decided to go out the front way. Before he could move, the young woman came out of the house, looked at him, and proceeded out the front gate. Alley figured, "This is it. I'll make my stand here." Soon she returned. A soldier stepped through the gate after her. "I had my gun on him and he had his on me." They recognized each other; he was from the 505th.

"Where the hell am I?" Alley demanded. He was told, "Ste. Mère-Eglise." He joined up with the 505th. At about daybreak he ran into Paul Rogers and Earl McClung from Easy. They spent the day, and the better part of the week that followed, fighting with the 505th.

All across the peninsula, throughout the night and into the day of D-Day, paratroopers were doing the same—fighting skirmishes, joining together in ad hoc units, defending positions, harassing the Germans, trying to link up with their units. This was exactly what they had been told to do. Their training and confidence thus overcame what could have been a disaster, and thereby turned the scattered drop from a negative into a plus. The Germans, hearing reports of action here, there, everywhere, grossly overestimated the number of troopers they were dealing with, and therefore acted in a confused and hesitant manner.

• • •

Winters had come down on the edge of Ste. Mère-Eglise. He could see the big fire near the church, hear the church bell calling out the citizens to fight the fire. He could not find his leg bag. The only weapon he had was his bayonet, stuck into his boot. His first thought was to get away from the machine-gun and small arms fire in the church square. Just as he started off, a trooper landed close by. Winters helped him out of his chute, got a grenade from him, and said, "Let's go back and find my leg bag." The trooper hesitated. "Follow me," Winters ordered and started off. A machine-gun opened up on them. "To hell with the bag," Winters said. He set out to the north to bypass Ste. Mère-Eglise before turning east to the coast. In a few minutes, he saw some figures and used his cricket. He got a reassuring double *click-clack* from Sergeant Lipton.

Lipton had landed in a walled-in area behind the *hôtel de ville* (city hall) in Ste. Mère-Eglise, a block from the church. Like Winters, he had lost his weapon when he lost his leg bag. In his musette bag he had two grenades and a demolitions kit, plus his trench knife. He climbed over a gate and worked his way down the street, away from the church and the fire. At the edge of town there was a low, heavy concrete signpost with the name of the village on it. Lipton put his face up close to the letters and moved along them, reading them one by one, until he knew that the sign read "Ste. Mère-Eglise."

Paratroopers were coming down around him. Not wanting to get shot by a nervous American, when he saw two coming down close together, he ran right under them. When they hit the ground, before they could even think about shooting, Lipton was already talking to them. They were from the 82d Airborne, 10 kilometers away from where they were supposed to be. Sergeant Guarnere joined up, along with Don Malarkey, Joe Toye, and Popeye Wynn. A few minutes later, Lipton ran into Winters.

"I saw a road sign down there," Lipton reported. "Ste. Mère-Eglise."

"Good," Winters answered. "I know where that is. I can take it from here." He set out at the head of the group, objective Ste. Marie-du-Mont. They joined a bunch from the 502d. About 0300 hours they spotted a German patrol, four wagons coming down the road. They set up an ambush, and there Guarnere got his first revenge for his brother, as he blasted the lead wagons. The other two got away, but E Company took a few prisoners.

A German machine-gun opened fire on the group. When it did, the prisoners tried to jump the Americans. Guarnere shot them with his pistol. "No remorse," he said when describing the incident forty-seven years later. "No pity. It was as easy as stepping on a bug." After a pause, he added, "We are different people now than we were then."

At about 0600 hours they ran into Capt. Jerre Gross of D Company and forty of his men. They joined forces to head toward Ste. Marie-du-Mont, some 8 kilometers southeast. In a few minutes they ran into the 2d Battalion staff with about forty more men. Winters found an M-1, then a revolver, belt, canteen, and lots of ammunition, "so I was feeling ready to fight—especially after I bummed some food from one of the boys." Lipton found a carbine. The others armed themselves.

• • •

As the Americans moved toward Ste. Marie-du-Mont, so did the commander of the German unit defending the area, Col. Frederick von der Heydte of the 6th Parachute Regiment. He was an experienced soldier, having been in the German Army since the mid-1920s and having led men in combat in Poland, France, Russia, Crete, and North Africa. Colonel von der Heydte was the senior German officer present, as the division commanders were in Rennes, on the Seine River, for a war game. He had one battalion in and around Ste. Mère-Eglise, another near Ste. Marie-du-Mont, the third in Carentan. All his platoons were standing too, some were trying to engage the Americans, but confusion caused by reports of landings here, there, seemingly everywhere had made concerted counterattacks impossible.

Colonel von der Heydte wanted to see for himself. He drove his motorcycle from Carentan to Ste. Marie-du-Mont, where he climbed to the top of the church steeple, 50 or 60 meters above the ground. There he had a magnificent view of Utah Beach.

What he saw quite took his breath away. "All along the beach," he recalled in a 1991 interview, "were these small boats, hundreds of them, each disgorging thirty or forty armed men. Behind them were the warships, blasting away with their huge guns, more warships in one fleet than anyone had ever seen before."

Around the church, in the little village and beyond in the green fields crisscrossed by hedgerows, all was quiet. The individual firefights of the night had tapered off with the coming of light. Von der Heydte could see neither American nor German units.

Climbing down from the steeple, the colonel drove his motorcycle a couple of kilometers north to Brécourt Manor, where the German artillery had a battery of four 105 mm cannon dug in and camouflaged. There were no artillery men around; evidently they had scattered in the night after the airborne landings began. Von der Heydte roared back to Carentan, where he ordered his 1st Battalion to occupy and hold Ste. Marie-du-Mont and Brécourt, and to find some artillerymen to get that battery working. It was perfectly placed to lob shells on the landing craft on Utah Beach, and to engage the warships out in the Channel.

• • •

By this time, about 0700, E Company consisted of two light machine-guns, one bazooka (no ammunition), one 60 mm mortar, nine riflemen, and two officers. As the 2d Battalion moved into a group of houses in a tiny village called Le Grand-Chemin, just three kilometers or so short of Ste. Marie-du-Mont, it drew heavy fire from up front. The column stopped; Winters and his men sat down to rest. Ten or fifteen minutes later, battalion S-1 Lt. George Lavenson, formerly of E Company, came walking down the road. "Winters," he said, "they want you up front."

Captain Hester, S-3, and Lieutenant Nixon, S-2,

both close friends of Winters, told him there was a four-gun battery of German 105 mm cannon a few hundred meters across some hedgerows and open fields, opposite a large French farmhouse called Brécourt Manor. Intelligence had not spotted the cannon, as they were dug into the hedgerow, connected by an extensive trench system, covered by brush and trees. There was a fifty-man platoon of infantry defending the position (part of Colonel von der Heydt's 1st Battalion); the cannon had just gone into action, firing on Utah Beach, some 4 or 5 kilometers to the northeast.

The 2d Battalion was less than 100 men strong at that point. Lieutenant Colonel Strayer had responsibilities in all four directions from Le Grand-Chemin. He was trying to build his battalion up to somewhere near its full strength of 600 men, and to defend from counterattacks. He could only afford to send one company to attack the German battery. Hester told Winters to take care of that battery.

• • •

It was 0830. Captain Sobel was about to get a little revenge on Hitler, the U.S. Army was about to get a big payoff from its training and equipment investment, the American people were about to get their reward for having raised such fine young men. The company that Sobel and the Army and the country had brought into being and trained for this moment was going into action.

• • •

Winters went to work instinctively and immediately. He told the men of E Company to drop all the equipment they were carrying except weapons, ammunition, and grenades. He explained that the attack would be a quick frontal assault supported by a base of fire from different positions as close to the guns as possible. He set up the two machine-guns to give covering fire as he moved the men forward to their jump-off positions.

The field in which the cannon were located was irregular in shape, with seven acute angles in the hedgerow surrounding it. This gave Winters an opportunity to hit the Germans from different directions.

Winters placed his machine-guns (manned by Pvts. John Plesha and Walter Hendrix on one gun, Cleveland Petty and Joe Liebgott on the other) along the hedge leading up to the objective, with instructions to lay down covering fire. As Winters crawled forward to the jump-off position, he spotted a German helmet—the man was moving down the trench, crouched over, with only his head above ground. Winters took aim with his M-1 and squeezed off two shots, killing the Jerry.

Winters told Lieutenant Compton to take Sergeants Guarnere and Malarkey, get over to the left, crawl through the open field, get as close to the first gun in the battery as possible, and throw grenades into the trench. He sent Sergeants Lipton and Ranney out along the hedge to the right, alongside a copse of trees, with orders to put a flanking fire into the enemy position.

Winters would lead the charge straight down the hedge. With him were Pvts. Gerald Lorraine (of regimental HQ; he was Colonel Sink's jeep driver) and Popeye Wynn and Cpl. Joe Toye.

Here the training paid off. "We fought as a team

without standout stars," Lipton said. "We were like a machine. We didn't have anyone who leaped up and charged a machine-gun. We knocked it out or made it withdraw by maneuver and teamwork or mortar fire. We were smart; there weren't many flashy heroics. We had learned that heroics was the way to get killed without getting the job done, and getting the job done was more important."

When Ranney and Lipton moved out along the hedge, they discovered they could not see the German positions because of low brush and ground cover. Lipton decided to climb a tree, but there were none of sufficient size to allow him to fire from behind a trunk. The one he picked had many small branches; he had to sit precariously on the front side, facing the Germans, exposed if they looked his way, balancing on several branches. About 75 meters away, he could see about fifteen of the enemy, some in the trenches, others prone in the open, firing toward E Company, too intent on the activity to their front to notice Lipton.

Lipton was armed with a carbine he had picked up during the night. He fired at a German in the field. The enemy soldier seemed to duck. Lipton fired again. His target did not move. Not certain that the carbine had been zeroed in, Lipton aimed into the dirt just under the man's head and squeezed off another round. The dirt flew up right where he aimed; Lipton now knew that the carbine's sights were right and his first shot had killed the man. He began aiming and firing as fast as he could from his shaky position.

Lieutenant Compton was armed with a Thompson submachine-gun that he had picked up during the night (he got it from a lieutenant from D Company who had broken his leg in the jump). Using all his athletic skill, he successfully crawled through the open field to the hedge, Guarnere and Malarkey alongside him. The Germans were receiving fire from the machine-gun to their left, from Lipton and Ranney to their rear, and from Winters's group in their front. They did not notice Compton's approach.

When he reached the hedge, Compton leaped over and through it. He had achieved complete surprise and had the German gun crew and infantry dead in his sights. But when he pulled the trigger on the borrowed tommy-gun, nothing happened. It was jammed.

At that instant, Winters called, "Follow me," and the assault team went tearing down the hedge toward Compton. Simultaneously, Guarnere leaped into the trench beside Compton. The German crew at the first gun, under attack from three directions, fled. The infantry retreated with them, tearing down the trench, away from Compton, Guarnere, and Malarkey. The Easy Company men began throwing grenades at the retreating enemy.

Compton had been an All-American catcher on the UCLA baseball team. The distance to the fleeing enemy was about the same as from home plate to second base. Compton threw his grenade on a straight line—no arch—and it hit a German in the head as it exploded. He, Malarkey, and Guarnere then began lobbing grenades down the trench.

Winters and his group were with them by now, firing their rifles, throwing grenades, shouting, their blood pumping, adrenaline giving them Superman strength.

Wynn was hit in the butt and fell down in the trench, hollering over and over, "I'm sorry, Lieutenant, I goofed off, I goofed off, I'm sorry." A German potato masher sailed into the trench; everyone dived to the ground.

"Joe, look out!" Winters called to Toye. The grenade had landed between his legs as he lay face down. Toye flipped over. The potato masher hit his rifle and tore up the stock as it exploded, but he was uninjured. "If it wasn't for Winters," Toye said in 1990, "I'd be singing high soprano today."

Winters tossed some grenades down the trench, then went tearing after the retreating gun crew. Private Lorraine and Sergeant Guarnere were with him. Three of the enemy infantry started running cross-country, away toward Brécourt Manor.

"Get 'em!" Winters yelled. Lorraine hit one with his tommy-gun; Winters aimed his M-1, squeezed, and shot his man through the back of his head. Guarnere missed the third Jerry, but Winters put a bullet in his back. Guarnere followed that up by pumping the wounded man full of lead from his tommy-gun. The German kept yelling, "Help! Help!" Winters told Malarkey to put one through his head.

A fourth German jumped out of the trench, about 100 yards up the hedge. Winters saw him, lay down, took careful aim, and killed him. Fifteen or twenty seconds had passed since he had led the charge. Easy had taken the first gun.

Winters's immediate thought was that there were plenty of Germans farther up the trench, and they would be counterattacking soon. He flopped down, crawled forward in the trench, came to a connecting trench, looked down, "and sure enough there were two of them setting up a machine-gun, getting set to fire. I got in the first shot and hit the gunner in the hip; the second caught the other boy in the shoulder."

Winters put Toye and Compton to firing toward the next gun, sent three other men to look over the captured cannon, and three to cover to the front. By this time Lipton had scrambled out of his tree and was working his way to Winters. Along the way he stopped to sprinkle some sulfa powder on Wynn's butt and slap on a bandage. Wynn continued to apologize for goofing off. Warrant Officer Andrew Hill, from regimental HQ, came up behind Lipton.

"Where's regimental HQ?" he shouted.

"Back that way," Lipton said, pointing to the rear. Hill raised his head to look. A bullet hit him in the forehead and came out behind his ear, killing him instantly.

After that, all movement was confined to the trench system, and in a crouch, as German machine-gun fire was nearly continuous, cutting right across the top of the trench. But Malarkey saw one of the Germans killed by Winters, about 30 yards out in the field, with a black case attached to his belt. Malarkey thought it must be a Luger. He wanted it badly, so he ran out into the field, only to discover that it was a leather case for the 105 mm sight. Winters was yelling at him, "Idiot, this place is crawling with Krauts, get back here!" Evidently the Germans thought Malarkey was a medic; in any case the machine-gunners did not turn on him until he started running back to the trench. With bullets kicking up all around him, he dived under the 105.

Winters was at the gun, wanting to disable it but without a demolition kit. Lipton came up and said he had one in his musette bag, which was back where the attack began. Winters told him to go get it.

Time for the second gun, Winters thought to himself. He left three men behind to hold the first gun, then led the other five on a charge down the trench, throwing grenades ahead of them, firing their rifles. They passed the two Jerries at the machine-gun who had been wounded by Winters and made them prisoners. The gun crew at the second gun fell back; Easy took it with only one casualty.

With the second gun in his possession, and running low on ammunition, Winters sent back word for the four machine-gunners to come forward. Meanwhile six German soldiers decided they had had enough; they came marching down the connecting trench to the second gun, hands over their heads, calling out "No make dead! No make dead!"

Pvt. John D. Hall of A Company joined the group. Winters ordered a charge on the third gun. Hall led the way, and got killed, but the gun was taken. Winters had three of his men secure it. With eleven men, he now controlled three 105s.

At the second gun site, Winters found a case with documents and maps showing the positions of all the guns and machine-gun positions throughout the Cotentin Peninsula. He sent the documents and maps back to battalion, along with the prisoners and a request for more ammunition and some reinforcements, because "we were stretched out too much for our own good." Using grenades, he set about destroying the gun crews' radio, telephone, and range finders.

Captain Hester came up, bringing three blocks of TNT and some phosphorus incendiary grenades. Winters had a block dropped down the barrel of each of the three guns, followed by a German potato-masher grenade. This combination blew out the breeches of the guns like half-peeled bananas. Lipton was disappointed when he returned with his demolition kit to discover that it was not needed.

Reinforcements arrived, five men led by Lt. Ronald Speirs of D Company. One of them, "Rusty" Houch of F Company, raised up to throw a grenade into the gun positions and was hit several times across the back and shoulders by a burst from a machine-gun. He died instantly.

Speirs led an attack on the final gun, which he took and destroyed, losing two men killed.

Winters then ordered a withdrawal, because the company was drawing heavy machine-gun fire from the hedges near Brécourt Manor, and with the guns destroyed there was no point to holding the position. The machine-gunners pulled back first, followed by the riflemen. Winters was last. As he was leaving he took a final look down the trench. "Here was this one wounded Jerry we were leaving behind trying to put a MG on us again, so I drilled him clean through the head." It was 1130. About three hours had passed since Winters had received the order to take care of those guns.

•　•　•

With twelve men, what amounted to a squad (later reinforced by Speirs and the others), Company E had destroyed a German battery that was looking straight down causeway No. 2 and onto Utah Beach. That battery had a telephone line running to a forward observer who was in a pillbox located at the head of causeway No. 2. He had been calling shots down on the 4th Infantry as it unloaded. The significance of what Easy Company had accomplished cannot be judged with any degree of precision, but it surely saved a lot of lives, and made it much easier—perhaps even made it possible in the first instance—for tanks to come inland from the beach. It would be a gross exaggeration to say that Easy Company saved the day at Utah Beach, but reasonable to say that it made an important contribution to the success of the invasion.

Winters's casualties were four dead, two wounded. He and his men had killed fifteen Germans, wounded many more, and taken twelve prisoners; in short, they had wiped out the fifty-man platoon of elite German paratroops defending the guns, and scattered the gun crews. In an analysis written in 1985, Lipton said, "The attack was a unique example of a small, well-led assault force overcoming and routing a much larger defending force in prepared positions. It was the high morale of the E Company men, the quickness and audacity of the frontal attack, and the fire into their positions from several different directions that demoralized the German forces and convinced them that they were being hit by a much larger force."

There were other factors, including the excellent training the company had received, and that this was their baptism of fire. The men had taken chances they would not take in the future. Lipton said he never would have climbed that tree and so exposed himself had he been a veteran. "But we were so full of fire that day."

"You don't realize, your first time," Guarnere said. "I'd never, never do again what I did that morning." Compton would not have burst through that hedge had he been experienced. "I was sure I would not be killed," Lipton said. "I felt that if a bullet was headed for me it would be deflected or I would move."

(Paul Fussell, in *Wartime*, writes that the soldier going into combat the first time thinks to himself, "It *can't* happen to me. I am too clever / agile / well-trained / good-looking / beloved / tightly laced, etc." That feeling soon gives way to "It *can* happen to me, and I'd better be more careful. I can avoid the danger by watching more prudently the way I take cover / dig in / expose my position by firing my weapon / keep extra alert at all times, etc."[1]

In his analysis, Winters gave credit to the Army for having prepared him so well for this moment ("my apogee," he called it). He had done everything right, from scouting the position to laying down a base of covering fire, to putting his best men (Compton, Guarnere, and Malarkey in one group, Lipton and Ranney in the other) on the most challenging missions, to leading the charge personally at exactly the right moment.

Winters felt that if Sobel had been in command, he would have led all thirteen men on a frontal assault and lost his life, along with the lives of most of the men. Who can say he was wrong about that? But then, who can say that the men of Easy would have had the discipline, the endurance (they had been marching since 0130, after a night of little or no real sleep; they were battered and bruised from the opening shock and the hard landing) or the weapons skills to carry off this fine feat of arms, had it not been for Sobel?

Sink put Winters in for the Congressional Medal of Honor. Only one man per division was to be given that ultimate medal for the Normandy campaign; in the 101st it went to Lt. Col. Robert Cole for leading a bay-

---

[1]Fussell, *Wartime*, 282.

onet charge; Winters received the Distinguished Service Cross. Compton, Guarnere, Lorraine, and Toye got the Silver Star; Lipton, Malarkey, Ranney, Liebgott, Hendrix, Plesha, Petty, and Wynn got Bronze Stars.

•   •   •

A month or so later, Winters was called into regimental HQ. Sink, Strayer, and the staff were sitting in a tent. At the head of a table was S. L. A. Marshall, the Army's combat historian. The atmosphere around the table was "electric," Winters remembered. "Those West Pointers would have 'killed' to have the opportunity I had to be sitting in the chair across from Marshall."

"O.K., Lieutenant," Marshall said, "tell me what you did out there on D-Day. You took that battery of 105s, didn't you?"

"Yes, sir, that's right."

"Tell me how you did it."

"Well, sir, I put down a base of fire, we moved in under the base of fire, and we took the first gun. And then we put down another base of fire and we moved to the second gun and the third gun and the fourth gun."

"O.K., anything else?"

"No, sir, that's basically it." As a junior officer facing all that brass, Winters figured he had better not lay it on too thick. So he made it sound like a routine training problem.

When Marshall wrote his book *Night Drop*, to Winters's disgust he left out Easy Company, except to say "the deployed [2d] battalion had kept the German battery entertained at long range. . . ." He did give a full account of the capture of a battery at Holdy, near causeway No. 1, by the 1st Battalion, 506th. Marshall wrote that the battalion had 195 men lined up to take the battery. Winters commented, "With that many E Co. men, I could have taken Berlin!"[2]

•   •   •

At about 1215, Sgt. Leo Boyle joined up. He had been dropped in the 82d's DZ, gotten lost, figured out where he was, marched toward Ste. Marie-du-Mont, and found his company. "The first man I met was Winters. He was tired. I reported in to him. He grunted and that's all I got out of him. I thought maybe he'd be a little more happy to see me, but he'd been under tremendous stress."

The men were congratulating one another, talking about what they had accomplished, trying to piece together the sequence of events. They were the victors, happy, proud, full of themselves. Someone found some cider in a cellar. It got passed around. When the jug got to Winters, he decided he was "thirsty as hell, and needed a lift." He shocked his men by taking a long pull, the first alcohol he had ever tasted. "I thought at the time it might slow down my thoughts and reactions, but it didn't."

Lieutenant Welsh reported for duty. He had been in various firefights alongside some men from the 82d. In his backpack he was carrying his reserve parachute; he

---

[2]S. L. A. Marshall, *Night Drop: The American Airborne Invasion of Normandy* (Boston: Little, Brown, 1962), 281–86. Marshall has come in for considerable criticism for the mistakes in his work, especially from paratroopers who were there. I have sympathy for him; writing accurately about a battle for which you have conflicting testimony from the eyewitnesses and participants is a challenge, and then some. Military historians do the best they can.

carried it throughout the Normandy campaign. "I wanted to send it back to Kitty to make a wedding gown for our marriage after the war. (Optimism?)"

German machine-gun fire from the hedgerow across the road from Brécourt Manor was building up. Winters put his machine-gunners to answering with some harassing fire of their own. Malarkey found his mortar tube, but not the base plate or tripod. Setting the tube on the ground, he fired a dozen rounds toward the Manor. Guarnere joined him, working another mortar tube. They discovered later that every round hit its target. "That kind of expertise you don't teach," Winters commented. "It's a God-given touch." When Malarkey ran out of mortar rounds, his tube was almost completely buried. An old French farmer got a shovel to help him dig it out.

Along about noon, infantry from the 4th Division began to pass Le Grand-Chemin. Welsh remembered "the faces of the first foot soldiers coming up from the beach while they puked their guts out from the sight of the distorted and riddled bodies of dead troopers and Germans."

There were about fifty E Company men together by then. No one knew of Lieutenant Meehan's fate, but Winters had become the de facto company commander.

Lieutenant Nixon came forward, with four Sherman tanks following. He told Winters to point out the enemy position to the tankers, then use E Company to provide infantry support for an attack. Winters climbed onto the back of the first tank and told the commander, "I want fire along those hedgerows over there, and there, and there, and against the Manor. Clean out anything that's left."

The tanks roared ahead. For the tankers, this was their first time in combat, their first chance to fire their weapons at the enemy. They had a full load of ammunition, for their 50-caliber and their 30-caliber machine-guns, and for their 75 mm cannon.

"They just cut those hedgerows to pieces," Welsh remembered. "You thought they would never stop shooting."

By midafternoon, Brécourt Manor was secured. The de Vallavieille family came out of the house, headed by Colonel de Vallavielle, a World War I veteran, along with Madame and the two teenage sons, Louis and Michel. Michel stepped into the entry into the courtyard with his hands raised over his head, alongside some German soldiers who had remained behind to surrender. An American paratrooper shot Michel in the back, either mistaking him for a German or thinking he was a collaborator. He lived, although his recovery in hospital (he was the first Frenchman evacuated from Utah Beach to England) took six months. Despite the unfortunate incident, the brothers became close friends with many of the E Company men. Michel became mayor of Ste. Marie-du-Mont, and the founder and builder of the museum at Utah Beach.

* * *

By late afternoon, the Germans had pulled out of Ste. Marie-du-Mont, as Easy and the rest of 2d Battalion moved in, then marched south-southwest a couple of kilometers to the six-house village of Culoville, where Strayer had 2d Battalion's CP. Winters got the men settled down for the night, with his outposts in place. The men ate their K rations. Winters went on a patrol by himself. Outside the village, he heard troops marching down a cobbled road. The sound of hobnailed boots told him they were Krauts. He hit the ditch; the German squad marched past him. He could smell the distinct odor of the Germans. It was a combination of sweat-soaked leather and tobacco. That's too close for comfort, Winters thought.

Lieutenant Welsh remembered walking around among the sleeping men, and thinking to himself that "they had looked at and smelled death all around them all day but never even dreamed of applying the term to themselves. They hadn't come here to fear. They hadn't come to die. They had come to win."

Before Lipton went to sleep, he recalled his discussion with Sergeant Murray before they jumped on what combat would be like and what they would do in different situations. He drifted off feeling "gratified and thankful that the day had gone so well."

As Winters prepared to stretch out, he could hear "Germans shooting their burp guns, evidently in the air, for they did no harm, and hollering like a bunch of drunk kids having a party," which was probably what was happening.

Before lying down, Winters later wrote in his diary, "I did not forget to get on my knees and thank God for helping me to live through this day and ask for his help on D plus one." And he made a promise to himself: if he lived through the war, he was going to find an isolated farm somewhere and spend the remainder of his life in peace and quiet.

6

"Move Out!"

CARENTAN

June 7–July 12, 1944

A T FIRST LIGHT on June 7, Captain Hester came to see Winters with a message. "Winters," he said, "I hate to do this to you after what you went through yesterday, but I want E Company to lead off the column toward Vierville."

The battalion had achieved its D-Day objectives, the 4th Division was well ashore, the causeways secured. Its next task was to move south, toward Carentan, on the other side of the Douve River, for the linkup with American forces coming west from Omaha Beach. The route was from Culoville through Vierville to St. Côme-du-Mont, then across the river into Carentan.

The 2d Battalion managed to clear Vierville, then move on to Angoville-au-Plain, with Easy now in reserve. The remainder of the day was spent beating off German counterattacks from Colonel von der

Heydte's 6th Parachute Regiment. The following day 1st Battalion of the 506th took St. Côme-du-Mont, about 3 kilometers north of Carentan, on the last high ground overlooking the Douve Valley and Carentan beyond. Colonel Sink set up his CP at Angoville-au-Plain, with Easy Company taking position to defend regimental HQ. That remained its task for the next three days.

* * *

Easy used the time to catch its breath and build its strength. Men joined up in a steady stream, coming from all over the Cotentin Peninsula. Sleep was still hard to come by, because of sniper fire, occasional counterattacks, artillery, and mortar fire. Burying dead bodies, human and animal, was a problem, as the bodies were beginning to bloat and smell.

Another problem emerged, one that was to plague the airborne forces throughout the next year. Every liberated village in France, and later in Belgium, Holland, Germany, and Austria, was full of wine, cognac, brandy, and other fine liquor, of a quality and in a quantity quite unknown to the average enlisted man. Pvt. Shifty Powers and a friend found a wine shop in St. Côme-du-Mont. They broke in and began sampling the bottles, "to find the kind we liked." They took a bottle each and went out back to drink in peace. "Every once in a while there's a sniper trying to shoot us, and he's trying to ricochet one in on us, and we would hear that bullet hit and ricochet around, we kind of enjoyed that."

Lieutenant Welsh found a barrel of cognac, "and I think he was trying to drink it all by himself," Winters recalled. "There were times when I talked to Harry and I realized later that he hadn't heard a word I'd said, and it was not because his hearing was bad. We got that problem straightened out in a few days." It didn't stay straightened out. There was just too much booze around, and the young warriors were under too much tension, for any simple solution.

On June 10 Pvt. Alton More asked Malarkey to join him on an expedition to Ste. Mère-Eglise to look through some musette bags that he had seen stacked up there in a vacant lot. More was a rugged John Wayne type, son of a saloonkeeper in Casper, Wyoming. He had married his high school sweetheart, and their first child had been born while he was in England. Malarkey agreed to go, but when they arrived, he felt a bit uneasy when he realized the musette bags had been removed from dead troopers. Nevertheless he joined More in emptying the bags upside down, picking up candy bars, toilet articles, rations, and money.

Suddenly Alton dropped to his knees and, in an almost inaudible voice, said, "Let's get the hell out of here." Malarkey glanced over and saw More looking at a knitted pair of baby booties. They dropped what they had collected and returned to St. Côme-du-Mont, resolving that in the future they would be more respectful of their dead comrades.

German dead were another matter. Souvenir hunting went on whenever there was a lull. Lugers were a favorite item, along with watches, daggers, flags, anything with a swastika on it. When Rod Strohl finally joined up, on D-Day plus four, Liebgott saw him and came running up. "Hey, Strohl, Strohl, I've got to show you mine." He produced a ring he had cut off the finger of a German he had killed with his bayonet.

• • •

By this time the 29th Division, coming west from Omaha Beach, had taken Isigny, 12 kilometers from Carentan. Carentan, with a population of about 4,000, lay astride the main highway from Cherbourg to Caen and St. Lô. The Paris-Cherbourg railroad ran through it. The German 6th Parachute Regiment, having failed to hold the high ground to the north, was now defending Carentan. Colonel von der Heydte had orders from Field Marshal Erwin Rommel to "defend Carentan to the last man."[1]

On June 10, the 29th Division coming from Omaha linked up with the 101st, northeast of Carentan. This made the beachhead secure, but it could not be developed or extended inland until the Americans drove the Germans out of Carentan. Progress was excruciatingly slow, for three major reasons: the lack of sufficient armor or artillery, the skill and determination of the defenders, and the hedgerows. Often 6 feet high or even more, with narrow lanes that were more like trenches, so solid that they could stop a tank, each hedgerow was a major enemy position. And there were so damn many of them. Take one hedgerow, after an all-out effort, and there was another one 50 meters or less away. This was about as bad a place to mount an infantry assault as could be imagined, as bad as clearing out a town house-by-house or room-by-room, as bad as attacking a World War I trench system. But it had to be done.

General Collins had VII Corps attacking north, in the direction of Cherbourg (the largest port in Normandy and a major strategic objective) and west,

---

[1]Rapport and Northwood, *Rendezvous with Destiny*, 166.

toward the coast (in order to cut off the Germans in the Cotentin from their line of communications), but gains were limited and little progress could be expected until the bottleneck at Carentan had been broken. The task fell to the 101st.

General Taylor decided to attack from three directions simultaneously. The 327th Glider Infantry Regiment would come in from the north, the 501st from the northeast, while the 506th would undertake a night march, swinging around the almost surrounded Carentan to the southwest. Coordinated attacks were scheduled to begin at dawn, 0500, June 12.

• • •

Captain Sobel had seen to it that Easy Company had spent months of training at night. Forced night marches cross-country, through woods, night compass problems, every conceivable problem of troop movement and control of troops at night. The men were completely at ease working at night, indeed some of them insisted they could see better in the dark than in daylight.

According to Winters (who was by now the acting company commander; Meehan was still listed as missing in action rather than KIA), the ones who could not handle the night were the regimental staff officers. They had "crapped out" on the training problems and had not done the field work night after night that the troops and junior line officers had undergone. It had shown up on D-Day night, Winters said: "They were the ones who had the problems getting oriented and finding their objectives. They had the big problem getting through hedgerows. The junior officers and enlisted men, completely on their own, had found their way around and found their objective with little problem and no maps."

The deficiency showed up again on the night march of June 11–12. F Company led the way, with E following. They set out for Carentan across a marsh, over a bridge, then west across fields to the railroad. It was rough going through swampy areas and hedgerows. The companies kept losing contact. F Company would hit a tough section, work its way through, then take off at a fast pace, with no consideration for the rear elements breaking through that same bottleneck. Regimental HQ kept changing orders for the boundaries of the 1st and 2d Battalions. The companies would stop, dig in, set up machine-guns, then get orders to move out again.

There had been major fighting over the route the 2d Battalion was following. The area was strewn with bodies, American and German, weapons and equipment, difficult to see clearly in the dark. Once over the Douve River, heading toward the railroad track, Easy lost contact with F Company. "I knew we would not be able to find our way to our objective over the strange terrain on our own," Lipton recalled, "and that we were strung out in a defenseless formation."

Winters tried to raise battalion on the radio. The operators spoke in muffled undertones. A German MG 42 (the best machine-gun in the world) opened up with several short bursts from somewhere off to the left. Lipton moved over to his machine-gunner and whispered to him to set up his gun facing toward the incoming fire. As Lipton moved quietly off to position the rest of his platoon, he remembered, "I almost jumped out of my skin when [the man] full-loaded his gun. The sound of a light machine-gun being full-loaded, two times pulling back and releasing the bolt, can be heard a half-mile away on a still night. All our attempts at being quiet and surprising the Germans gone for nothing." But there was no further attack, and Lipton breathed a bit easier.

Contact was reestablished. Easy moved out again. Along the path it followed there was a dead German, his right hand extended into the air. Everyone stepped over him until Pvt. Wayne "Skinny" Sisk got there. Sisk reached out and shook the hand, meanwhile stepping on the bloated stomach. The corpse went "Bleh."

"Sorry, buddy," Sisk whispered and moved on.

The path took an abrupt turn to the right. Carson recalled that "there was a German there with a rifle pointed right at you. He must have scared half the company. I said to myself, 'Why the hell doesn't he shoot and get it over with?' But he was dead and rigor mortis had set in, he was just like a statue there."

Easy reached the railroad line and set up another defensive position. The word came to expect German armor. Lipton put Tipper and his bazooka on the bank, with no line of retreat possible: a do-or-die situation.

"Tipper," Lipton whispered, "we're depending on you. Don't miss."

"I won't."

Tipper soon had a problem. His ammunition carrier, Pvt. Joe Ramirez, seemed awfully nervous. "We'll be O.K., Joe," Tipper told him. "Just be sure you have two bazooka rounds ready to go, with absolutely no time lost, not a fraction of a second." Ramirez went back and returned with two bazooka rounds, stumbling and crashing around. To Tipper's horror, he said he had removed the pins (with the safety pin gone, an armed bazooka rocket would explode if dropped from two or three feet).

"Stick those pins back in," Tipper whispered. "I'll tell you when I want them out."

"I don't know where they are," Ramirez answered, holding the rounds stiffly out away from his body. "I tossed them away."

"Good God Almighty! Find them." Ramirez could not. Tipper got down on his hands and knees to help look. They found the pins. Ramirez's arms were twitching as Tipper carefully reinserted the pins. "When the disarming was accomplished," Tipper said, "Joe calmed down and his twitching stopped. Mine started at that point."

No attack developed. This was because Colonel von der Heydte, short on ammunition after six days of heavy fighting with no supplies reaching him, had pulled most of his force out of Carentan. He left behind one company to hold the city as long as possible, while he got resupplied and prepared a counterattack from the southwest. The fifty-man company in Carentan had a machine-gun position to shoot straight up the road leading to the southwest, and 80 mm mortars zeroed in on the critical T-junction on the edge of town.

Easy moved out again, headed northeast. By 0530, the 2d Battalion of the 506th was in position to attack Carentan. The objective was the T-junction defended by the company from the 6th Parachute Regiment. The last 100 or so meters of the road leading to the T-junction was straight, with a gentle downward slope. There were shallow ditches on both sides. F Company was on the left flank, with E Company going straight down the road and D Company in reserve. The orders

were to move into Carentan and link up with the
327th coming in from the north.

All was quiet, no action. Lieutenant Lavenson, formerly of E Company, now battalion S-1, went into a
field to take a crap. The men could see his white fanny
in the early dawn light. A German sniper fired one
shot and hit Lavenson in the butt. (He was evacuated
to England; later, as he was being flown back to the
States, his plane went down over the Atlantic.)

By this time, Winters was furious. It had taken all
night for regiment to get the men in position. Stop,
move out, stop, move out, so many times that the men
were worn out. "It shouldn't have been," Winters said.
"It wasn't that difficult. We had screwed away the
night, just getting into position." There was no time
for a reconnaissance; Easy had no idea what lay ahead.
There was no artillery preparation, or air strikes.

The order came down: attack at 0600.

Winters had his old platoon, the 1st, under
Lieutenant Welsh, on the left side of the road, just past
where the road curved and then straightened out, with
2d platoon on the right and 3d platoon in reserve. The
men lay down in the ditches by the side of the road,
awaiting orders. The German defenders had not
revealed their machine-gun position or fired any mortars. Everything was quiet.

At 0600 Winters ordered, "Move out." Welsh kicked
off the advance, running down the road toward the
T-junction some 50 meters away, his platoon following. The German machine-gun opened fire, straight
down the road. It was in a perfect position, at the perfect time, to wipe out the company.

The fire split the platoon. The seventh man behind
Welsh stayed in the ditch. So did the rest of the pla-

toon, almost thirty men. They were face down in the ditches on both sides of the road, trying to snuggle in as close as they could.

Winters jumped into the middle of the road, highly agitated, yelling, "Move out! Move out!" It did no good; the men remained in place, heads down in the ditch.

From his rear, Winters could hear Lieutenant Colonel Strayer, Lieutenants Hester and Nixon, and other members of the battalion HQ hollering at him to "get them moving, Winters, get them moving."

Winters threw away his gear, holding on to his M-1, and ran over to the left side, "hollering like a mad man, 'Get going!'" He started kicking the men in the butt. He crossed to the other side and repeated the order, again kicking the men.

"I was possessed," Winters recalled. "Nobody'd ever seen me like that." He ran back to the other side, machine-gun bullets zinging down the street. He thought to himself, My God, I'm leading a blessed life. I'm charmed.

He was also desperate. His best friend, Harry Welsh, was up ahead, trying to deal with that machine-gun. If I don't do something, Winters thought to himself, he's dead. No question about it.

But the men wouldn't move. They did look up. Winters recalled, "I will never forget the surprise and fear on those faces looking up at me." The German machine-gun seemed to be zeroing in on him, and he was a wide open target. "The bullets kept snapping by and glancing off the road all around me."

"Everybody had froze," Strohl remembered. "Nobody could move. And Winters got up in the middle of the road and screamed, 'Come on! Move out! Now!'"

That did it. No man in the company had ever before

heard Winters shout. "It was so out of character," Strohl said, "we moved out as one man."

According to Winters, "Here is where the discipline paid off. The men got the message, and they moved out."

As Sergeant Talbert passed Winters, he called out, "Which way when we hit the intersection?"

"Turn right," Winters ordered.

(In 1981, Talbert wrote Winters: "I'll never forget seeing you in the middle of that road. You were my total inspiration. All my boys felt the same way.")

Welsh, meanwhile, was neutralizing the machine-gun. "We were all alone," he remembered, "and I couldn't understand where the hell everybody was." Thanks to the distraction caused by Winters running back and forth, the machine-gunner had lost track of Welsh and his six men. Welsh tossed some grenades at the gun, followed by bursts from his carbine. The men with him did the same. The machine-gun fell silent.[2]

• • •

The remainder of Easy Company drove into the intersection at a full run, and secured it. Winters sent the 1st platoon to the left, the 2d to the right, clearing out the houses, one man throwing grenades through windows while another waited outside the door. Immediately after the explosion, the second man

---

[2]Winters wrote in 1990: "Later in the war, in recalling this action with Major Hester, he made a comment that has always left me feeling proud of Company E's action that day. As S-3, Hester had been in a position to see another company in a similar position caught in M.G. fire. It froze and then got severely cut up. E Company, on the other hand, had moved out, got the job done, and had not been cut up by that M.G."

kicked in the door to look for and shoot any survivors.

Tipper and Liebgott cleared out a house. As Tipper was passing out the front door, "A locomotive hit me, driving me far back inside the house. I heard no noise, felt no pain, and was somehow unsteadily standing and in possession of my M-1." The German rear guard was bringing its prepositioned mortars into play. Liebgott grabbed Tipper and helped him to a sitting position, called for a medic, and tried to reassure Tipper that he would be O.K.

Welsh came up and got some morphine into Tipper, who was insisting that he could walk. That was nonsense; both his legs were broken, and he had a serious head wound. Welsh and Liebgott half dragged him into the street, where "I remember lying at the base of the wall with explosions in the street and shrapnel zinging against the wall above my head." Welsh got Tipper back to the aid station being set up in a barn about 20 meters to the rear.

Mortars continued coming in, along with sniper fire. Lipton led 3d platoon to the intersection and peeled off to the right. There were explosions on the street; he huddled against a wall and yelled to his men to follow him. A mortar shell dropped about 2 meters in front of him, putting shell fragments in his left cheek, right wrist, and right leg at the crotch. His rifle clattered to the street. He dropped to the ground, put his left hand to his cheek and felt a large hole, but his biggest concern was his right hand, as blood was pumping out in spurts. Sergeant Talbert got to him and put a tourniquet on his arm.

Only then did Lipton feel the pain in his crotch. He reached down for a feel, and his left hand came away bloody.

"Talbert, I may be hit bad," he said. Talbert slit his pants leg with his knife, took a look, and said, "You're O.K."

"What a relief that was," Lipton remembered. The two shell fragments had gone into the top of his leg and "missed everything important."

Talbert threw Lipton over his shoulder and carried him to the aid station. The medics gave Lipton a shot of morphine and bandaged him up.

Malarkey recalled that during "this tremendous period of fire I could hear someone reciting a Hail Mary. I glanced up and saw Father John Maloney holding his rosary and walking down the center of the road to administer last rites to the dying at the road juncture." (Maloney was awarded the DSC.)

Winters got hit, by a ricochet bullet that went through his boot and into his leg. He stayed in action long enough to check the ammunition supply and consult with Welsh (who tried to remove the bullet with his knife but gave it up) to set up a defensive position in the event of a counterattack.

By this time it was 0700, and the area was secured. F Company, meanwhile, had hooked up with the 327th. Carentan had been captured. Lieutenant Colonel Strayer came into town, where he met the commander of the 3d Battalion of the 327th. They went into a wine shop and opened a bottle to drink to the victory.

Winters went back to the battalion aid station. Ten of his men were there, receiving first aid. A doctor poked around Winters's leg with a tweezers, pulled the bullet, cleaned out the wound, put some sulfa powder on it, and a bandage.

Winters circulated among the wounded. One of them was Pvt. Albert Blithe.

"How're you doing, Blithe? What's the matter?"

"I can't see, sir. I can't see."

"Take it easy, relax. You've got a ticket out of here, we'll get you out of here in a hurry. You'll be going back to England. You'll be O.K. Relax," Winters said, and started to move on.

Blithe began to get up. "Take it easy," Winters told him. "Stay still."

"I can see, I can see, sir! I can see you!"

Blithe got up and rejoined the company. "Never saw anything like it," Winters said. "He was that scared he blacked out. Spooky. This kid just completely could not see, and all he needed was somebody to talk to him for a minute and calm him down."

• • •

The Germans were certain to counterattack, and it was sure to come from the southwest, down the road Easy had followed into town. Terrain dictated the axis of the advance; a peninsula of high ground led into Carentan from that direction. To the north, beyond the railroad track, was flooded ground, as also to the south of the road. General Taylor decided to push out several kilometers to the west and set up a defensive position on the high ground.

Winters got his orders. Easy would be on the far right, alongside the railroad track. He checked for ammunition. Leo Boyle and some others from 1st platoon found and "liberated" a two-wheel farm cart loaded with ammunition, and brought it to the barn on the edge of town that was serving as the aid station. As Boyle was preparing to bring it forward, he heard the cry, "Enemy tank!"

"I looked cautiously out of the doorway and saw

the vague outline of a turret of a tank in a hedgerow a few yards away. Before I could react, a bullet from the machine-gun in the tank penetrated my left leg above the knee and knocked me to the ground." Boyle was taken by truck back to Utah Beach, for evacuation to England. Along the way, "we met Captain Sobel, who was ferrying supplies to the front by jeep."

Bazooka fire drove the tank off. Winters got the company reorganized and pushed off to the southwest, alongside the railroad track. The company moved 3 kilometers without significant resistance. Winters set up a defensive position behind a hedgerow.

The Germans were directly in front, behind the next hedgerow, laying down harassing fire. Anyone who moved drew aimed fire. As the light faded, the company received a resupply of food and ammunition and settled in for the evening. Winters got orders from battalion to jump off on an attack at first light, 0530.

At about 0030 hours, June 13, the Germans sent a patrol into the field between the hedgerows. Not a silent patrol to get intelligence, but a couple of squads, evidently drunk, shooting their machine pistols and shouting oaths at the Americans. "It scared the hell out of us," Winters remembered, "it didn't make any sense." He feared a night attack, but just that quickly the Germans fell back.

Gordon with his machine-gun, Sisk, and Guth were on outpost, on the far right, against the railroad track. Gordon was "uncomfortable and quite frightened," as there was little concealment, and he felt "very exposed." Sergeant Talbert checked on the men, decided they were too exposed, and pulled them back to the main line of defense.

Sergeant Talbert was up and down the line all night,

shifting the men back and forth so that they could catch a few minutes' sleep. He had the riflemen fix their bayonets. It was a cool evening; Talbert picked up a German poncho and put it on. About 0300 he prodded Pvt. George Smith with his revolver, to awaken him for duty. Smith was almost comatose. When he finally awakened, he saw in the pale moonlight this figure in a German poncho hovering over him and prodding him with a pistol.

Smith jumped up with his rifle with the fixed bayonet and began lunging at Talbert. Talbert tried to stop him, hollering, "Smith, it's Tab, don't!" but Smith kept thrusting until he succeeded in bayoneting Talbert in the chest. Fortunately he missed the lungs and heart, but Talbert was out of action. He had to be dragged away and carried the 3 kilometers back to the aid station.

By 0530, Winters had the company ready to attack. Just as he gave the order to move out, Colonel von der Heydte launched his 6th Parachute Regiment on its counterattack. Both sides cut loose with artillery, mortar, machine-gun, and rifle fire, everything they had. There was mass confusion. Fire coming in, dead-tired men who had used up their adrenaline long since, Taylor urging speed, men shouting, at one point a firefight between Easy and another company of the 101st, some Sherman tanks coming up in support firing into friendly units on the left, chaos.

Under the intense incoming fire, F Company on Easy's left flank broke and fell back. (The C.O. of the company was relieved on the spot by Colonel Strayer.) That exposed D Company's right flank, so it fell back too. That left Easy all alone, isolated, its right flank up against the track, its left flank in the air.

Easy stood to its guns. Gordon set his machine-gun up on a gate at the opening of the hedgerow into the field (he had lost the tripod on D-Day) and blasted away. A mortar round dropped 10 meters in front of him. Gordon went down with shrapnel in his shoulder and leg. The same mortar wounded Rod Strohl. Still they stayed in the line, continuing to fire. Winters, Compton, Welsh, and the other officers were running up and down the line, encouraging the men, straightening things out, making sure everything was done that could be done to stop the Germans.

A German tank started to break through the hedgerow on Easy's left flank, exactly where F Company should have been. Welsh told Pvt. John McGrath to bring his bazooka and come on. They raced out into the open field, crouched down, armed the bazooka, and Welsh told McGrath to fire. The shot hit the turret, but bounced off. The German tank turned its 88 mm cannon toward Welsh and McGrath and fired. The shell zoomed over their heads, missing by a few feet. The tank gunner could not depress his cannon sufficiently, because the tank driver was climbing the hedgerow in an effort to break through.

Welsh started reloading the bazooka. McGrath was saying, over and over, "Lieutenant, you're gonna get me killed. You're gonna get me killed." But he held his place, took careful aim at the tank, which was at the apex of its climb, cannon pointing skyward, the huge vehicle just about to tip forward as it broke through, and fired. He hit exactly where he wanted, the unarmored belly of the tank, and it exploded in a great burst of flame and fire.

That was the critical moment in the battle. German tank drivers lined up behind the one McGrath had hit, put their gear in reverse and began to back off. Meanwhile battalion headquarters had stopped the retreat of D and F companies, pulled them together, and pushed them forward about 150 meters, closing the gap somewhat on the left flank.

Still the Germans came on. They tried a flanking movement on the far (north) side of the railroad track. Winters got some mortar fire going, which stopped that attempt. Easy held its ground. The company had taken ten casualties on June 12 in the attack on Carentan, and nine more on June 13 in the defense of Carentan.

• • • •

Gordon dropped out of the line and found Winters. A piece of shrapnel had gone into the calf of his leg on one side and come out on the other; he was also bleeding from the shrapnel wound in his shoulder. But what bothered him was a boil that had developed on his shin right above his boot. The pain was unbearable. He told Winters he had to have the boil lanced. Winters told him to hobble his way back to the aid station.

The medic took one look at this man bleeding from the leg and shoulder, looking like someone who had not slept for three days and had just come in from an intense battle, and asked, "Are you hurt?"

"Well, yes," Gordon replied, "but that's not the problem. My problem is this boil. Get the boil." The medic lanced the boil, then looked at the other wounds. He said the shoulder would be all right, "but your leg wound is bad." Each side of the wound had closed, and Gordon's leg was turning blue. "You're going to have some real problems with that," the medic said. "We've got to evacuate you."

"No way," Gordon protested. "I'll didn't tell Lieutenant Winters."

"I'll get word back to him, don't worry about that." So Gordon finally agreed to be evacuated.

• • •

At 1630, sixty tanks from the 2d Armored, accompanied by fresh infantry from the 29th Division, came up to relieve Easy. Winters recalled "what a wonderful sight it was to see those tanks pouring it to the Germans with those heavy 50-caliber machine-guns and just plowing straight from our lines into the German hedgerows with all those fresh infantry soldiers marching along beside the tanks."

"Oh, what a mess they made!" Welsh remembered, rubbing his hands with glee as he thought about it forty-seven years later.

• • •

At 2300 Easy and the rest of the 506th was withdrawn into division reserve in Carentan. The officers found billets for the men in undestroyed houses. Winters found a deserted hotel for his billet. Before going to bed, the officers checked on the men. Welsh returned to the hotel from his rounds, sat down on the steps, and fell asleep right there. Winters slept between sheets. It was a sleep he never forgot.

The following day, June 14, the barber shops had opened for business, and the men were queuing up for haircuts (they would help themselves to liquor, food, or whatever in abandoned shops and homes, but they paid for services). Winters went to the aid station to have his leg wound attended to; for the next five days he took it easy. It was during this period that he wrote the diary entries about his D-Day experiences, quoted in the preceding chapter. Welsh ran the company. Colonel Sink dropped by to thank Winters for the job Easy had done on June 13, when it held the right flank and prevented a German breakthrough that might well have been decisive in the struggle for Carentan. Sink also said he was recommending Winters for the Congressional Medal of Honor for the action at Brécourt Manor on D-Day. Winters thought that was very nice, but wondered what about medals for the men.

As for the action at Carentan, Colonel Sink told reporter Walter McCallum of the Washington *Star*, "It was Lt. Winters's personal leadership which held the crucial position in the line and tossed back the enemy with mortar and machine-gun fire. He was a fine soldier out there. His personal bravery and battle knowledge held a crucial position when the going was really rough."[3]

* * *

The company went into a defensive position south of Carentan. The second day in this static situation, someone came down the hedgerow line asking for Don Malarkey and Skip Muck. It was Fritz Niland. He found Muck, talked to him, then found Malarkey, and had only enough time to say good-bye; he was flying home.

A few minutes after Niland left, Muck came to Malarkey, "his impish Irish smile replaced by a frown." Had Niland explained to Malarkey why he was going home? No. Muck told the story.

---

[3]Washington *Star*, June 25, 1944.

The previous day Niland had gone to the 82d to see his brother Bob, the one who had told Malarkey in London that if he wanted to be a hero, the Germans would see to it, fast, which had led Malarkey to conclude that Bob Niland had lost his nerve. Fritz Niland had just learned that his brother had been killed on D-Day. Bob's platoon had been surrounded, and he manned a machine-gun, hitting the Germans with harassing fire until the platoon broke through the encirclement. He had used up several boxes of ammunition before getting killed.

Fritz Niland next hitched a ride to the 4th Infantry Division position, to see another brother who was a platoon leader. He too had been killed on D-Day, on Utah Beach. By the time Fritz returned to Easy Company, Father Francis Sampson was looking for him, to tell him that a third brother, a pilot in the China-Burma-India theater, had been killed that same week. Fritz was the sole surviving son, and the Army wanted to remove him from the combat zone as soon as possible.

Fritz's mother had received all three telegrams from the War Department on the same day.

Father Sampson escorted Fritz to Utah Beach, where a plane flew him to London on the first leg of his return to the States.

• • •

The company dug in. Neither side was making infantry assaults south of Carentan, but the incoming and outgoing mail was tremendous, since both sides were receiving reinforcements in artillery and heavy weapons, the Americans from the beach and the Germans from the French interior.

In their foxholes, the men of Easy stayed underground, ready to repel any ground attack, but otherwise remaining out of sight during daylight hours. Lieutenant Nixon, battalion intelligence officer (S-2), wanted to know the strength of the German infantry opposite Easy's position. Winters came down the line, asking for a volunteer to take out a high noon patrol. No one responded. He told Guarnere that he was nominated to lead the patrol. Guarnere got a briefing from Nixon, who gave him a map showing all the hedgerows and a cluster of farm buildings that seemed to be a German command post, almost a kilometer away.

Guarnere, Privates Blithe and Joseph Lesniewski of Erie, Pennsylvania, and two others set out. Using the hedgerows for concealment, they moved forward. Blithe was at the point. He reached the last hedgerow leading to the farm buildings. A German sniper put a bullet into his neck.

"Get the hell out of here," Guarnere shouted. As the patrol fell back, German machine pistols opened up. When the patrol got back to Easy's lines, the company's machine-guns answered the fire.

Later, Malarkey led another patrol in another attempt to get information on the enemy. On this patrol Private Sheehy, at the point, moved up next to a hedgerow. Malarkey joined him there, but as he moved forward he stepped on a tree limb, breaking it. Immediately a German helmet raised up right across the hedgerow. Sheehy got him full in the face with a blast from his tommy-gun.

Seeing more Germans, Malarkey pulled the patrol back at a full run. Rob Bain, carrying a 300 radio, had trouble keeping up. After they had gotten back safely,

Bain's comment was, "Apparently patrols are quite necessary, but it appears to me to be a good way to get your tail shot off."

•   •   •

The next day was relatively quiet. Fat Norman cattle were grazing in the field behind the company's position. Pvt. Woodrow Robbins, 1st squad machine-gunner, was dug in about 15 feet from Christenson's foxhole.

"Hey, Chris," he called out, "let's get some of that meat in the field!" Christenson did not want to leave his foxhole, but Bill Howell joined Robbins as he crawled up to a cow and shot her. They butchered the animal, then returned with a hind quarter. Robbins cut up steaks for the whole squad. They fried the meat over open fires in their foxholes. That night, Robbins and Howell tied the remainder of the carcass to a tree to the rear.

They covered it with a poncho; the squad figured to be eating beef rather than K rations for a few days. What they had not figured on was all the shrapnel flying around from the incessant artillery barrages. It perforated the meat. At the next feast, the men of the squad were continually cutting their gums on shrapnel.

•   •   •

June 23. A sniper fired at Christenson, from 600 meters. Chris ducked behind a hedgerow and shouted to Robbins to spray the area from which the bullet came. Robbins fired fifty rounds at the distant trees. "I could hear a nervous grumbling from the men down the line," Christenson remembered. "Tension always grew when out of complete silence a machine-gun fires that many rounds." In the far distance, the sound of mortars belched, *waump, waump, waump, waump.* "This nerve-racking sound confirmed that four mortar bombs were heading in our direction. The suspense of waiting is eerie. Indescribable. Miserable. Then *'Boom,'* the first one exploded not more than 7 feet in front of Robbins's and Howell's gun."

Howell jumped out of his position and ran to Christenson's foxhole, as the second mortar round exploded almost on top of the first, "so close that you could taste the pungent gunpowder." Howell leaped into Christenson's foxhole. "I was all bent over and unable to move," Chris said, "because of my doubled up, cramped position. It was difficult to breathe, yet I was laughing hysterically for Howell's eyes were as big as tea cups. He was muttering things like, 'Christ-sake, oh my God,' at each shell burst. The pressure this big man was putting on me suddenly threw me into a state of panic, for I was suffocating." Fortunately the shelling stopped.

• • •

After two weeks on the main line of resistance (MLR), the men of Easy stank. They had not had a bath or shower or an opportunity to shave. Many had dysentery; all were continually drenched with sweat. Their hair was matted from dirt and dust made worse by the profuse sweating caused by wearing their helmets constantly, and by the impregnated clothes they had been wearing since June 6. They looked like Bill Mauldin's Willy and Joe characters.

On June 29, the 83d Infantry Division came up to relieve the 101st. "They were so clean looking," Christenson remembered, "with a full complement of men in each unit. Even the paint on their helmets looked as if they had just been unpacked. The impact of seeing such a disheveled motley group as we were was a shock to them."

For Easy, to get off the front line, even if it was only for a few days, was a deliverance. The thought of an uninterrupted full night's sleep, not being harassed by gunfire or being sent out on patrol, to get something hot to eat, to sleep dry, and most of all to get a shower, was good beyond description.

• • •

Easy had jumped into Normandy on June 6 with 139 officers and men. Easy was pulled out of the line on June 29 with 74 officers and men present for duty. (The 506th had taken the heaviest casualties of any regiment in the campaign, a total of 983, or about 50 percent.) The Easy men killed in action were Lts. Thomas Meehan and Robert Mathews, Sgts. William Evans, Elmer Murray, Murray Robert, Richard Owen, and Carl Riggs, Cpls. Jerry Wentzel, Ralph Wimer, and Hermin Collins, Pvts. Sergio Moya, John Miller, Gerald Snider, William McGonigal, Ernest Oats, Elmer Telstad, George Elliott, and Thomas Warren.

• • •

For the 101st, Carentan was the last action of the Normandy campaign. The division was gradually pulled back to a field camp north of Utah Beach, complete with radio, telephone, bulletin board, policing the area, keeping weapons clean, parade ground formations, and a training schedule. To compensate, there were hot showers and nearly unlimited opportunities for scrounging.

Pvt. Alton More was the master scrounger in Easy Company. He found a way to get into the main supply depot near Utah. On his first foray, he returned carrying two cardboard boxes, one of fruit cocktail and the other of pineapple. "It tasted like the best thing you ever ate in your life," Harry Welsh remembered, "and I was never so sick in my life. We weren't used to that food." Thereafter, More brought in a more varied diet from his daily expeditions.

General Taylor stopped by, to congratulate the company on its lonely stand on the far right flank at Carentan. The men wanted to know what about his "give me three days and nights of hard fighting and I'll have you out of here" pre-D-Day promise.

Gen. Omar Bradley appeared for an awards ceremony. Standing on a little platform in the field, he read out the citations for the Distinguished Service Cross for eleven men, including General Taylor, Chaplain Maloney, and Lieutenant Winters. "That was a proud moment," Winters said. He recalled that after the ceremony, Bradley had the troops break formation and gather round him. "Are there any reporters here, any correspondents?" he asked. "If there are, I don't want this recorded.

"What I want to say," he went on, "is that things are going very well, and there is a possibility at this point, as I see it, that we could be in Berlin by Christmas."

Winters thought to himself, God, I can make it till Christmas. Just let me go home for Christmas.

On July 1, Winters received news of his promotion to captain. On July 10, the company moved down to Utah Beach, to prepare to embark for England. "Seeing the beach for the first time," Winters recalled, "with that armada of ships as far as the eye could see in every direction, and seeing the American flag on the beach, left me feeling weak in the knees for a few moments and brought tears to my eyes."

Private More pulled one last raid on that vast supply dump. He broke into the main motor pool and stole a motorcycle, complete with sidecar. He hid it behind a sand dune, then asked Captain Winters if he could put it on the LST and take it back to England. "Up to you," Winters replied.

The next day, as the company marched up the ramp of the gigantic LST, More moved the motorcycle up the inland side of the forward dune. He had arranged with Malarkey for a hand signal when everyone was aboard and it was time to go. Malarkey tipped off the Navy personnel. At the proper moment, standing on the ramp, Malarkey gave the signal and More came roaring over the dune and up the ramp.

On the LST, the skipper said to Welsh, "Lieutenant, what would your men like to have: chicken or steak? ice cream? eggs?"

Sailing in convoy, the LST got back to Southampton the night of July 12. The next morning, a train took the men (except More and Malarkey, who rode their motorcycle) to Aldbourne. "It was wonderful to be back," Winters remembered. "Everybody was glad to see us. It was just like home."

7

Healing Wounds and
Scrubbed Missions

ALDBOURNE

July 13–September 16, 1944

"IT'S THE ONLY TIME I ever saw the Army do anything right," Gordon Carson said. "They put us on those LSTs, brought us into Southampton, took us back to Aldbourne, gave us two sets of complete, all-new uniforms, all our back pay, $150 or more, and a seven-day pass, and by seven, eight in the morning we're on our way to London."

The men of Easy have little memory of that week in London. The American paratroopers were the first soldiers to return to England from Normandy; the papers had been full of their exploits; everyone in town wanted to buy them a meal or a beer—for the first day or so. But the young heroes overdid it. They drank too much, they broke too many windows and chairs, they got into too many fights with nonparatroopers. It was one of the wildest weeks in London's history. One newspaper compared the damage done to the Blitz. A joke went around: the M.P.s in London were going to receive a presidential citation for duty above and beyond during the week the 101st was in town.

Not everyone went to London. Harry Welsh traveled to Ireland, to see relatives. Winters stayed in Aldbourne to rest, reflect, and write letters to the parents of men killed or wounded. Gordon and Lipton, after recovery from their wounds, went to Scotland to see the sights.

* * *

In the hospital after his evacuation from Normandy, Gordon had been given skin grafts, then had his leg enclosed in a cast that ran from hip to toe. He was the only combat wounded man in his ward; the others were ill or had been hurt in accidents in England. He was therefore "an object of great respect. They were in awe of me." Three times officers came in to pin a Purple Heart on his pillow. "I would lower my eyes modestly and murmur thanks to the small group who had gathered to see the hero." Then he would hide the medal and wait for the next one.

After eight weeks in the hospital, he returned to E Company. (It was Airborne policy to return recovered men to their original company; in the infantry, when wounded became fit for duty, they went wherever they were needed. The former was, in the opinion of every paratrooper, one of the wisest things the Airborne did; the latter policy was, in everyone's opinion, one of the dumbest things the Army did.)

Sergeant Talbert got back to Easy at the same time Gordon did. As his wound had been inflicted by Private

Smith's bayonet, rather than by a German, he was disqualified from receiving the Purple Heart. Gordon told him not to worry, he could fix him up with one of his extra ribbons. The 3d platoon got together and conducted an appropriate ceremony for Talbert. Gordon and Rogers had written a poem to immortalize Talbert, Smith, "and the bayonet that came between them." The title was "The Night of the Bayonet"; fortunately for posterity, the poem has not survived (or at least the authors refused to give it to me for this book). The indignant Talbert declared, "I could have shot the little bastard six times as he lunged toward me, but I didn't think we could spare a man at the time."

Some of the wounded were worried about permanent disability. Malarkey found this out when he and Don Moone were sitting in the mess hall as Lipton passed by. "Hi, crip," Malarkey called out. Lipton turned and grabbed the two men by their throats, lifted them from their chairs, and declared that he would take them on one at a time or together. They went pale and said they didn't mean anything by the crack. Later Lipton returned, red faced, and said he was sorry to lose his temper, but he feared that the wound to his hand had inflicted permanent damage that would prevent him from playing college football.

•   •   •

Underlying the release of tension in London, or Gordon's feeble attempts at some humor, was the reality these men had faced and their apprehension about what they would be facing.

Sergeant Martin looked around the 1st platoon barracks the first night back from Normandy, and half the men who had been there from September 1943 to May

1944 were gone. He said to Guarnere, "Jesus, Bill, here we've got a half a hut full of guys, and we aren't even started in the war yet. We don't have a Chinaman's chance of ever getting out of this thing."

"If we lost half the barracks in one goddamn little maneuver in Normandy," Guarnere replied, "forget it, we'll never get home."

They took their leave in Scotland, where they got tattoos, figuring what the hell, "losing that many men in one deal like that and the whole war ahead of us, why not?"

Pvt. David Kenyon Webster had jumped with 2d Battalion's HQ Company on D-Day, been wounded a few days later, evacuated to England, and returned to Aldbourne before the battalion returned. He hid in the shadows of the Red Cross hut as "the thin, tired column of survivors marched into the area," hoping that no one would look him in the face and ask, "Where the hell were you, Webster, when the Krauts made the big counterattack the other side of Carentan and F Company gave ground and E Company's flank was exposed?"

His embarrassment aside, Webster was overjoyed to see his friends return. "You know everybody in the Battalion by sight," he wrote, "if not by name, and you feel like part of a big family. You are closer to these men than you will ever be to any civilians."

He applied for a transfer back to E Company, because with HQ Company he had been an ammunition carrier most of the time, had fired his machinegun only once in Normandy, and "I craved action. I wanted to get the war over with; I wanted to fight as a rifleman in a line company." He became a member of 1st platoon.

Webster's attitude was, as he wrote his parents, "I am living on borrowed time. I do not think I shall live through the next jump. If I don't come back, try not to take it too hard. I wish I could persuade you to regard death as casually as we do over here. In the heat of battle you expect casualties, you expect somebody to be killed and you are not surprised when a friend is machine-gunned in the face. You have to keep going. It's not like civilian life, where sudden death is so unexpected."

When his mother wrote to express her considerable alarm at this attitude (and her worries about his younger brother, who had just joined the paratroopers), Webster was blunt in his reply: "Would you prefer for somebody else's son to die in the mud? You want us to win the war, but you apparently don't want to have your sons involved in the actual bloodshed. That's a strangely contradictory attitude.

"Somebody has to get in and kill the enemy. Somebody has to be in the infantry and the paratroops. If the country all had your attitude, nobody would fight, everybody would be in the Quartermaster. And what kind of a country would that be?"

Lipton felt that "when men are in combat, the inevitability of it takes over. They are there, there is nothing they can do to change that, so they accept it. They immediately become callused to the smell of death, the bodies, the destruction, the killing, the danger. Enemy bodies and wounded don't affect them. Their own wounded and the bodies of their dead friends make only a brief impression, and in that impression is a fleeting feeling of triumph or accomplishment that it was not them. [Thank God it was him and not me is a feeling common to many combat soldiers when their comrades fall; later it can produce guilt feelings.] There is still work to be done, a war to be won, and they think about that."

Once out of the line, back in a rest camp, Lipton goes on, "they begin to think. They remember how their friends were wounded or killed. They remember times when they were inches or seconds from their own death. Far from combat, death and destruction are no longer inevitable—the war might end, the missions might be cancelled. With these thoughts men become nervous about going back in. As soon as they are back in, however, those doubts and that nervousness are gone. The callousness, the cold-bloodedness, the calmness return. Once more there's a job to be done, the old confidence comes back, the thrill of combat returns, and the drive to excel and win takes over again."

If that sounds idealized, it can't be helped; that is the way Lipton and many others in Easy, and many others in the Airborne and throughout the American Army—and come to that, in the German and Red Armies too—fought the war. But by no means does Lipton's analysis apply to all soldiers. Millions of men fought in World War II. No one man can speak for all of them. Still, Lipton's insights into the emotional state of the combat soldier provide guidance into attempting to understand how men put up with combat.

• • •

Coming out of Normandy, many of the men of Easy were fighting mad at the Germans and absolutely convinced the Allies would win the war. "I hope to go back soon," Webster told his parents, "for I owe the Germans several bullets and as many hand grenades as I can throw." The Germans had cut the throats of paratroops caught in their harnesses, bayoneted them, stripped them, shot them, wiped out an aid station. Because of these atrocities, "we do not intend to show them mercy." As to the outcome, "after seeing that beachhead, a breathtaking panorama of military might, I know we cannot lose. As for the paratroopers, they are out for blood. I hope to be back in on the kill."

• • •

Promotions were made. Welsh and Compton moved up from 2d to 1st lieutenant. Regiment needed new junior officers, to replace casualties; Winters recommended Sgt. James Diel, who had acted as company 1st sergeant in Normandy, for a battlefield commission. Colonel Sink approved, so Diel became a 2d lieutenant and was assigned to another company in the 506th. Winters moved Lipton up to replace him as company 1st sergeant. Leo Boyle became staff sergeant at Company HQ. Bill Guarnere became a staff sergeant. Don Malarkey, Warren Muck, Paul Rogers, and Mike Ranney jumped from private to sergeant (Ranney had been a sergeant but was busted to PFC during the Sobel mutiny). Pat Christenson, Walter Gordon, John Plesa, and Lavon Reese were promoted from private to corporal.

• • •

Webster was an aspiring novelist, an avid reader of the best in English literature, a Harvard man, a combat veteran who praised and damned the Army on the basis of personal observation and keen insight. His long letters home provide snapshots of some of the men of Easy Company, following its first combat experience.

Pvt. Roy Cobb, who had been hit on Harry Welsh's

plane over Normandy and thus did not make the jump, "was an old soldier with some nine years to his credit. He managed to keep one long, easy jump ahead of the Army. His varied and colorful wartime career had thus far included: 1. An assault landing in Africa with the 1st Armored Division; 2. A siege of yellow jaundice and an evacuation to America on a destroyer after his troopship had been torpedoed; 3. Several months' training at the Parachute School; 4. A timely leg wound from flak over Normandy. Tall, lean, thirsty, and invariably good-natured."

The first squad of the 1st platoon was "headed by little Johnny Martin, an excellent soldier, a premier goldbrick, and a very fast thinker who could handle any combat or garrison problem that arose, always had the equipment, the food, and the good living quarters."

The second squad leader was "Bull" Randleman, who was constantly bitching but who could "be very G.I., as I once discovered when he turned me in to the first sergeant for laughing at him when he told me to take off my wool-knit hat in the mess hall. Bull was considered a very acceptable noncom by the officers, who frowned on Sergeant Martin's flip attitude."

Webster's squad leader was Sgt. Robert Rader. "I don't think Rader ever goldbricked in his life; he was the ideal garrison soldier, the type that knows all the commands for close-order drill and takes pride in a snappy manual of arms, that is impatient with men who ride the sick book and slip away from night problems."

The assistant squad leaders, Cpls. William Dukeman, Pat Christenson, and Don Hoobler, "generally let the buck sergeants do the work. Dukeman had a way of beating night problems and skipping off to

London every weekend that was truly marvelous to behold." Christenson was Randleman's assistant, which Webster considered a "snap job" because Randleman, like Rader, was very conscientious. Christenson was "of medium height and athletic build, with curly golden hair, E Company's only glamour boy. Hoobler was his opposite in every way. Hoobler was the only person I met who actually enjoyed fighting; he got a kick out of war. A happy-go-lucky, gold-toothed boy, he volunteered for all the patrols in combat and all the soft jobs in garrison. He was one of the best and most popular soldiers in the company."

In Webster's opinion (and he had been around a lot as a member of HQ Company), the members of 1st platoon, E Company, were "younger, more intelligent than those in other companies." For the first time in the Army, and to his delight, he found men who talked about going to college after the war, including Corporal Dukeman and Sergeants Muck, Carson, and Malarkey.

All these men were what Webster called "new-army noncoms." Their average age was twenty-one. They did not know the Articles of War backward and forward, they didn't care about "the Book that ruled the lives of so many regular-army men." They mingled with their men, they had not served in Panama or Hawaii or the Philippines. "They were civilian soldiers. They were the ones who saved America."

Webster was also impressed by some of the officers. He described Winters as "a sizable, very athletic individual who believed in calisthenics in garrison and aggressiveness in combat." Welsh was now Winters's executive officer; Webster described him as "small, dark, lazy, quick-thinking, the only officer in the 2d

Battalion who could give an interesting and informative current events' lecture." He thought Lieutenant Compton, leader of the 2d platoon, a friendly and genial man who was everyone's favorite. He had convinced the college-bound group that UCLA was the only place to go for an education.

First platoon was led by Lt. Thomas Peacock, a replacement officer. Webster wrote that "he always obeyed an order without question, argument, or thought." Webster felt that Peacock "was highly esteemed by his superior officers and cordially disliked by his men. He was too G.I." Once the platoon came back to Aldbourne from a ten-hour cross-country march; Peacock made the men play a baseball game, because that was what was on the schedule. "Peacock believed in the book; he was in his element in Normandy as battalion supply officer, but as a platoon leader his men hated even to look at him."

Peacock's assistant was Lt. Bob Brewer. Very young, a superb athlete, Webster described him as "overgrown, boyish."

•   •   •

In the summer of 1944, Easy Company had excellent billets. The officers were in a lovely brick house near the village green; in back there were stables, which the men cleaned out and used. The stables consisted of a series of box stalls in each of which four men lived in comfort and a dark, welcome privacy. There they could hide; so many did so when night training exercises resumed that Winters was forced to make a habit of checking the individual stalls to be certain no one was hiding behind the bunks or standing in the clothes hanging from the hooks. Beyond cover and concealment, each stall had a stove, a large, thick, soundproof door, and a high, airy ceiling. There was sufficient room to hang uniforms and barracks bags and still play poker or craps.

For entertainment, the men listened to Armed Forces Network (AFN) radio. It was on from 0700 to 2300 with an occasional rebroadcast of a Bob Hope show, BBC news every hour, and swing music. The men much preferred it to BBC broadcasts, even though they had to endure SHAEF exhortations to keep clean, salute more often, or refrain from fighting. ("Remember, men, if you're looking for a fight, wait till you meet the Germans!")

When they didn't like the tune being played on AFN, they could turn to German radio and listen to Axis Sally and Lord Haw Haw. These propagandists played popular tunes, intermixed with messages that were so crudely done they always brought a laugh.

In addition to the radio, there were movies twice a week, usually cowboy thrillers, seldom a recent release. Occasionally a United Services Organization (USO) show came to the area, but generally the big stars stuck to London.

Glenn Miller was an exception. For Malarkey, "the big thrill of the summer" came on July 25, when he was one of six men in the company to get a ticket to a concert given by Miller and his Army Air Force Band in Newbury. Forty-seven years later, Malarkey could remember the program; Miller started with "Moonlight Serenade" ("the most thought-provoking theme song ever written," according to Malarkey), followed by "In the Mood."

On weekends, when they were not in a marshaling area or on an alert, the men got passes. Malarkey and More would jump on their motorcycle and head for the south coast—Brighton, Bournemouth, or Southampton—for swimming and sun bathing. Upon returning from one such excursion, they got a message from Captain Sobel. He wanted Malarkey and More to know that he knew they had the motorcycle and that it was stolen, but he was not going to do anything about it, except that he intended to confiscate it when the company next went into combat. Malarkey figured that Sobel's relatively reasonable attitude was a result of his unwillingness to confront Captain Winters.

What was not so pleasant as the billets or the radio or the weekends was the training. "I got the impression we were being punished for going to Normandy," Webster wrote. There was a dreary list of parades, inspections, field problems, night problems, and trips to the firing range.

Winters had smuggled some live ammunition back to Aldbourne from Normandy. He used it to give the replacements the feel of advancing in an attack under covering fire. There was a risk involved, obviously to the men on maneuvers, but also to Winters himself, as it was unauthorized, and if anyone had been wounded, it would have been his fault. But he felt the risk was worthwhile, because he had learned on June 6 at Brécourt Manor that the key to a successful attack was to lay down a good, steady base of fire and then advance right under it. Done correctly, the job got accomplished with few casualties.

The training exercises were necessary in order to give the replacements in the company (nearly half the company was made up of recruits by this time, just over from the States after completing jump school) the feel of live fire, and to integrate them into the company. But, necessary or not, they were hated. Still, compared to the 1943 experience in Aldbourne, the summer of 1944 was a joy. Malarkey explained: "We were no longer subject to the discipline and vindictiveness of Herbert Sobel and Sergeant Evans. With Dick Winters fairness and compassion replaced the unreasonableness of his predecessor. The esprit de corps in the company increased tremendously."

* * *

It helped morale that, however rigorous the training program, Easy was spending the summer in Aldbourne rather than Normandy. "I thank God and General Eisenhower that we returned to England," Webster wrote his parents, "whenever I think of the Pacific boys, living in jungles and on barren coral reefs, and of the infantry in France, grinding forward without music or entertainment of any kind until they are killed or wounded." All the men in Aldbourne were keenly aware that the 4th Infantry Division, their partners on D-Day, was still on the line, taking casualties, sleeping in foxholes, eating K rations, never bathing.

Rumors were constant. On August 10, Eisenhower himself inspected the division, which convinced everyone that the next combat jump was coming immediately, a conviction reinforced on August 12 when brand-new equipment was handed around. Some were sure it was off for the South Pacific, others thought India, others Berlin.

Those rumors were ridiculous, of course, but what fed them was the fact that the division made plans for sixteen operations that summer, each one of which was canceled. The problem was that through to the end of July, the front line in Normandy was nearly static;

then Bradley's First Army broke out at St. Lo, Patton's Third Army went over to Normandy, and the American ground forces overran proposed drop zones before the paratroopers could complete their plans and make the jump.

On August 17, Easy was alerted and briefed for a drop near Chartres, to set up roadblocks to cut off supplies and reinforcements for the Germans in Normandy, and to block their escape route. The company, along with the rest of the battalion, took buses to the marshaling area, at Membury airdrome, outside Aldbourne. They were fed steak and eggs, fried chicken, white bread, milk, ice cream. They checked their weapons and equipment, went over their briefing, discussed their objective.

The recruits were excited, tense, eager, nervous. The veterans were worried. "I hate to think of going again," Webster wrote in his diary. What worried him most of all was the thought of being killed in his chute as he came down, swinging helplessly in the air, or getting caught in a tree or on a telephone pole and being bayoneted or shot before he could free himself. He had acquired a .45 automatic pistol, but it was no match for a distant machine-gun. He felt that if he could live through the jump, he could take the rest as it came.

Talking to the subdued veterans around him at the airdrome, he noticed that "the boys aren't as enthusiastic or anxious to get it over with as they were before Normandy. Nobody wants to fight anymore."

Some hope was expressed that with Patton racing across France, the Allies on the offensive in Italy, the Red Army moving forward relentlessly on the Eastern Front, and the Wehrmacht high command in turmoil after the July 20 attempt on Hitler's life, Germany might collapse any day. Most of the men would have welcomed such a development, but not Webster, who wrote his parents:

"I cannot understand why you hope for a quick end of the war. Unless we take the horror of battle to Germany itself, unless we fight in their villages, blowing up their houses, smashing open their wine cellars, killing some of their livestock for food, unless we litter their streets with horribly rotten German corpses as was done in France, the Germans will prepare for war, unmindful of its horrors. Defeat must be brought into Germany itself before this mess can come to a proper end; a quick victory now, a sudden collapse, will leave the countryside relatively intact and the people thirsty for revenge. I want the war to end as quickly as anybody wishes, but I don't want the nucleus of another war left whole."

August 19 was D-Day for Chartres. It was scheduled to be a daylight drop. All around Membury that morning, men were getting up at first light, after a more-or-less sleepless night spent mainly sweating on their cots, imagining all sorts of possibilities. They dressed silently. They were detached and gloomy. No one was cutting Mohawk haircuts. There were no shouts of "Look out, Hitler! Here we come!" It was more a case of "Momma, if you ever prayed for me, pray for me now."

Joyous news over the radio! Patton's Third Army tanks had just taken the DZ at Chartres! The jump was canceled! The men shouted. They jumped up and down. They laughed. They blessed George Patton and his tankers. They cheered and danced. That afternoon, they returned to Aldbourne.

• • •

On Sunday morning, August 28, the 506th held a memorial service for the men killed in Normandy. When it was announced that the men would have to give up their Sunday morning, there was terrific moaning and groaning; as one trooper put it, he would honor the dead on Saturday morning or all day Monday, but he'd be damned if he'd honor the dead on his own time. But that was just talk, a soldier exercising his inalienable right to grouse. He put on his class A uniform and went along with the rest.

Easy Company was taken by buses to regimental HQ on the estate of Lord Wills at Littlecote, outside Chilton Foliat, where it joined the other companies on a soft green field. A band played the dead march in such a slow cadence that everyone got out of step, but once the regiment was in place, the 2,000 young American warriors spread like a solid brown carpet on the lawn, the grand castle before them, it made an inspiring sight.

Chaplain McGee gave a talk, saying the dead really were heroic, America really was worth dying for, those who died did not die in vain, and so on. The men were more impressed by the regimental prayer, written by Lt. James Morton and read by the chaplain:

"Almighty God, we kneel to Thee and ask to be the instrument of Thy fury in smiting the evil forces that have visited death, misery, and debasement on the people of the earth. . . . Be with us, God, when we leap from our planes into the dark abyss and descend in parachutes into the midst of enemy fire. Give us iron will and stark courage as we spring from the harnesses of our parachutes to seize arms for battle. The legions of evil are many, Father; grace our arms to meet and defeat them in Thy name and in the name of the freedom and dignity of man. . . . Let our enemies who have lived by the sword turn from their violence lest they perish by the sword. Help us to serve Thee gallantly and to be humble in victory."

General Taylor came next, but his speech was drowned out by a formation of C-47s passing overhead. Then the roster of the dead and missing was read out. It seemed to drone on endlessly—there were 414—and each name brought a sharp intake of breath from the surviving members of the soldier's squad, platoon, company. Each time he heard the name of a man he knew, Webster thought of "his family sitting quietly in a home that will never be full again." The reading ceased abruptly with a private whose name began with Z. The regiment marched off the field to the tune of "Onward Christian Soldiers."

• • •

The 101st Airborne Division was now a part of the First Allied Airborne Army, which included the U.S. 17th, 82d, and 101st Airborne (together the U.S. units constituted the XVIII Airborne Corps), the Polish 1st Parachute Brigade, and the British 1st and 6th Airborne Divisions plus the 52d Lowlanders (air-transported). Gen. Matthew Ridgway commanded the XVIII Corps; Gen. Lewis Brereton commanded the Airborne Army. General Taylor remained in command of the 101st; Gen. James Gavin commanded the 82d.

All these generals, and their senior subordinates, were itching to get the Airborne Army into action, but every time they made a plan, briefed the men, transported them to their marshaling areas, and prepared to load up, the ground troops overran the DZ and the mission was canceled.

It happened again at the end of August. On the thirtieth, at midnight, Taylor ordered company formations. The men were told to pack their bags for an 0800 departure for Membury. At the airdrome, along with all the other activity, a money exchange took place; English pounds for Belgian francs. Thus the men knew the objective even before the briefing (finance officers told those who did not have a pound note, "tough").

The DZ was to be near Tournai, Belgium, just across the border from the French city of Lille. The aim was to open a path for the British Second Army in its drive across the Escaut Canal and into Belgium. Two days of intense briefings, hectic preparations, and marvelous food followed. But on September 2 the Guards Armored Division of the British Second Army captured Tournai, and the operation was canceled. There was the same relief as when the Chartres drop was canceled, but the determination of the high command to get the paratroopers into the action was so obvious to the men that even as they rode the bus back to Aldbourne, they acknowledged to each other that one of these times they would not be coming back from the airport.

• • • •

The Allied armies continued to roll through France and Belgium. The Airborne Army's high command grew ever more desperate to get into the battle. It had the best troops in ETO, the best commanders, the highest morale, unmatched mobility, outstanding equipment. Officers and men were proved veterans who wanted another chance to show what paratroopers could do in modern war. The Airborne Army was by far Eisenhower's greatest unused asset. He wanted to keep the momentum of the advance going, he wanted to seize the moment to deliver a decisive blow before the Germans could recover from their six-week-long retreat from France. When Montgomery proposed to utilize the Airborne Army in a complex, daring, and dangerous but potentially decisive operation to get across the Lower Rhine River, Eisenhower quickly agreed, to the immense delight of the Airborne Army command.

Code name was MARKET-GARDEN. The objective was to get British Second Army, with the Guards Armored Division in the van, through Holland and across the Rhine on a line Eindhoven-Son-Veghel-Grave-Nijmegen-Arnhem. The British tanks would move north along a single road, following a carpet laid down by the American and British paratroopers, who would seize and hold the many bridges between the start line and Arnhem.

The British 1st Airborne Division, reinforced by the Poles, would be at the far end of the proposed line of advance, at Arnhem. The 82d Airborne would take and hold Nijmegen. The 101st's task was to land north of Eindhoven, with the objective of capturing that town while simultaneously moving through Son toward Veghel and Grave, to open the southern end of the line of advance. The task of the 2d Battalion of the 506th PIR was to take the bridge over the Wilhelmina Canal at Son intact, then join the 3d Battalion in attacking Eindhoven, where it would hold the city and its bridges until the Guards Armored Division passed through.

It was a complicated but brilliant plan. Success would depend on execution of almost split-second timing, achieving surprise, hard fighting, and luck. If everything worked, the payoff would be British armored forces on the north German plain, on the far side of the Rhine, with an open road to Berlin. If the operation failed, the cost would be the squandering of the asset of the Airborne Army, failure to open the port of Antwerp (Eisenhower had to agree to put off the commitment of troops needed to open that port in order to mount MARKET-GARDEN), a consequent supply crisis throughout ETO, and a dragging out of the war through the winter of 1944–45.

In addition to putting off the opening of Antwerp, Eisenhower had to stop Patton east of Paris to get sufficient fuel for the British Second Army to mount MARKET-GARDEN. In short, the operation was a roll of the dice, with the Allies putting all their chips into the bet.

• • •

On September 14, Easy took the buses back to the Membury marshaling area. On the fifteenth, the company got its briefing. It was reassuring. The men were told this was to be the largest airborne landing in history, three divisions strong. It would be a daylight landing. Unlike Normandy, it would come as a surprise to the Germans. Flak would be light, the initial ground opposition almost nonexistent.

In the marshaling area, waiting to go, there was a great deal of gambling. One of the recruits, Pvt. Cecil Pace, was a fanatic gambler. To the chagrin of the veterans, he won $1,000 at craps.

Colonel Sink gave the regiment a pep talk. "You'll see the British tanks," he said, "some of them Shermans and the others Cromwells. Don't mistake the Cromwells for German tanks.

"And those Guards divisions—they're good outfits. Best in the British army. You can't get in 'em unless you've got a 'Sir' in front of your name and a pedigree a yard long. But don't laugh at 'em. They're good fighters.

"Another thing," he went on, rubbing his face. "I don't want to see any of you running around in Holland in wool-knit caps. General Taylor caught a 506th man wearing one of those hats in Normandy and gave me hell for it. Now, I don't want to catch hell, see, and I know you don't, so if you've got to wear a wool-knit cap, keep it under your helmet. And don't let General Taylor catch you with that helmet off.

"I know you men can do all right, so I don't have to talk about fighting. This is a good enough outfit to win a Presidential Citation in Normandy. Now, you old men look after the replacements, and we'll all get along fine."

Webster recorded that it was always a pleasure to listen to Sink, because he had a sensible, realistic, humorous approach to combat. General Taylor was his opposite; in Webster's opinion Taylor had a "repellently optimistic, cheerleading attitude. Colonel Sink knew the men hated to fight. Up to the end of the war, General Taylor persisted in thinking that his boys were anxious to kill Germans. We preferred Colonel Sink."

• • •

On September 16 Private Strohl, who had been in the hospital since June 13, got a one-day pass from the doctors. He hitched a ride to Aldbourne, where he ran into Captain Sobel, who was ferrying baggage back to Membury. Sobel told Strohl that the company was about to go into action; Strohl said he wanted to join up and asked for a ride to the airdrome.

Sobel warned him, "You're going to be AWOL." Strohl responded that he did not think he would get into big trouble by choosing to go into combat with his company, so Sobel told him to hop in.

"It was a stupid thing to do," Strohl said four decades later. "I was as weak as a pussy cat." But he wasn't going to let his buddies go into action without him. He got himself equipped and climbed into a C-47.

Popeye Wynn, who had been shot in the butt helping to destroy the battery at Brécourt Manor on June 6, had been operated on and was recuperating in a hospital in Wales when he was told that if he was absent from his company for more than ninety days, when he was listed fit for combat, he would be assigned to a different outfit. Wynn wanted none of that. He persuaded a sergeant who was in charge of releasing the patients to send him back to Aldbourne with light-duty papers. He arrived on September 1, threw away the papers, and rejoined the 3d platoon.

He was not fully recovered. During the flight to Holland, he stood up in the back of the stick, as he was too sore to sit. But he was there, where he wanted to be, going into combat with his buddies in Easy Company.

8

"Hell's Highway"

HOLLAND

September 17–October 1, 1944

I T WAS A BEAUTIFUL end-of-summer day in northwest Europe, with a bright blue sky and no wind. The Allied airborne attack came as a surprise to the Germans; there were no Luftwaffe planes to contest the air armada. Once over Holland, there was some antiaircraft fire, which intensified five minutes from the DZ, but there was no breaking of formation or evasive action by the pilots as there had been over Normandy.

Easy came down exactly where it was supposed to be. So did virtually all the companies in the division. The landing was soft, on freshly plowed fields, in the memory of the men of Easy the softest they ever experienced. Webster wrote his parents, "It was the most perfectly flat jump field I've ever seen. Basically, Holland is just a big, glorified jump field." The official history of the 101st declared that this was "the most successful landing that the Division had ever had, in either training or combat."[1]

The only problem Winters could recall was the need to get off the DZ as soon as possible to avoid getting hit by falling equipment and landing gliders. "It was just raining equipment," he said: "Helmets, guns, bundles." Malarkey remembered running off the field to the assembly area (marked by smoke grenades). He heard a crash overhead; two gliders had collided and came plummeting to earth. There was no German opposition on the ground; the company assembled quickly and set off toward its objective.

• • •

The objective was the bridge over the Wilhelmina Canal at Son. The route was over a north-south road that ran from Eindhoven to Veghel to Nijmegen to Arnhem. The road was part asphalt, part brick, wide enough for two automobiles to pass each other but a tight squeeze for two trucks. Like most roads in Holland, it was a meter or so above the surrounding fields, meaning that anything moving on it stood out against the horizon.

The road was the key to Operation MARKET-GARDEN. The task for the American airborne troops was to take control of the road and its many bridges to open a path for the British XXX Corps, with the Guards Armored Division in the van, to drive through to Arnhem and thus over the Lower Rhine River.

Easy landed about 30 kilometers behind the front line, some 15 kilometers north of Eindhoven. The 506th's initial objective was Son, then Eindhoven,

---

[1]Rapport and Northwood, *Rendezvous with Destiny,* 269.

which meant the initial march was south. The regiment moved out with 1st Battalion going through the field to the west of the road, 2d Battalion down the road, 3d Battalion in reserve. Second Battalion order of march was D Company leading, then E Company, Battalion HQ, and F Company following.

The column entered Son. The residents were drawn up on each side of the road, as for a parade. Unlike Normandy, where the French villagers mainly stayed out of sight, the Dutch were ecstatic to be liberated. The parish priest, Hussen of Son, handed out cigars. Orange flags, forbidden by the German occupiers, flew from the windows. People gave the passing paratroopers apples and other fruit. Bartenders opened their taps and handed out glasses of beer. Officers had a hard time keeping the men moving.

Emerging from Son, less than a kilometer from the bridge, the column was fired on by a German 88 and by a machine-gun, both shooting straight down the road. There were no casualties. D Company covered the right side of the road, E Company the left. They pushed forward, firing rifles and lobbing mortar shells, which silenced the opposition. But the Germans had done their job, delaying the advance long enough to complete their preparations for blowing the bridge.

When the lead American elements were 25 meters or less from the bridge, it blew in their faces. There was a hail of debris of wood and stone. Winters, with Nixon beside him, hit the ground, big pieces of timber and large rocks raining down around him. Winters thought to himself, What a hell of a way to die in combat!

Colonel Sink ordered 2d Battalion to lay down a covering fire while 1st Battalion looked for a way to get over the canal. Cpl. Gordon Carson of Easy spotted a couple of waterlogged rowboats on the far side and decided on immediate action. He stripped stark naked, made a perfect racing dive into the water, swam across, and fetched a boat that carried some men from the first squad about halfway over the canal before it sank. Other men from 1st Battalion, more practical, took the doors off a nearby barn and with the help of Sergeant Lipton and several E Company men laid them across the bridge pilings. The German rear guard, its mission accomplished, withdrew. Engineers attached to the regiment improved the footbridge over the canal, but it was so weak that it could bear only a few men at a time. It took the battalion hours to get across.

It was getting dark. Sink got word that the Guards Armored Division had been held up by 88s a few kilometers south of Eindhoven, and he did not know the state of German defenses in the city. He ordered a halt for the night.

The platoon leaders posted outposts. Those not on duty slept in haystacks, woodsheds, whatever they could find. Privates Hoobler and Webster of Sergeant Rader's 2d squad, 1st platoon, found a farmhouse. The Dutch farmer welcomed them. He led them through the barn, already occupied with regimental Headquarters Company ("You shoot 'em, we loot 'em" was its motto), who resented their presence. On to the kitchen, where the Dutchman gave them half a dozen Mason jars filled with preserved meat, peaches, and cherries. Hoobler gave him some cigarettes, and Webster handed him a D-ration chocolate bar. He sucked in the smoke greedily—the first decent cigarette he had enjoyed in five years—but saved the candy for his little boy, who had never tasted chocolate.

Webster decided on the spot that he liked the Dutch much better than the British or French.

* * *

In the morning the march resumed, with 2d Battalion following 1st Battalion on the road south. On the edge of Eindhoven, a city of 100,000 that rose abruptly from the rich black soil, Colonel Sink spread his regiment, sending 2d Battalion out to the left, with Easy on the far left flank. Winters gave the order over his radio: "Lieutenant Brewer, put your scouts out and take off." Brewer spread 1st platoon out in textbook formation, scouts to the front, no bunching up, moving fast. The platoon advanced through truck gardens and freshly plowed fields toward the houses on the edge of the city.

There was only one thing wrong. Brewer was in front, with his map case at his side, his binoculars hanging around his neck, obviously an officer. Worse, he was well over 6 feet tall. Gordon thought he looked like a field marshal on parade. He was a perfect target.

Winters shouted over his radio, "Get back. Drop back. Drop back!" but Brewer could not hear him. He kept moving ahead. Every man in the company, every man in battalion, could see what was sure to happen.

A shot rang out. A sniper had fired from one of the houses. Brewer went down "like a tree felled by an expert lumberman." He had been shot in the throat just below the jaw line. Gordon and a couple of other enlisted men ran over to him, even though their orders were to keep moving and leave any wounded for the medics. They looked down at Brewer, bleeding profusely from his wound.

"Aw, hell, forget him," someone said. "He's gone, he's

gonna die." They moved on, leaving Brewer lying there.

He heard it all, and never forgot it, and never let the men forget it when he recovered and rejoined the company.

After that there was only light, scattered resistance, mainly from snipers. The 506th got into Eindhoven without further difficulty. The Dutch were out to welcome them. Many spoke English.

"So nice to see you!" they called out. "Glad you have come!" "We have waited so long!" They brought out chairs, hot tea, fresh milk, apples, pears, peaches. Orange flags and orange armbands hidden for years blossomed on all the houses and shirtsleeves. The applause was nearly deafening; the men had to shout to each other to be heard. "It was the most sincere thanksgiving demonstration any of us were to see," Webster wrote, "and it pleased us very much." It took most of the rest of the day to push through the crowds to secure the bridges over the Dommel River. It did not matter; the British tankers did not show up until late that afternoon. They promptly stopped, set up housekeeping, and proceeded to make tea.

Winters set up outposts. Those not on duty joined the celebration. They posed for pictures, signed autographs (some signing "Monty," others "Eisenhower"), drank a shot or two of cognac, ate marvelous meals of fresh vegetables, roast veal, applesauce, and milk. The civilians continued to mob them as if they were movie stars. Winters still shakes his head at the memory: "It was just unbelievable."

• • •

The company spent the night in hastily dug foxholes in Tongelre, a suburb on the east side of Eindhoven.

On the morning of September 19, Winters got orders to march east, to Helmond, in order to broaden the Eindhoven section of the corridor and to make contact with the enemy. A squadron of Cromwell tanks from the Hussars accompanied Easy. Some of the men rode on the backs of the Cromwells. The tanks, Webster wrote, "barked, spluttered, clanked, and squeaked in their accustomed manner as we set out."

Winters led a forced march to Nuenen, about 5 kilometers, encountering no opposition but once again cheering Dutch, offering food and drink. Webster remarked that this was the village in which Vincent van Gogh had been born. "Who the hell's that?" Rader asked.

Beyond Nuenen, the picnic ended. The Germans had recovered from their surprise and were beginning to mount counterattacks. "Kraut tanks! Kraut tanks!" Webster heard Pvt. Jack Matthews call out.

Oh, Jesus Christ! Webster thought to himself, as he and the others jumped off the Cromwells to dive into a ditch. Less than 400 meters away the first in a column of German tanks "slithered through the bushes like an evil beast."

The 107th Panzerbrigade, stationed in Helmond, was attacking west, toward Nuenen, with some fifty tanks—"more than we had ever seen at one time," Winters recalled. Sergeant Martin saw a German tank almost hidden in a fence row about 100 meters away. A British tank was coming up. Martin ran back to it, climbed aboard, and told the commander there was an enemy tank just below and to the right. The tank continued to move forward. Martin cautioned the commander that if he continued his forward movement the German tank would soon see him.

"I caunt see him, old boy," the commander replied, "and if I caunt see him, I caunt very well shoot at him."

"You'll see him damn soon," Martin shouted as he jumped down and moved away.

The German tank fired. The shell penetrated the British tank's armor. Flame erupted. The crew came flying out of the hatch. The gunner pulled himself out last; he had lost his legs. The tank, now a flaming inferno, continued to move forward on its own, forcing Bull Randleman to move in the direction of the enemy to avoid it. A second British tank came forward. It too got blasted. Altogether four of the British tanks were knocked out by the German 88s. The two remaining tanks turned around and began to move back into Nuenen. Easy Company fell back with them.

Sergeant Rogers had been hit. He was bleeding badly. "They kinda pinked you a little, didn't they, Paul," Lipton said. "Rogers let out a string of profanity that lasted a full minute," Lipton remembered. "Most unusual for him."

Lt. Buck Compton got hit in the buttocks. Medic Eugene Roe went to Compton's aid. Malarkey, Pvt. Ed Heffron, and a couple of others came forward to help.

As Heffron reached to help, Compton looked up and moaned, "She always said my big ass would get in the way."

He looked at the five men gathered around him. "Take off," Compton ordered. "Let the Germans take care of me."

He was such a big man, and the fire was so intense, that the troopers were tempted to do just that. But Malarkey, Guarnere, and Joe Toye pulled a door off a farm outbuilding and laid Compton face down on it. Then they skidded him up the roadside ditch to one of the retreating British tanks and loaded him, face down, onto the back end.

The bullet that hit Compton had gone into the right cheek of his buttocks, out, into the left cheek, and out. Lipton looked at him and couldn't help laughing. "You're the only guy I ever saw in my life that got hit with one bullet and got four holes," he told Compton.

Compton growled, "If I could get off this tank, I'd kill you."

Other men joined Compton on the backs of the withdrawing tanks. Strohl and Gordon, who had been out on the flank, Strohl with a mortar and Gordon with his machine-gun, had to run across an open field to rejoin the outfit. The weight of their weapons slowed them down. Bullets were kicking up the dirt at their feet. There was a 3-foot-high wooden fence between them and the road. "We hurdled it like two horses," Strohl said. Safely on the other side, they paused to catch their breath.

"That's one thing you and I will never do again," Strohl said.

"I don't think we did it the first time," Gordon replied.

They took off again for the tanks, caught up, and Gordon pulled himself onto the back of one. But Strohl was dead beat. He put his hand up; Gordon grabbed it as Strohl passed out. Gordon hauled him aboard and got him secured.

Randleman, who had been in the van, got hit in the shoulder and cut off from his squad. He ducked into a barn. A German soldier came running in behind him. Randleman bayoneted the man, killed him, and covered

his body with hay. Then he covered himself up with hay
and hid out.

• • •

Once in town, men found shelter in buildings that
they used as cover to move around and set up some
semblance of a return fire. Easy managed to hold up
the Germans but was unable to force them back. Sgt.
Chuck Grant got hit, among many others. Pvt. Robert
Van Klinken was killed by a machine-gun burst when
he tried to run forward with a bazooka. Pvt. James
Miller, a nineteen-year-old replacement, was killed
when a hand grenade went off on his kidneys.

Pvt. Ray Cobb had the shakes. Webster heard
Sergeant Martin comforting him, "the way a mother
talks to a dream-frightened child: 'That's all right,
Cobb, don't worry, we're not going back out there. Just
relax, Cobb, take it easy.'"

Martin went over to a Cromwell, hiding behind a
building. He pointed out the church steeple and asked
the commander to take it out, as the Germans were
using it as an observation post.

"So sorry, old man, we can't do it," the commander
replied. "We have orders not to destroy too much property. Friendly country, you know."

The Germans kept pressing. Their aim was to get
through to the highway leading from Eindhoven to
Nijmegen—"Hell's Highway," as the 101st named it—
and cut it. But they could not get through Nuenen.

Winters had decided to withdraw under the cover of
darkness, but before giving ground he wanted a prisoner for interrogation. He called for volunteers for a
patrol. No one volunteered.

"Sergeant Toye," he called out.

"Yes, sir, I'm here."

"I need two volunteers."

Toye selected Cpl. James Campbell and a private and set out. They were tripping over British and American bodies as they made their way to a nearby wood. A German soldier fired at them. Toye told his men to stay put. He crept into the woods, went around the German, got behind him, and gently placed his bayonet against the man's back. The soldier gave Toye no trouble. Pushing the German ahead of him, Toye returned through the woods and delivered his prisoner.

The company retreated to Tongelre. Winters noticed that the Dutch people who had been cheering them in the morning, were closing their shutters, taking down the orange flags, looking sad and depressed, expecting the Germans to reoccupy Eindhoven. "We too were feeling badly," Winters remarked. "We were limping back to town."

After getting his men settled down and fed, Winters went to battalion HQ. He found Lieutenant Colonel Strayer and his staff laughing it up, eating a hearty supper, in a jovial mood. Strayer saw Winters, turned, and with a big smile asked, "How did it go today, Winters?"

Tight-lipped, Winters replied, "I had fifteen casualties today and took a hell of a licking." The conversation in the room came to an abrupt stop.

Easy got one break that day. The company bedded down in Tongelre, so it watched, rather than endured, a seventy-plane Luftwaffe bombing mission against the British supply column in Eindhoven. As the Allies had no antiaircraft guns in the city, the Germans were able to drop bright yellow marker flares and then make run after run, dropping their bombs. The city was severely damaged. Over 800 inhabitants were wounded, 227 killed.

The next morning, Strayer moved his other two companies into Nuenen. They found Sergeant Randleman holding the fort. The German tanks had moved out, to the northwest, toward Son. Company E set up close-in defenses around Eindhoven and stayed there two days.

• • •

On the morning of September 22, Winters got orders to mount his men on trucks. The 506th was moving to Uden, on Hell's Highway, to defend the town against a Panzer attack that the Dutch underground warned was coming from Helmond. Regimental HQ Company, with Lt. Col. Charles Chase (the 506th Regimental X.O.) in command, accompanied Easy and three British tanks in an advance party. There were only enough trucks for the 100 or so men of HQ Company plus a platoon of Easy. Winters, Lieutenant Welsh, and Captain Nixon joined the convoy.

The trucks got through Veghel and into Uden without encountering resistance. Winters and Nixon climbed to the top of the church steeple to have a look. When they got to the belfry, the first thing they saw was German tanks cutting the highway between Veghel and Uden. Then Winters spotted a patrol coming toward Uden. He ran down the stairs, gathered the platoon, and said, "Men, there's nothing to get excited about. The situation is normal; we are surrounded." He organized an attack, moved out to meet the German patrol, and hit it hard, driving it back. Colonel Chase told Winters to set up a defense. Easy, with help from HQ Company, set up roadblocks on all roads leading into Uden.

Winters told Sergeant Lipton to take every man he could find, regardless of unit, and put him into the line. Lipton saw two British soldiers walking by. He grabbed one by the shoulder and ordered, "You two come with me."

The man looked Lipton up and down calmly and said, "Sergeant, is that the way you address officers in the American army?" Lipton took a closer look and saw that on his British combat uniform was the insignia of a major. "No, sir," he stammered. "I'm sorry." The major gave him a bit of a half-smile as he walked away.

The Germans did not come on. Had they realized that there were fewer than 130 men in Uden and only three tanks, they surely would have overrun the town, but evidently Winters's quick counterattack against their lead patrol convinced them that Uden was held in strength. Whatever the reason, they shifted the focus of their attack from Uden to Veghel.

Winters and Nixon climbed to the belfry again. They had a clear view of Veghel, 6 kilometers south. "It was fascinating," Winters recalled, "sitting behind the German lines, watching tanks approach Veghel, German air force strafing, a terrific exchange of fire-power." The members of Easy who were in Veghel remember it as pure hell, the most intense shelling they had ever experienced.

It was a desperate battle, the biggest the 506th had yet experienced. It was also critical. "The enemy's cutting the road did not mean simply his walking across a piece of asphalt," the history of the division points out. "That road was loaded with British transport vehicles of every type. Cutting the road meant fire and destruction for the vehicles that were caught. It meant clogging the road for its entire length with vehicles that suddenly had nowhere to go. For the men at Nijmegen and Arnhem, cutting the road was like severing an artery. The stuff of life—food, ammunition, medical supplies, no longer came north."[2]

Webster was in Veghel. When the German artillery began to come in, he took shelter in a cellar with a half-dozen Easy men, plus some Dutch civilians. "It was a very depressing atmosphere," he wrote, "listening to the civilians moan, shriek, sing hymns, and say their prayers."

Pvt. Don Hoobler was with the 3d squad, 1st platoon, hiding in a gateway. He decided to have some fun with Pvt. Farris Rice, so he whistled a perfect imitation of an incoming shell. Rice fell flat on his face. That put Hoobler in stitches: "Ha! Ha! Ha! Ha! Boy, sure sucked you in on that one!"

"Goddamn you, Hoobler, that's bad on a guy."

BzzYoo . . . BAM! A real shell came in. Hoobler stopped laughing.

Colonel Sink came roaring up in a jeep, jumped out, and began barking orders right and left. He got the men of Easy, and those of D and F Companies, to establish a perimeter defense with orders to shoot at anything moving.

Webster and the others climbed out of the cellar and went into an orchard. Webster and Pvt. Don Wiseman frantically dug a foxhole, 2 feet wide, 6 feet long, 4 feet deep. They wanted to go deeper but water was already seeping in.

[2]Rapport and Northwood, *Rendezvous with Destiny*, 359.

Sitting helplessly under intense artillery fire is pure hell, combat at its absolute worst. The shells were coming in by threes. "Wiseman and I sat in our corners and cursed. Every time we heard a shell come over, we closed our eyes and put our heads between our legs. Every time the shells went off, we looked up and grinned at each other.

"I felt sick inside. I said I'd give a foot to get out of that place. We smelled the gunpowder as a rancid thunderhead enveloped our hole. A nasty, inch-square chunk of hot steel landed in Wiseman's lap. He smiled.

"Three more. And then three, and then three. No wonder men got combat exhaustion." Webster later wrote his parents, "Artillery takes the joy out of life."

Things quieted down sufficiently for the supply people to bring up some British rations. Webster shouted at Hoobler to throw him a can. Hoobler was sitting above ground, laughing and joking, having a picnic with four or five others. "Come and get it," he called back. "The 88s are taking a break."

An 88 came in. Hoobler leaped into his hole, with his buddies piling in on top of him.

The men spent the night in their foxholes. There was a drizzle, the air was frosty. They sat with their heads on their knees, pulled their raincoats around their shoulders, and nodded off the best they could.

• • •

Back in Uden, Winters and Nixon lost their front-row seat. A German sniper spotted them and fired away. He hit the bell in the belfry. The ringing noise and the surprise sent the two officers flying down the steps. "I don't think our feet touched the steps more than two or three times," Winters declared.

He sat up his CP at a store on the road junction on the south end of town. The owners, the Van Oer family, who lived there, welcomed them, then went down to the cellar. Winters had his men move the furniture and rugs to one side, then brought in the machine-guns, ammunition, Molotov cocktails, and explosives and prepared to defend against any attack. His plan was, if the Germans came on with tanks, to drop composition C charges and Molotov cocktails on the tanks from the second floor windows—the Russian style of tank defense.

With that position set, Winters went to the other end of town, the northwest corner. On the left side of the road coming into town there was a manor house, with a tavern on the other side. Winters told Welsh to put the roadblock between the two buildings, backed up by one of the British tanks. He indicated he wanted Welsh to set up his CP in the manor.

Winters checked his other roadblocks, then at 2200 he returned to the northwest corner for one last look around. The British tank was where it was supposed to be, but there was no one in it or around it. Nor were there any E Company men at the roadblock. Highly agitated, Winters ran over to the manor and knocked on the door. A maid answered. She spoke no English, he spoke no Dutch, but somehow she figured out that he wanted to see "the soldiers." She escorted him down a hallway and opened the door to a large, lavishly furnished living room.

"The sight that greeted my eyes left me speechless," Winters recalled. "Sitting on the floor, in front of a large, blazing fire in a fireplace, was a beautiful Dutch girl, sharing a dinner of ham and eggs with a British lieutenant." She smiled at Winters. The lieutenant turned his head and asked, "Is my tank still outside?" Winters exploded. The lieutenant got moving.

Winters went back to the street to look for Welsh and his men. "Where the hell can Harry be?" He looked at the tavern across the street and his question answered itself. He went in and found Welsh and his men sacked out on the top of the bar.

"Harry and I talked this whole situation over," was the polite way Winters put it. "Satisfied that we would have a roadblock set up to my satisfaction, and that I could get a good night's sleep and not worry about a breakthrough, I left."

•   •   •

In Veghel, the Germans continued to attack through the night and into the next morning. British planes and tanks finally drove them off. The 506th moved out again, getting to Uden on the afternoon of September 24. The Easy Company men who had been trapped in Veghel assumed that the small force isolated in Uden had been annihilated; those in Uden likewise assumed that the rest of the company in Veghel had been annihilated. When the two parts reunited and learned that the entire company had survived the encounter in good shape, there was mutual elation.

The company prepared to spend the night in Uden. The men who had been there were amazed when the men who had undergone the shelling in Veghel dug foxholes 4 feet deep; they had only dug 6 inches or so into the ground and let it go at that. The officers had billets in houses in Uden. Lieutenant Peacock of 1st platoon approached Webster's foxhole and told him to come along. Webster climbed out, and they walked to

Peacock's billet above a liquor store on the village square.

"Take that broom and sweep this room out," Peacock ordered.

"Yes, sir," Webster replied, thinking to himself, What kind of a man is this? He decided, "I would rather starve to death as a bum in civilian life than be a private in the army."

* * *

The Germans had lost Uden and Veghel, but they hardly had given up. On the evening of September 24, they attacked Hell's Highway from the west, south of Veghel, and managed to drive a salient across it. Once again the road was cut.

It had to be reopened. Although the strategic objective of MARKET-GARDEN had been lost by now (on September 20 the Germans had retaken the bridge at Arnhem from Col. John Frost's battalion of the British 1st Airborne Division, and the division as a whole had been thrown on the defensive and the Guards Armored Division had been halted on September 22 some 5 kilometers south of Arnhem), it was still critical to keep the road open. Tens of thousands of Allied troops were dependent on it totally for their supplies. The units north of Veghel included the U.S. 101st at Uden and the 82d at Nijmegen, the British 1st Airborne north of the Lower Rhine, outside Arnhem, the Guards Armored and the 43d Wessex Divisions, the Polish parachute regiment, and the British 4th Dorset and 2d Household Cavalry regiments, all between Nijmegen and Arnhem. If the 101st could not regain control of the road and keep it open, what was already a major defeat would turn into an unmitigated disaster of catastrophic proportions.

General Taylor ordered Colonel Sink to eliminate the German salient south of Veghel. At 0030, September 25, Sink ordered his battalions to prepare to move out. At 0445 the 506th began marching, in a heavy rain, south from Uden toward Veghel. The order of march was 1st Battalion on the right, 3d Battalion on the left, 2d Battalion in reserve. At about 0700 the weary men passed through Veghel. At 0830 the 1st and 3d Battalions began the attack on the salient. Initially the advance went well, but soon the German artillery and mortar fire thickened. German tanks, brand-new Tiger Royals with 88 mm guns, dug in along the road, added their own machine-gun and shell fire. They were supported by Colonel von der Heydte's 6th Parachute Regiment, Easy's old nemesis at Ste. Marie-du-Mont and Carentan. The concentration on the narrow front was murderous. About noon, the battalions were forced to halt and dig in.

Sink ordered Lieutenant Colonel Strayer to have 2d Battalion make an end run, a flanking move to the left. It would be supported by British Sherman tanks. There was a wood of young pine trees along the left (east) side of the highway to provide a screen for the flanking movement. Company E led the way for the battalion.

Company E's first attack in Holland had been to the south, toward Son and then Eindhoven. The second had been to the east, toward Nuenen. The third had been to the north, into Uden. Now it would be attacking to the west, thus completing the points of the compass. That is the way surrounded troops fight. That was the way the airborne had been trained to fight.

•   •   •

Nixon joined Winters to scout the terrain. They found a pathway on the edge of the woods that was solid and firm, providing traction for the tanks. Good enough so far, but the woods ran out 350 meters from the highway, giving way to open ground that provided no cover whatsoever for the final assault.

Winters put the company into formation: scouts out, two columns of men, spread out, no bunching up. They got halfway across the field when the Germans opened up with machine-gun fire. Everyone hit the ground.

Guarnere and Malarkey got their 60 mm mortar into action. Guarnere called out range and direction; Malarkey worked the mortar. He was the only man in the field at that point who was not flat on his stomach. His first round knocked out a German machine-gun post.

Winters was shouting orders. He wanted machine-guns to go to work. The crews found a slight depression in the ground and set up the gun. They began to lay down a base of fire. Winters spotted a Tiger Royal dug in hull-defilade on the other side of the road and told the machine-gunners to take it under fire.

Turning to his right, Winters noticed Nixon examining his helmet, a big smile on his face. A German machine-gun bullet from the first burst had gone through the front of his helmet and exited out the side at such an angle that the bullet simply left a burn mark on his forehead. It did not even break the skin.

The German fire was too intense; Winters decided to pull the company back to the woods. The process would be to maintain the base of fire from the machine-guns while the riflemen backed off the field; when the riflemen reached the woods, they would begin firing to permit the machine-gunners to pull back.

When Lipton reached Winters, on the edge of the woods, Winters told him, "They [the machine-gunners] will need more ammo. Get some out there to them." Lipton ran to a Sherman tank (all the tanks were behind the woods, out of sight from the Germans—much to the disgust of the men of Easy). Shermans used 30-caliber machine-guns, the same as Easy Company's machine-guns. Lipton got four boxes of ammunition from the British. He gave two to Sergeant Talbert and took two himself. They ran out to the machine-guns in the middle of the field, which were firing continuously, dropped the boxes, circled around, and ran back to the edge of the field as fast as they could run. "The Germans were poor shots," Lipton remembered. "We both made it."

Just as the German parachute troops began to drop mortars on the machine-gun positions, Easy's riflemen went to work and the machine-gunners were able to withdraw.

Winters ran back to the tanks. He climbed on the lead tank "to talk nose to nose with the commander." He pointed out that there was a Tiger Royal dug in on the far side of the road. "If you pull up behind the bank on the edge of the woods, *you* will be hull-defilade, and you can get a shot at him." As Winters climbed down, that tank and the one to its left cranked up and began plowing straight through that stand of small pine trees, knocking them down.

As the first tank got to the far edge of the woods, it wheeled left to line up for a shot at the Tiger. *Wham!* The Tiger laid an 88 into it. The shot hit the cannon barrel and glanced off the hull. Evidently the German commander had fired blind, lining up on the falling tops of the trees.

The British commander threw his tank into reverse, but before he could back out, the Tiger put a second round dead center through the turret. It penetrated the armor. The commander's hands were blown off. He tried to pull himself up through the hatch with his arms, but his own ammunition began to explode. The blast killed him and blew his body up and out. The remainder of his crew died inside. The tank burned through the afternoon and into the night, its ammunition exploding at intervals.

The Tiger turned its 88 on the second tank and knocked it out with one shot.

• • •

Easy spent the remainder of the day, and all that night, in a miserable constant rain, raking the roadway with mortar fire. Headquarters Company brought up some 81 mm mortars to add to the fire. Artillery at Veghel joined in, but cautiously, because elements of the 502d PIR were attacking the salient from the south.

It was a long, miserable, dangerous night for the company, but the battalion S-2, Captain Nixon, had a lovely evening. He found a bottle of schnapps somewhere, and drank it himself. He knew he had a perfect excuse—his close call that afternoon when the bullet went through his helmet. He got roaring drunk and spent the night singing and laughing until he passed out.

In the early hours of September 26, the Germans withdrew from the salient. At first light, the 506th advanced on the road, unopposed. Once again, the

American paratroopers occupied the ground after a fierce firefight with German paratroopers.

That afternoon, in the rain, the regiment marched back to Uden. Easy Company arrived after dark, dead tired. The following afternoon, the men received their first mail since leaving England ten days earlier. This strengthened a general feeling that for the Americans at least, the campaign in Holland was over.

• • •

That supposition turned out to be wrong, but it was true that the offensive phase of the campaign had ended. And failed.

For Easy, as for the 101st, the 82d, and the British armored and infantry outfits involved in MARKET-GARDEN, it had been a dispiriting experience. For the British 1st Airborne Division, it had been a disaster. It had landed on the north side of the Lower Rhine on September 17 with 10,005 men. It evacuated on September 26 only 2,163. Nearly 8,000 men were killed, wounded, or captured. Not only had there been no strategic or tactical gain to compensate for such losses, now the Allies had a salient leading nowhere that had to be defended. It was a narrow finger pointed into German lines, surrounded on three sides by a superior German force, dependent on the vulnerable Hell's Highway for supplies.

Ten days earlier, the euphoria in the Allied camp had been running very high. One more operation and the war would be over had been the feeling. The Germans had been on the run ever since the breakout in Normandy, from the beginning of August right on through to the middle of September. It had been assumed that their unit cohesion was gone, their armor was gone, their ammunition was gone, their morale was gone. Those assumptions proved to be one of the great intelligence failures of the war.

In fact, by mid-September the Germans were well on their way to pulling off what came to be called the Miracle of the West. They put their units back together, resupplied and refitted them, brought in replacements, established a coherent defensive line. Eisenhower learned from the experience; in March 1945 he wrote his wife, "I never count my Germans until they're in our cages, or are buried!"[3]

MARKET-GARDEN was a high risk operation that failed. It was undertaken at the expense of two other possible offensives that had to be postponed because Eisenhower diverted supplies to MARKET-GARDEN. The first was the Canadian attack on the approaches to Antwerp, Europe's greatest port and essential to the support of any Allied offensive across the Rhine. In the event, Antwerp was not opened and operating until the end of 1944, which meant that through the fall the Allied Expeditionary Force (AEF) fought with inadequate supplies. The second postponed offensive was that of Patton's Third Army, south of the Ardennes. Patton believed that if *he* had gotten the supplies that Monty got for MARKET-GARDEN, he could have crossed the Rhine that fall and then had an unopposed path open to Berlin. That seems doubtful, but we will never know because it was never tried.

To the end of his life, Eisenhower insisted that MARKET-GARDEN was a risk that had to be run. In my interviews with him, between 1964 and 1969, we

---

[3]John S. D. Eisenhower, ed., *Letters to Mamie* (Garden City, N.Y.: Doubleday & Co., 1978), 244.

discussed the operation innumerable times. He always came back to this: the first rule in the pursuit of a defeated enemy is to keep after him, stay in contact, press him, exploit every opportunity. The northern approach to Germany was the shortest, over the terrain most suitable to offensive operations (once the Rhine had been crossed). Eisenhower felt that, given how close MARKET-GARDEN came to succeeding, it would have been criminal for him not to have tried.

Until I undertook this study of Easy Company, I agreed with his analysis. Now, I wonder. Easy Company was as good as any company in the AEF. It had won spectacular victories in Normandy. Its morale was high, its equipment situation good when it dropped into Holland. It had a nice mix of veterans and recruits, old hands and fresh men. Its officers were skilled and determined, as well as being brave. The N.C.O.s were outstanding.

Despite this, in the first ten days in Holland, just as Winters told Strayer the night of the attack at Neunen, it took a hell of a licking. It failed to get the bridge at Son, it failed to get through at Nuenen on its way to Helmond and for the first time was forced to retreat, it failed in the drive to Uden, it failed in its initial attack on the German salient south of Veghel.

The causes of these failures were many. First and most critical, in every case the German opposition outmanned and outgunned the company. The airborne troops did not have the artillery or the manpower necessary to launch a successful attack against German armor. Second, these were crack German troops, including their elite parachute regiment. They did not outfight the men of Easy, but they fought as well as the Americans did. Third, the coordination between the British tankers and the American infantry was poor. Neither Easy Company nor the Guards Armored Division had any training in working with each other. This shortcoming hurt Easy at Nuenen, at Uden, and again south of Veghel. At Brécourt Manor and at Carentan in Normandy, Easy had worked effectively with American tanks. In Holland, it worked ineffectively with British tanks.

On a larger scale, the trouble with MARKET-GARDEN was that it was an offensive on much too narrow a front. The pencil-like thrust over the Rhine was vulnerable to attacks on the flanks. The Germans saw and took advantage of that vulnerability with furious counterattacks all along the length of the line, and hitting it from all sides.

In retrospect, the idea that a force of several divisions, consisting of British, American, and Polish troops, could be supplied by one highway could only have been accepted by leaders guilty of overconfidence. Easy was one of 150 or so companies that paid the price for that overconfidence. It jumped into Holland on September 17 with 154 officers and men. Ten days later, it was down to 132.

9

The Island

HOLLAND

October 2–November 25, 1944

ASY COMPANY, like all units in the American airborne divisions, had been trained as a light infantry assault outfit, with the emphasis on quick movement, daring maneuvers, and small arms fire. It had been utilized in that way in Normandy and during the first ten days in Holland. From the beginning of October until almost the end of November 1944, however, it would be involved in static, trench warfare, more reminiscent of World War I than World War II.

The area in which it fought was a 5-kilometer-wide "island" that lay between the Lower Rhine on the north and the Waal River on the south. The cities of Arnhem, on the Lower Rhine, and Nijmegen, on the Waal, marked the eastern limit of the 101st's lines; the small towns of Opheusden on the Lower Rhine and Dodewaard on the Waal were the western limit. The

Germans held the territory north of the Lower Rhine and west of the Opheusden-Dodewaard line.

The Island was a flat agricultural area, below sea level. Dikes that were 7 meters high and wide enough at the top for two-lane roads held back the flood waters. The sides of the dikes were sometimes steep, more often sloping so gradually as to make the dikes 200 or even 300 feet wide at the base. Crisscrossing the area were innumerable drainage ditches. Hills rose on the north side of the Lower Rhine, giving the Germans a distinct advantage in artillery spotting. They had apparently unlimited ammunition (the German industrial heartland was only 50 kilometers or so up the Rhine River), enough at any rate to enable them to fire 88s at single individuals caught out in the open. All movement on the Island was by night; during daylight hours, men stayed in their foxholes, observation posts, or houses and barns. The fall weather in northwest Europe was, as usual, miserable: cold, humid, rainy, a fit setting for a World War I movie.

There were whole regiments of British artillery on the Island, firing in support of the 101st. This meant that Island battles were artillery duels in which the main role of the infantry was to be prepared to hurl back any assault by the German ground troops and to serve as forward artillery observers. Patrols went out every night, to scout and to maintain contact with the enemy. For the most part, however, Easy and the other companies in the 101st sat there and took it, just as their fathers had done in 1918. A man's inability to do anything about the artillery fire added to the widespread, overwhelming feeling of frustration.

But of course it was not 1918. On the Island, the

men of Easy first saw jet airplanes in action. They watched vapors from the V-2s, the world's first medium-range ballistic missile, as they passed overhead on the way to London. Still, as had been true of soldiers on the Western Front in 1914–17, they fought without tank support, as a tank was much too conspicuous a target on the Island.

The rations added to the sense that Easy was in a World War I movie rather than a real 1944 battle. The company drew its rations from the British, and they were awful. The British 14-in-1s, according to Corporal Gordon, "will support life, but not morale." Bully beef and heavy Yorkshire pudding were particularly hated, as was the oxtail soup, characterized as "grease with bones floating in it." Most men took to throwing everything in the 14-in-1s into a single large pot, adding whatever vegetables they could scrounge from the countryside, and making a sort of stew out of it. Fortunately there was fresh fruit in abundance, mainly apples and pears. Cows that desperately needed milking were relieved of the contents of their bulging udders, and that helped, but there was no coffee and the men quickly tired of tea.

Worst of all were the English cigarettes. Cpl. Rod Bain described them as "a small portion of tobacco and an ungodly amount of straw." Best of all was the daily British rum ration. Next best was finding German rations. The hard biscuits were like concrete, but the canned meat and tubes of Limburger cheese were tasty and nutritious.

As had been true of the villages of France on both sides of the line on the Western Front 1914–1918, the civilian residents of the Island were evacuated (and Holland is the most densely populated country on earth). This gave the men almost unlimited opportunities for looting, opportunities that were quickly seized. Webster wrote, "Civilians dwell under the misapprehension that only Germans and Russians go through drawers, closets, and chicken coops, whereas every G.I. of my acquaintance made a habit of so doing." Watches, clocks, jewelry, small (and large) pieces of furniture, and of course liquor quickly disappeared—that is, what was left, as the British had already stripped the area.

The Island was most like World War I in its stagnated front. Easy spent nearly two months there, in daily combat. It sent out almost 100 patrols. It repelled attacks. It fired an incredible amount of ammunition. It took casualties. But when it was finally relieved, it turned over to the relieving party front-line positions that had hardly moved one inch.

• • •

The company moved onto the Island on October 2, by truck, over the magnificent bridge at Nijmegen (still standing) that had been captured by the 82d on September 20 at 2000. Once over the Waal, the trucks took the men some 15 kilometers, past dozens of camouflaged British artillery pieces, to the village of Zetten.

They arrived at night, to relieve the British 43d Division. The 506th regiment was taking over a stretch of front line that had been held by a full division. It was over 6 miles in length. The 2d Battalion was on the right (east) end of the line, with Easy on the far right with the 501st PIR to its right. Easy had to cover almost 3 kilometers with only 130 men.

British soldiers met the company in Zetten and

escorted the leading elements to their new positions. "What's it like up here?" Webster asked.

"It's a bloody rest position, mate," was the reply. The numerous craters from 105s and 88s looked fresh to Webster, who doubted that he was being given straight scoop. After a three-hour march, the patrol reached its destination, a clump of houses nestled beside a huge dike. The Lower Rhine was on the other side of the dike, with a kilometer or so of flat, soggy grazing land between it and the dike. The area was littered with dead animals, burned houses, and empty machine-gun belts and ammo boxes. This was no-man's-land.

To cover his assigned section of the front, Winters put the 2d and 3d platoons on the line, along the south side of the dike, with the 1st platoon in reserve. He did not have sufficient troops to man the line properly, so he placed outposts along the dike at spots that he calculated were most likely enemy infiltration points. He kept in contact with the outposts by means of radio, wire, and contact patrols. He also sent three-man patrols to the river bank, to watch for enemy movement and to serve as forward artillery observers. He set up his CP at Randwijk.

• • •

At 0330, October 5, Winters sent Sgt. Art Youman out on a patrol, with orders to occupy an outpost in a building near a windmill on the south bank of the dike. With Youman were Pvts. James Alley, Joe Lesniewski, Joe Liebgott, and Rod Strohl. The building was beside a north-south road that ran to a ferry crossing on the river to the north, back to the small village of Nijburg to the south.

When the patrol reached the road, Youman told Lesniewski to go to the top of the dike to look things over. When he reached the top, hugging the ground as he had been taught, Lesniewski saw an unexpected sight, the outline of a German machine-gun set up at the point where the road coming from the ferry crossed the dike. Behind it, in the dark, he could just make out a German preparing to throw a potato-masher grenade at Youman's patrol, down at the south base of the dike.

Simultaneously the other members of the patrol heard German voices on the north side of the dike. Liebgott, who was trailing, called out, "Is that you, Youman?"

The German threw the grenade as Lesniewski called out a warning. Other Germans pitched grenades of their own over the dike. Lesniewski got hit in the neck by shrapnel. Alley got blown to the ground by a blast of shrapnel that left thirty-two wounds in his left side, face, neck, and arm. Strohl and Liebgott took some minor wounds; Strohl's radio was blown away.

They had run into a full company of SS troops. It had come across the river by ferry earlier that night and was attempting to infiltrate south of the dike, to make a diversionary assault in support of a major attack the 363d Volksgrenadier Division was sched-uled to launch at first light against the left flank of the 506th at Opheusden. Although the patrol did not know it, another SS company had crossed the dike and was on the loose behind American lines. Although division did not yet know it, the attack on 1st and 2d Battalions of the 506th was much more than just a local counterattack; the German objective was to clear the entire Island area of Allied troops.

After the skirmish with the first SS company, the E Company patrol fell back. It was a full kilometer to Winters's CP. "Come on, Alley," Strohl kept saying. "We've got to get our asses out of here."

"I'm coming, I'm coming," the limping Alley replied.

At 0420 Strohl got back to the CP to report the German penetration.[1] Winters immediately organized a patrol, consisting of a squad and a half from the 1st platoon, which was in reserve, plus Sgt. Leo Boyle from HQ section with a radio.

Sergeant Talbert ran back to the barn where his men were sleeping. "Get up! Everybody out!" he shouted. "The Krauts have broken through! God damn you people, get out of those beds." Webster and the others shook themselves awake, grabbed their rifles, and moved out.

Winters and his fifteen-man patrol moved forward quickly, along the south side of the dike. As they approached the SS company, he could see tracer bullets flying off toward the south. The firing made no sense to him; he knew there was nothing down that way and guessed that the Germans must be nervous

---

[1] When I did a joint interview with Strohl and Winters in the summer of 1990, the conversation went as follows:

Ambrose: So Rod comes back and tells you, "We've got a penetration here." Now pick up the story.

Winters: Let me tell you when he comes in, he's been in combat. He is breathless and you take one look at him and you know here's a guy that has just faced death. No question about it.

Strohl: I didn't look that bad.

Winters: You don't have to be ashamed of it. Somebody shooting at you.

Strohl: He's saying I shit my pants. I never.

and confused. He decided to stop the patrol and make his own reconnaissance.

Leaving the patrol under Sergeant Boyle's command, he crawled to the top of the dike. On the other (north) side, he saw that there was a 1-meter-deep ditch running parallel to the dike. It would provide some cover for an approach to the road. He returned to the patrol, ordered two men to stay where they were as rear and right flank protection, and took the remainder up and over the dike to the ditch on the north side. The group then moved forward cautiously down the ditch toward the road.

When he was 200 meters from the road, Winters stopped the patrol again and moved forward alone, to scout the situation. As he neared the road—which was raised a meter or so above the field—he could hear voices on the other side. Looking to his right, he could see German soldiers standing on top of the dike by the machine-gun position, silhouetted against the night sky. They were wearing long winter overcoats and the distinctive German steel helmets. Winters was about 25 meters from them, down in the drainage ditch. He thought to himself, This is just like the movie *All Quiet on the Western Front.*

He crawled back to the patrol, explained the situation, and gave his orders. "We must crawl up there with absolutely no noise, keep low, and hurry, we won't have the cover of night with us much longer."

The patrol got to within 40 meters of the machine-gun up on the dike. Winters went to each man and in a whisper assigned a target, either the riflemen or the machine-gun crew. Winters whispered to Christenson to set up his 30-caliber machine-gun and concentrate on the German MG 42. Behind Christenson, Sergeant

Muck and PFC Alex Penkala set up their 60 mm mortar.

Stepping back, Winters gave the order, "Ready, Aim, Fire!" in a low, calm, firing-range voice. Twelve rifles barked simultaneously. All seven German riflemen fell. Christenson's machine-gun opened up; he was using tracers and could see he was shooting too high, but as he depressed his fire Muck and Penkala dropped a mortar round smack on the German machine-gun. Sergeant Boyle was "astounded at the heavy, accurate fire that we delivered at the enemy." He later told Lipton he thought it was the best shooting he had ever seen.

The patrol began to receive some light rifle fire from across the road running from the dike to the ferry. Winters pulled it back down the ditch for about 200 meters, to a place where the ditch connected with another that ran perpendicular to it, from the dike to the river. Out of range of the Germans, he got on Boyle's radio and called back to Lieutenant Welsh.

"Send up the balance of the 1st platoon," he ordered, "and the section of light machine-guns from HQ Company attached to E Company."

As the patrol waited for the reinforcements, Sgt. William Dukeman stood up to shout at the men to spread out (as Gordon Carson, who recalled the incident, remarked, "The men will congregate in a minute"). Three Germans hiding in a culvert that ran under the road fired a rifle grenade. Dukeman gave a sigh and slumped forward. He was the only man hit; a chunk of steel went in his shoulder blade and came out through his heart, killing him. The survivors opened up with their rifles on the Germans in the culvert and killed them in return.

While waiting for the remainder of the platoon to come forward, Winters went out into the field between the two lines to be alone and to think things through. Three facts struck him: the enemy was behind a good solid roadway embankment, while his men were in a shallow ditch with no safe route for withdrawal; the enemy was in a good position to out-flank the patrol to the right and catch it in the open field; there was nothing south of the bank to stop the Germans from moving down the road unmolested to the 2d Battalion CP at Hemmen. Under the circum-stances, he decided he had no choice but to attack. It was now full daylight.

Returning to the patrol, he found that the reinforce-ments had arrived. Now he had some thirty men. He called Lts. Frank Reese and Thomas Peacock and Sgt. Floyd Talbert together and gave his orders: "Talbert, take the third squad to the right. Peacock, take the first squad to the left. I'll take the second squad right up the middle. Reese, put your machine-guns between our columns. I want a good covering fire until we reach that roadway. Then lift your fire and move up and join us." He told Talbert and Peacock to have their men fix bayonets.

As his subordinates went off to carry out his orders, Winters called the 2d squad together and explained the plan. Private Hoobler was standing right in front of him. When Winters said, "Fix bayonets," Hoobler took a big swallow. Winters could see his Adam's apple move up and down his throat. His adrenaline was flowing.

"My adrenaline was pumping too," Winters remem-bered. On his signal the machine-guns began laying a base of fire, and all three columns started to move as fast as they could across the 200 meters of level but spongy-soft field between them and the road, doing their best to keep low.

At this point, Winters had no firm idea on how many Germans were on the other side of the road running from the dike to the ferry, which was just high enough to block his view. Nor did the Germans know the Americans were coming; inexcusably, after losing their machine-gunners and riflemen in the first volley, they had failed to put an outpost on the road or up on the dike.

In the lead, Winters got to the road first. He leaped up on it. Right in front of him, only a few feet away, was a German sentry with his head down, ducking the incoming fire from Reese's machine-guns. To his right, Winters could see out of the corner of his eye a solid mass of men, more than 100, packed together, lying down at the juncture of the dike and the road. They too had their heads down to duck under the machine-gun fire. They were all wearing their long winter overcoats and had their backpacks on. Every single one of them was facing the dike; he was behind them. They were only 15 meters away.

Winters wheeled and dropped back to the west side of the road, pulled the pin of a hand grenade, and lobbed it over toward the lone sentry. Simultaneously the sentry lobbed a potato masher back at him. The instant Winters threw his grenade he realized he had made a big mistake; he had forgotten to take off the band of tape around the handle of the grenade he kept there to avoid an accident.

Before the potato masher could go off, Winters jumped back up on the road. The sentry was hunched down, covering his head with his arms, waiting for

Winters's grenade to go off. He was only 3 yards away. Winters shot him with his M-1 from the hip.

The shot startled the entire company. The SS troops started to rise and turn toward Winters, en masse. Winters pivoted to his right and fired into the solid mass.

Winters described what happened next: "The movements of the Germans seemed to be unreal to me. When they rose up, it seemed to be so slow, when they turned to look over their shoulders at me, it was in slow motion, when they started to raise their rifles to fire at me, it was in slow, slow motion. I emptied the first clip [eight rounds] and, still standing in the middle of the road, put in a second clip and, still shooting from the hip, emptied that clip into the mass."

Germans fell. Others began aiming their rifles at Winters. Others started running away from him. But all their movements were awkward, hampered by those long overcoats. He dropped back to the west side of the road. Looking to his right he could see Talbert running crouched over leading his column. It was still 10 meters from the road. Winters's own column, in the middle, was struggling through the field. Peacock's column on the left was 20 meters short of the road, held up by some wires running across the field.

Winters put in a third clip and started popping up, taking a shot or two, then dropping back down. The Germans were running away as best they could when the other American columns reached the road.

"Fire at will," Winters called out.

It was a duck shoot. The Germans were fleeing. The Easy Company riflemen were shooting them unmolested. "I got one!" Webster heard Hoobler call out.

"Damn, I got one!" According to Webster, "Hoobler was in his element, he ate this stuff up."

A bunch of Germans were cut off, hiding in some tall weeds. Christenson spotted them. "Anybody here speak German?" he called out. Webster came up. *"Heraus!"* he yelled. *"Schnell! Hände hoch! Schnell! Schnell!"* One by one, eleven Germans came out. Husky, hard-boiled, they claimed they were Poles. Christenson motioned them to the rear.

Webster went back to the road to get in on the shooting. A German turned to fire back. "What felt like a baseball bat slugged my right leg," Webster recalled, "spun me around, and knocked me down." All he could think to say was, "They got me!" which even then seemed to him "an inadequate and unimaginative cliché." (Like all writers, he was composing his description of the event as it happened.)

It was a clean wound. The bullet went in and out Webster's calf, hitting no bone. A million dollar wound. I got it made, he thought to himself. When medic Eugene Roe got to him, Webster had a big grin on his face. Roe patched the wound and told Webster to retire. Webster gave his bandoliers to Martin, "who was still very calm and unconcerned, the calmest, most fearless person I ever saw," and his grenades to Christenson. He kept his pistol and M-1 and began limping to the rear.

• • •

Winters could see more German soldiers about 100 yards away, pouring over the dike from the south side, the previously unnoticed SS company. They joined their retreating comrades in a dash to the east, away from the Easy Company fire. This made the target bigger. Lieutenant Reese had brought the machine-guns forward by this time; Private Cobb set his up and began putting long-distance fire on the routed German troops.

The surviving German troops reached a grove of trees, where there was another road leading to the river. As Winters observed, they swung left and began to follow that road to the river.

Winters got on the radio and called for artillery. British guns began pounding away at the main force of retreating Germans. Winters wanted to push down to the river on his road, to cut off the Germans at the river, but thirty-five men against the 150 or so surviving Germans was not good odds. He got on the radio again to 2d Battalion HQ for support. HQ promised to send a platoon from Fox Company.

Waiting for the reinforcements, Winters made a head count and reorganized. He had one man dead (Dukeman) and four wounded. Eleven Germans had surrendered. Liebgott, slightly wounded in the arm, was a walking casualty. Winters ordered him to take the prisoners back to the battalion CP and then get himself tended by Doc Neavles.

Then he remembered that Liebgott, a good combat soldier, had a reputation of "being very rough on prisoners." He also heard Liebgott respond to his order with the words, "Oh, Boy! I'll take care of them."

"There are eleven prisoners," Winters said, "and I want eleven prisoners turned over to battalion." Liebgott began to throw a tantrum. Winters dropped his M-1 to his hip, threw off the safety, pointed it at Liebgott, and said, "Liebgott, drop all your ammunition and empty your rifle." Liebgott swore and grumbled but did as he was ordered.

"Now," said Winters, "you can put *one* round in your rifle. If you drop a prisoner, the rest will jump you." Winters noticed a German officer who had been pacing back and forth, obviously nervous and concerned over Liebgott's exuberance when he first got the assignment. Evidently the officer understood English; when he heard Winters's further orders, he relaxed.

Liebgott brought all eleven prisoners back to battalion HQ. Winters knew that for certain, as he checked later that day with Nixon.

• • •

The ferry crossing the Germans had used to get over, and now would need to get back, was at the end of the road Easy Company was on. Winters wanted to get there before they did. When the platoon from Fox Company arrived, bringing more ammunition, Winters redistributed the ammo and then gave his orders. He set up a base of fire with half the sixty or so men under his command, then had the other half move forward 100 meters, stop and set up its own base of fire, and leapfrog the first group down the road. He intended to repeat this maneuver the full 600 or so meters to the river.

About 200 meters short of the river, Winters's unit reached some factory buildings. German artillery had started to work. The SS troops, desperate to get to the ferry, mounted a seventy-five-man attack on the right rear flank of the Americans. Winters realized he had overreached. It was time to withdraw to be able to fight another day. The unit leapfrogged in reverse back to the dike.

Just as the last men got over the dike, the Germans cut loose with a terrific concentration of artillery fire on the point where the road crossed the dike. They had it zeroed in perfectly. The airborne men scattered right and left, but not before suffering many casualties.

Winters grabbed the radio and called battalion HQ to ask for medics and ambulances. Doc Neavles came on and wanted to know how many casualties.

"Two baseball teams," Winters replied.

Neavles knew nothing about sports. He asked Winters to put it in clear language.

"Get the hell off the radio so I can get some more artillery support," Winters shouted back, "or we'll need enough for three baseball teams."

Just at that moment, Boyle "heard some mortars coming. You could tell they were gonna be close." Boyle wasn't moving too fast, as he was exhausted, a result of a less than complete recovery from his wound received in Normandy. "I pitched forward on the dike. A shell hit just behind me on the left and tore into my left leg from the hip to the knee and that was it. A terrible blow but no pain." Just before he lost consciousness, Winters tapped him on the shoulder and told him he would be taken care of.

Guarnere and Christenson cut his pants leg off and sprinkled sulfa powder on the horrible wound (most of the flesh on Boyle's left thigh had been torn away). They gave him morphine and got stretcher bearers to carry him rearward.

•　•　•

Webster, alone, was trying to cross an open field to get to an aid station. He was crawling along a cow path, lower than he had ever gotten in training, crawling through mud and cow dung. He ripped his pants on a barbed-wire fence. On the far side, he risked getting up and limping the last 100 yards to safety. A German observer saw him and called down some 88s. Three explosions, one on each side, one behind, made Webster feel "terrified and self-conscious." He managed to get out of the field before the 88 completed the bracket.

Some F Company men helped him to a road junction. Two medics with a jeep, coming back from the dike, picked him up, laid him across the engine hood, "and told me to relax. They said we would be going fast, because the man on the rear stretcher, Sergeant Boyle, was badly wounded and in need of immediate medical attention."

Altogether, the two platoons from Easy and Fox Companies took eighteen casualties from that artillery bombardment. None killed.

•   •   •

Winters set up strong points to cover the place where the road crossed the dike. Captain Nixon came up. "How's everything going?" he asked. For the first time since the action began, Winters sat down. "Give me a drink of water," he said. As he reached for Nixon's canteen, he noticed that his hand was shaking. He was exhausted.

So was Christenson. He couldn't understand it, until he counted up. He realized that he had fired a total of fifty-seven clips of M-1 ammunition, 456 rounds. That night while trying to stay awake on outpost duty and trying to calm down after being so keyed up, Christenson pissed thirty-six times.

•   •   •

With thirty-five men, a platoon of Easy Company had routed two German companies of about 300 men.

American casualties (including those from Fox Company) were one dead, twenty-two wounded. Germans casualties were fifty killed, eleven captured, about 100 wounded.

Later, Winters realized that he and his men had been "very, very lucky." In an analysis, he said the main reason for success was the poor quality of German leadership. The Germans had let the 1st squad get away with sitting in the field waiting for reinforcements. They had bunched up in one big mass, inexcusable in Winters's view. They had allowed two machine-guns to pin them down while the three columns of Easy ran 200 yards across the field in the bayonet charge. They had reacted much too slowly when Winters fired on them from the road. They failed to put together an organized base of fire when the shooting started.

Easy, by contrast, did almost everything right. Winters called this "the highlight of all E Company actions for the entire war, even better than D-Day, because it demonstrated Easy's overall superiority in every phase of infantry tactics: patrol, defense, attack under a base of fire, withdrawal, and, above all, superior marksmanship with rifles, machine gun, and mortar fire."

More can be said. For example, the physical fitness of the Easy men was a sine qua non. They put out more energy than a heavyweight boxer in a fifteen-round title match, way more; they put out more energy than a man would playing sixty minutes in three consecutive football games. Also notable was the company's communication system, with radio messages, runners, and hand signals being used effectively. The leapfrog advances and retreats put into play the training they had undergone at Toccoa and were carried out in textbook fashion. The evacuation of the wounded was likewise carried out with calm efficiency. The coordination with British artillery was outstanding.

So was Winters. He made one right decision after another, sometimes instinctively, sometimes after careful deliberation. The best was his decision that to attack was his only option. He provided not only brains but personal leadership. "Follow me" was his code. He personally killed more Germans and took more risks than anyone else.

But good as Easy Company of the 506th was, and there was no better light infantry company in the Army, there was nothing it could do about that terror of the battlefield, modern artillery. Easy had to cross the dike to get home. It could not stay in the open field and get pounded. But in crossing the dike, the company exposed itself to zeroed-in German artillery. A few minutes of total terror, and the company had taken more casualties than it had in its encounters with German riflemen by the hundreds earlier in the day.

"Artillery is a terrible thing," Webster said. "God, I hate it."

•   •   •

The Public Relations Office of the 101st Airborne Division gave the action extensive publicity, in typical wartime jargon: "Winters's order had to be, and was, for a bayonet attack. At a result of that brave order two companies of SS were heavily battered and forced to withdraw without getting an opportunity to start their attack which was scheduled to start at almost that very instant."

Insofar as the German 363d Volksgrenadier Division launched a major attack at Opheusden at dawn that day, against the left flank of the 506th, the small action at the dike may have been crucial. Had the German SS companies proceeded unmolested south of the dike, they would have hit regimental HQ at exactly the moment Colonel Sink had to concentrate his attention on Opheusden.

Sink was appreciative. He issued a General Order citing 1st platoon of Easy for gallantry in action. After describing the bayonet charge, he wrote: "By this daring act and skillful maneuver against a numerically superior force" the platoon "inflicted heavy casualties on the enemy" and turned back the enemy's attempt to attack battalion HQ from the rear.

• • •

A couple of days after the bayonet attack, Colonel Sink paid Winters a visit. "Do you think you can handle the battalion?" he asked, indicating that he was considering making Winters the X.O. of 2d Battalion. (Maj. Oliver Horton had been killed in battle at Opheusden on October 5.)

Winters, twenty-six and a half years old, a captain and company commander for only three months, gulped and replied, "Yes, sir. I know I can handle our battalion in the field. Combat doesn't worry me. It's the administration. I've never had administration."

"Don't worry," Sink assured him. "I'll take care of that part." On October 9, he made Winters the X.O. of 2d Battalion.

• • •

Winters's replacement as Easy Company commander failed to measure up. He came in from another battalion. Pvt. Ralph Stafford was scathing in his description: "He really screwed up. He not only didn't know what to do, he didn't care to learn. He stayed in bed, made no inspections and sent for more plums." He was shortly relieved.

Other replacement officers had also failed. Christenson said of one, "Indecision was his middle name. . . . In combat his mind became completely disoriented, and he froze. We, the N.C.O.s of the platoon, took over and got the job done; and never did he complain, for he realized his inability to command under pressure."

Webster wrote about a platoon leader in the Nuenen fight: "I never saw him in the fracas. He never came to the front. He failed to live up to his responsibilities; the old men in the platoon never forgave him. For an enlisted man to fail in a grave situation was bad, but for an officer, who was supposed to lead his men, it was inexcusable."

Malarkey related that in that fight, Guarnere "was giving hell to some officer who had his head buried in the sand, telling him he was supposed to be leading the platoon. . . . The same officer was later seen at an aid station shot through the hand, suspected of being self-inflicted."

A combination of new officers and men who had not been trained up to the standard of the original Currahee group, the rigors of constant pounding by artillery and the danger of night patrols was taking a toll on Easy. The conditions exacerbated the situation.

Paul Fussell has described the two stages of rationalization a combat soldier goes through—it *can't* happen to me, then it *can* happen to me, unless I'm more careful—followed by a stage of "accurate perception: it *is going to* happen to me, and only my not being there [on the front lines] is going to prevent it."[2] Some men never get to the perception; for others, it comes almost at once. When it does come to a member of a rifle company in the front line, it is almost impossible to make him stay there and do his duty. His motivation has to be internal. Comradeship is by far the strongest motivator—not wanting to let his buddies down, in the positive sense, not wanting to appear a coward in front of the men he loves and respects above all others in the negative sense. Discipline won't do it, because discipline relies on punishment, and there is no punishment the Army can inflict on a front-line soldier worse than putting him into the front line.[3]

One reason for this is what Glenn Gray calls "the tyranny of the present" in a foxhole. The past and, more important, the future do not exist. He explains that there is "more time for thinking and more loneliness in foxholes at the front than in secure homes, and time is measured in other ways than by clocks and calendars."[4] To the soldier under fire who has reached his limit, even the most horrible army jail looks appealing. What matters is living through the next minute.

---

[2]Paul Fussell, *Wartime*, 282.

[3]Except certain death. The Wehrmacht in Normandy, for example, had German sergeants standing behind foreign conscripts. A Pole in the Wehrmacht at Omaha Beach managed to be taken prisoner. At his interrogation, he was asked how the front-line troops stood up to the air and naval pounding. "Your bombs were very persuasive," he replied, "but the sergeant behind me with a pistol in his hand was more so." But the American Army didn't do things that way.

[4]Gray, *The Warriors*, 119.

Gray speculates that this is why soldiers will go to such extraordinary lengths to get souvenirs. At Brécourt Manor, Malarkey ran out into a field being raked by machine-gun fire to get what he thought was a Luger from a dead German. In Holland, on October 5, as Webster was limping back to the rear, in an open field under fire from a German 88, he spotted "a German camouflaged poncho, an ideal souvenir." He stopped to "scoop it up." Gray explains the phenomenon: "Primarily, souvenirs appeared to give the soldier some assurance of his future beyond the destructive environment of the present. They represented a promise that he might survive." It is almost impossible to think of anything but survival in a life-threatening situation, which accounts for the opposite phenomenon to souvenir-grabbing—the soldier's casual attitude toward his own possessions, his indifferent attitude toward money. "In campaigns of extreme hazard," Gray writes, "soldiers learn more often than civilians ever do that everything external is replaceable, while life is not."[5]

What is not replaceable is the esteem of comrades, but to the replacement soldier, just arrived, there is no comradeship, so there is nothing to hold him to his post. Gray tells the story of a deserter he found in a woods in France in November 1944. The lad was from the Pennsylvania mountains, he was accustomed to camping out, he had been there a couple weeks and intended to stay until the war ended. "All the men I knew and trained with have been killed or transferred," the deserter explained. "I'm lonely. . . . The shells seem to come closer all the time and I can't

---

[5]Gray, *The Warriors*, 82.

stand them." He begged Gray to leave him. Gray refused, said he would have to turn him in, but promised he would not be punished. The soldier said he knew that; he bitterly predicted "they" would simply put him back into the line again—which was exactly what happened when Gray brought him in.[6]

At the front, not only spit-and-polish discipline breaks down. Orders can be ignored, as supervision is not exact where danger of death is present. "Old soldiers have learned by bitter experience to be independent and to make their own decisions," Webster wrote his parents shortly after he was wounded. "Once our lieutenant told my squad leader to take his eight men and knock out some anti-aircraft guns that were firing on a flight of gliders. Nine men with rifles fighting dual-purpose 88s and 40 mms! The sergeant said yes [censored]. By using his own judgment he saved our lives in a situation where a new man would have rushed in blindly. This same lieutenant later ordered two scouts into a German position, but they, knowing better, got [censored]."

Veterans tried to help replacements, but they also took care not to learn their names, as they expected them to be gone shortly. It was not that the old hands had no sympathy for the recruits. "Our new members," Webster wrote his parents, "representatives of the 18-year-old draft, were so young and enthusiastic-looking it seemed a crime to send them into battle. We paratroopers get the best men in the army, but it's a hell of a fate for somebody who's never been away from home or high school to come here."

No man in Easy had been in combat before June 6,

---

[6]Gray, *The Warriors*, 17–18.

1944, but by October all the men who took off from England on the evening of June 5 who were still alive in Holland had been through two combat jumps and two campaigns. Many of them had been wounded; some of the wounded had gone AWOL from the hospital to go to Holland. This was not because they had a love of combat, but because they knew if they did not go to war with Easy, they would be sent to war with strangers, as the only way out of combat for a rifleman in ETO was death or a wound serious enough to cost a limb. If they had to fight, they were determined it would be with their comrades.

Replacements could seldom reach this level of identification. Further, as the army was speeding up the training process to provide men for the battle, the replacements were not of the quality of the original Currahee men. At Veghal, Webster saw a replacement named Max "moaning and clutching his right hand."

"Help me! Help me! Somebody help me!"

"What's wrong? Shot anywhere else?"

"No, no. It hurts!"

"Why don't you get up and run?"

"He didn't feel like it. He was in shock so bad he just wanted to lie there and moan. . . . It's a funny thing about shock. Some boys can have their foot blown off and come limping back to the aid station under their own power, while others, like Max, freeze up at the sight of blood and refuse to help themselves. They say that shock is largely physical, but it seems to me that one's mental attitude has a lot to do with it. Max wasn't aggressive, he wasn't hard, he wasn't well-trained."

That officers and men broke under the constant

strain, tension, and vulnerability is not remarkable. What is remarkable is that so many did not break.

* * *

With Winters's replacement gone, 1st Lt. Fred "Moose" Heyliger took over the company. Heyliger was an OCS graduate who had led the HQ Company mortar platoon in Normandy (where he was promoted to 1st Lieutenant) and Holland. He had been in E Company back in the States. From the first, Winters liked him immensely.

Heyliger was a good C.O. He visited the outposts at night. He went on patrols himself. He saw to the men as best could be done. Like the men in the foxholes, he never relaxed. The tension was always there. His company was spread much too thin to prevent German patrols from penetrating the line, and the dangerous possibility of another breakthrough of the size of that of October 5 was in his mind constantly. He bore up under the responsibility well, took the strain, did his duty.

* * *

"The British are masters of intrigue," according to Cpl. Walter Gordon. "I wouldn't necessarily want them on my flank for an assault on some target, but I sure would like to have them plan it, because they are very good at planning."

He was referring to "the Rescue," which took place at midnight, October 22–23. A week earlier, Col. O Dobey (nicknamed "The Mad Colonel of Arnhem") of the British 1st Airborne Division, who had escaped from a German hospital after being made prisoner, had swum across the Rhine and contacted Colonel Sink.

Dobey said there were 125 British troops, some ten Dutch resistance fighters who were being sought by the Germans, and five American pilots hiding out with the Dutch underground on the north side of the Lower Rhine. He wanted to get them back, and he needed help. Sink agreed to cooperate. As the crossing point was across from Easy's position, Sink volunteered Heyliger to lead the rescue patrol. Or, as Gordon put it, "We would furnish the personnel, the British would furnish the idea and, I suppose, the Band-Aids. A fair swap, by British standards."

Dobey was in contact with the Dutch underground on the far side via telephone (for some reason, the Germans had never cut those lines). He designated the night of October 22–23 for the operation. The American 81st AA-AT Battalion would fire tracers over the river with their Bofors guns to mark the spot where the Dutch would bring the men waiting to be rescued. To allay German suspicion, for several nights before the operation, the 81st fired tracers at midnight.

On the appointed night, Heyliger, Lts. Welsh and Edward Shames, and seventeen men selected by Heyliger followed engineer tape from the dike down to the river, where British canvas collapsible boats had been hidden the previous evening. It was, as usual, a murky night, with a drizzle adding to the obscurity. The shivering men edged the boats into the river. At midnight, the Bofors fired the tracers straight north. The Dutch underground blinked the V-for-Victory signal with red flashlights from the north bank. Easy began paddling as silently as possible across the river.

The men crossed with pounding hearts but without

incident. They leaped out of the boats and moved forward. Gordon had the machine-gun on the left flank; he set it up and prepared to defend against attack. Cpl. Francis Mellett had the machine-gun on the right flank. Private Stafford was at the point for the column seeking contact with the Dutch underground, Heyliger immediately behind him.

Stafford moved forward stealthily. There was no firing, no illumination. This was enemy territory, completely unfamiliar to the Americans, and it was pitch black. "The absolute quiet was almost petrifying to me," Stafford remembered.

Stafford took another cautious step. A large bird flew up not more than a foot away from his face. "I am positive my heart stopped beating," Stafford recalled. "I flipped off the safety on my M-1 and was about to fire when Lt. Heyliger calmly said, 'Easy.'"

They continued on and shortly met the British troops. The first one Stafford saw "hugged me and gave me his red beret, which I still have." A British brigadier stepped forward and shook Heyliger's hand, saying he was the finest looking American officer he had ever seen.

Heyliger motioned for the British to move in column to the boats, urging them to keep silent. But they just could not. Pvt. Lester Hashey recalled one saying, "I never thought I'd be so glad to see a bloody Yank." Lieutenant Welsh, who was in charge down at the boats, grew exasperated with the Brits who kept calling out, "God bless you, Yank," and told them they would all get killed if they didn't shut up.

The British got into the boats; Heyliger pulled his men back in leapfrog fashion; soon everyone was ready to shove off. Gordon was the last one back, and in the trailing boat crossing the river. "There was a certain amount of excitement and urgency," he said, and he was certain the Germans would sink them all any moment. But they were never spotted. By 0130 the entire party were safely on the south bank and crossing no-man's-land on the way to the American front line behind the dike.

The next day Colonel Sink issued a citation for gallantry in action. He declared that "the courage and calmness shown by the covering force was a major factor in this successful execution. So well organized and executed was this undertaking that the enemy never knew an evacuation had taken place.

"All members of this covering force are commended for their aggression, spirit, prompt obedience of orders and devotion to duty. Their names appear below."

Gordon's name is there. When I suggested that he must be proud to have volunteered for and carried out so well such a hazardous operation, he said the only reason he went along was that Heyliger had selected him. "It was not a volunteer operation. I'm not saying I wouldn't have volunteered, I'm just saying I didn't volunteer."

•   •   •

On October 28, the 101st Division's area of responsibility was enlarged. The 506th shifted to the east on the river bank, just opposite Arnhem. Easy was in the line in the vicinity of the village of Driel, which put the company in the easternmost tip of the Allied advance toward Germany. It was replacing a British unit.

As the company moved into its new positions,

Sergeant Lipton and battalion X.O. Winters talked with the British commander. He said they could see Germans moving around and digging in along the railroad track to the east. (Easy was still on the right flank of the 506th, at Driel; that put it at the point where the line bent at an acute angle, meaning one platoon faced north, another east, with the third in reserve.)

"Well, when you see them, why don't you fire on them?" Winters asked.

"Because when we fire on them, they just fire back."

Winters and Lipton looked at each other in disbelief. Easy always tried to keep the German heads down and on the defensive whenever it occupied the front line.

It did so at Driel and kept up active patrolling. The artillery continued to pound away. The Germans still had the advantage of holding the high ground north of the river, so movement by day was impossible. The platoons in the front line lived in foxholes. The rain was all but constant. No one ever got really dry. No shaves, no showers, no relaxation. A miserable existence.

To the rear, at the CPs and further back, conditions improved somewhat. Artillery was a problem, of course, but there was hot food and other compensations. The men listened to "Arnhem Annie," a German propaganda broadcaster, over the radio. Between American songs, she invited them to cross the river, surrender, and live in comfort until the war was over. The supply people were able to bring copies of *Yank* and *Stars and Stripes* to the men. The 101st's daily news sheet, *The Kangaroo Khronicle*, resumed publishing. The Germans dropped some leaflets, *Why Fight for the Jews?* The 506th P.O.W. Interrogation

Team broadcast over a loudspeaker surrender invitations to the Germans.

The only effect of the propaganda, by both sides, was to bring a good laugh.

* * *

Winters was bored. Being X.O. "was a letdown, a tremendous letdown. The most fun I had in the Army, the most satisfying thing I did was company commander. Being a junior officer was a tough job, taking it from both sides, from the men and from Captain Sobel. But as company commander, I was running my own little show. I was out front, making a lot of personal decisions on the spot that were important to the welfare of my company, getting a job done."

But as battalion X.O., "I was an administrator, not making any command decisions or such, just recommendations to the battalion commander, to the battalion S-2."

I suggested that some people would feel a sense of relief at the change.

"I didn't," Winters replied.

* * *

1st Lt. Harry Welsh's 2d platoon had the sector of the line facing east. His CP was in a barn some 50 meters west of the railroad tracks, where the Germans had their outposts. His platoon strength was down to two dozen men; even if he kept half of them on alert, that meant twelve men to cover a front of 1,500 meters. With a more than 200-meter gap between outposts, it was relatively easy for German patrols to penetrate the line after dark. They did so regularly, not with the purpose of mounting an attack—like the Allies, they had accepted the static situation and their lines were thinly held, too—but to make certain the Americans were not building up.

After his experiences on October 5, Winters was worried about the porous situation at the front. When he heard a member of the rescue mission of October 22–23 describe the penetration of German lines without being spotted as "fantastic," he snorted: "The Germans did the same thing to us. They got two companies across and we never fired a shot at them until they got up on the dike. So what's the big deal?"

Winters was also frustrated in his new job. He craved action and fretted over the German penetrations. On the afternoon of October 31, he called Heyliger on the telephone to suggest that that night the two of them make their own inspection of the outposts. Heyliger agreed. At 2100 hours that evening, Winters arrived at Easy's CP. Heyliger telephoned Welsh to let him know that he and Winters were on their way out to see him.

"As Moose and I proceeded down the path leading to Welsh's CP," Winters related, "we were walking shoulder to shoulder, as the path was only about six feet wide, slightly raised. There was a drop of about three feet into a drainage ditch on each side."

Out of the darkness came an order, "Halt!"

Heyliger was a calm, easygoing man, a C.O. who did not get excited unnecessarily. So when Winters felt him take an extra hard deep breath, he tensed. Winters figured Heyliger had forgotten the password.

Heyliger started to say "Moose," but before he got the word half out, *blam, blam, blam*—an M-1 spat three bullets out from a distance of 10 yards.

Heyliger dropped to the road with a moan. Winters

dived into the ditch on the left side of the road. He feared they had run into a German patrol because the M-1 fire had been so rapid it could have been a German machine pistol. Then he heard footsteps running away.

Winters crawled back onto the path, grabbed Heyliger, and pulled him to the side. He had been hit in the right shoulder, a fairly clean wound, and in the left calf, a bad one—his calf looked like it had been blown away. Winters set to bandaging the leg.

A few minutes later Winters heard footsteps running his way. As he moved to grab his rifle, he heard Welsh calling in a low voice, "Moose? Dick?"

Welsh and two of his men helped bandage Heyliger. They gave him morphine shots and carried him back to the battalion CP. By then he had lost so much blood, and had had so many shots of morphine, he had a wax-like pallor that made Winters doubt he was going to make it.

He made it. Within a week he was back in a hospital in England. While there he was promoted to captain and given the British Military Cross for the rescue patrol. But for Heyliger, the war was over.

The soldier who shot Heyliger had been tense, frightened, unsure of himself. The incident broke him up. He was a veteran, not a recruit. Winters decided not to punish him. Soon thereafter, he was eased out of the company.

On November 7, Heyliger wrote Winters from his hospital bed. "Dear Dick: Here I am laying flat on my back taking it easy. I want to thank you for taking care of me that night I got hit. It sure is a stupid way to get knocked off.

"I arrived here naked as a jay bird. Didn't have a

thing. I know you have my wings and pistol, but I am sweating out the clothes in my bed roll and the rolls of film in my musette bag. . . .

"Jesus, Dick, they put casts right over my wounds and it smells as if a cat shit in my bed. I can't get away from that stink.

"Well, this is short, but my right arm is very weak. Remember me to all."

• • •

Heyliger's replacement as C.O. of Easy was 1st Lt. Norman S. Dike, Jr. He came over from division HQ. Tall, slim, good looking, he was well educated and talked in a military tone of voice. He made a good impression.

• • •

Being X.O. put Winters into daily contact with Nixon, by now battalion S-3. They hardly could have been more different. Winters grew up in a middle-class home; Nixon's father was fabulously wealthy. Winters had not gotten out of Pennsylvania in his teenage years; Nixon had lived in various parts of Europe. Winters was a graduate of a small college; Nixon came from Yale. Winters never drank; Nixon was an alcoholic. But they were the closest of friends, because what they had in common was a dedication to the job at hand, and a remarkable ability to do that job. Every member of Easy interviewed for this book said Winters was the best combat commander he ever saw, while Nixon was the most brilliant staff officer he knew in the war.

"Nixon was a hard man to get out of the sack in the morning," according to Winters. One day in November, Winters wanted to get an early start. Nixon, as usual, could not be talked into getting up. Winters went to his bed, grabbed his feet while he was still in his sleeping bag, and threw them over his shoulder.

"Are you going to get up?"

"Go away, leave me alone."

Winters noticed that the water pitcher was half-full. Still holding Nixon's feet on his shoulder, he grabbed the pitcher and started pouring the contents on Nixon's face. Nixon opened his eyes. He was horrified. "No! No!" he begged. Too late, the contents were on their way. Only then did Winters realize that Nixon had not gone outside to piss away the liquor he had drunk, but used the water pitcher instead.

Nixon yelled and swore, then started laughing. The two officers decided to go into Nijmegen to investigate the rumor that hot showers were available for officers there.

•   •   •

The campaign dragged on. Increasing cold added to the misery of the daily rains. Finally, in late November, Canadian units began to replace the 101st. Easy's turn came on the night of November 24–25, when it pulled out of the line. In the morning, the men boarded trucks for the trip back to France for rest, refitting, receiving replacements, and a shower, which the enlisted men had not had in sixty-nine days.

Easy had jumped on September 17 with 154 officers and men. It came out of Holland with 98 officers and men. Lieutenants Brewer, Compton, Heyliger, and Charles Hudson had been wounded, along with forty-five enlisted men. The Easy men killed in action were William Dukeman, Jr., James Campbell, Vernon

Menze, William Miller, James Miller, Robert Van Klinken. The company had taken sixty-five casualties in Normandy, so its total at the end of November was 120 (some of these men had been wounded in both campaigns), of whom not one was a prisoner of war.

As the trucks rolled back down Hell's Highway, the Dutch lined the roads to cheer their liberators. "September 17," they shouted, as the convoy moved through Nijmegen, Uden, Veghel, Eindhoven.

The men of Easy did not feel like conquering heroes. Sergeant Lipton summed it up: "Arnhem Annie said over the radio, 'You can listen to our music, but you can't walk in our streets.' She was right. We didn't get into Arnhem."

10

Resting, Recovering, and Refitting

MOURMELON-LE-GRAND

November 26–December 18, 1944

AT 0400 NOVEMBER 26, Easy arrived at Camp Mourmelon, outside the village of Mourmelon-le-Grand (nearby was the village of Mourmelon-le-Petit), some 30 kilometers from the cathedral town and champagne center of Reims. Mourmelon had been a garrison town for at least 1,998 years—Julius Caesar and his Roman legions had used it as a campground in 54 B.C. The French Army had had barracks there for hundreds of years, and still does in the 1990s. Located on the plain between the Marne River to the south and the Aisne River to the north, on the traditional invasion route toward Paris (or toward the Rhine, depending on who was on the offensive), Mourmelon was in an area that had witnessed many battles through the centuries. Most recently the area had been torn up between 1914 and 1918. The artillery craters and trenches from the last world war were everywhere. American Doughboys had fought in the vicinity in 1918, at Chàteau-Thierry and Belleau Wood.

The transition from front line to garrison duty was quick. The first day in camp featured a hot shower and a chance to launder clothes. The second day the company had a marching drill; the next day there was a regular retreat formation with cannon firing and inspection. On November 30, the mail caught up with the men, boosting morale 100 percent.

One might have thought that after more than two months on the front line, the paratroopers would have wanted to sleep for a week. But after one or two experiences of that miracle that is a soldier's night sleep, the boys needed a physical outlet for their energy and some nonsensical way to release the built-up tension. On December 1, everyone got a pass to Reims. So did the men of the 82d Airborne, camped nearby. The mix was volatile. Although Reims was crawling with M.P.s, because it was Eisenhower's HQ, there was plenty to drink, and thus plenty of drunks and plenty of men who wanted to fight.

"What's that eagle screaming for?" an 82d man would ask his buddies when they encountered someone wearing the Screaming Eagle shoulder patch.

"Help! Help! Help!" was the reply. And a fistfight would start. On December 4, all passes to Reims were canceled because, as one trooper put it, "the boys won't behave in town."

Division tried to work off some of the excess energy by ordering 5-mile marches, parades, and lots of calisthenics. It also organized games of baseball, basketball, and football. It borrowed football equipment from the Air Force, flown in from England. Tryouts were held for a Christmas Day Champagne Bowl game between the 506th and the 502d; those who made the team practiced for three hours and more a day. For other entertainment, Division set up three movie theaters, and opened a Red Cross club. The chow was superb.

Several days after arrival at Mourmelon, the men got paid in the mess hall at the conclusion of dinner. Sergeant Malarkey drew his pay and had started out the door when he noticed a crap game in progress. A hot shooter had piled up a big bankroll. Malarkey thought he could not possibly continue to throw passes so he started fading the shooter. In a few minutes he had blown three months' pay. He left the mess hall thinking how dumb he was—not to have gambled, but to have lost everything without once shooting the dice himself.

Back in barracks he ran into Skip Muck. There was a dice game going on. Malarkey asked Muck if he intended to get in it; no, Muck replied, he was tired of being broke all the time. Besides he only had $60 left after paying off his previous gambling debts. Malarkey thereupon talked him into a $60 loan and got into the game. In fifteen minutes he had built himself a bankroll of French francs, British pounds, U.S. dollars, Belgian francs, and Dutch guilders. (The arguments about the exchange rate around those crap games were intense; somehow these guys, most of whom had hated—and mostly flunked—math in high school, figured it out.)

Malarkey took his money over to the N.C.O. club and got into a game with some twenty players. He threw $60 of U.S. money into the game—the amount he had borrowed from Muck. He won. He let it ride and won again. And again. And again. On the last throw he had $3,000 riding. He won.

He was afraid to leave the game with more than $6,000, which was damn near the whole company payroll. He put the large francs in his pockets and stayed in the game until he had lost all the American, British, Dutch, and Belgian money. Returning to barracks, he gave Muck the $60 plus a $500 tip. He still had $3,600.

• • •

The men were put to work improving the barracks. The most recent occupants had been two divisions of German infantry plus several squadrons of light cavalry. German orders of the day, propaganda posters, and the like were on the walls. They came down, the leavings of the horses were cleaned up, bunks were repaired, latrines and roads improved. "And thru it all like a bright thread," the 506th scrapbook *Currahee* declared, "ran the anticipation of the Paris passes. Morning, noon, and night, anywhere you happened to be you could hear it being discussed."

Division policy was that the men would go into Paris by companies, one at a time. The ones who made it came back with tales that topped those their fathers told after visiting Paris in 1918–19. The ones who were waiting discussed endlessly what they were going to do when they got to the city.

Some individuals got passes. In a couple of cases, they were wasted. Dick Winters got a pass; he went to Paris, got on the Metro, rode to the end of the line, and discovered that he had taken the last run of the day. Darkness had fallen, the city was blacked out, he walked back to his hotel, got in well after midnight, and the next day returned by train to Mourmelon. "That was my big night in Paris." Pvt. Bradford Freeman, from Lowndes County, Mississippi, got a pass to Paris. Forty-six years later he recalled of his one day in the City of Lights, "I didn't care for what I saw, so I went back to camp."

There appeared to be no hurry about getting to Paris, as the general impression was that the paratroopers were going to stay in camp until the good campaigning weather returned in the spring. At that time they expected to jump into Germany, on the far side of the Rhine. The impression was reinforced when General Taylor flew back to the States to participate in conferences regarding proposed changes in organization and equipment of the American airborne divisions. It became a certainty on December 10, when Taylor's deputy, Brig. Gen. Gerald Higgins, flew to England with five senior officers from the 101st to give a series of lectures on MARKET-GARDEN. Command passed to Brig. Gen. Anthony McAuliffe, the division's artillery commander.

* * * *

Veterans were returning from hospital, new recruits coming in. Buck Compton rejoined the company, recovered from his wound in Holland. Lt. Jack Foley, who had hooked up as replacement during the last week in Holland, became assistant platoon leader of 2d platoon under Lieutenant Compton. The men, Foley remembered, "were a mixture of seasoned combat veterans, some with just Holland under their belt, and of course green replacements."

The replacements, eighteen- and nineteen-year-olds fresh from the States, were wide-eyed. Although the veterans were only a year or two older, they looked terrifying to the recruits. They were supposed to have handed in their live ammunition when they left

Colonel Robert F. Sink *(top left)*, first and only commander of the 506th Regiment; Captain Herbert Sobel *(below left),* first C.O. of Easy Company; and Lt. Richard Winters *(below)*, platoon commander in Easy. The company, brought into existence at Toccoa, Georgia, in July 1942, was trained and hammered into shape by

Army Signal Corps

these men. Sink and Winters were tough but fair and respected; Sobel was a martinet and widely disliked. Still, as Private Rod Strohl put it forty-nine years later, "Herbert Sobel *made* E Company." The rigorous training in the States saved many lives in combat in Europe.

Army Signal Corps

Forrest Guth

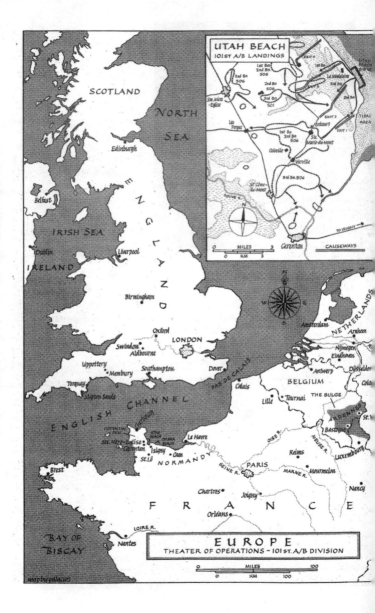

UTAH BEACH
101ST A/B LANDINGS

EUROPE
THEATER OF OPERATIONS – 101ST. A/B DIVISION

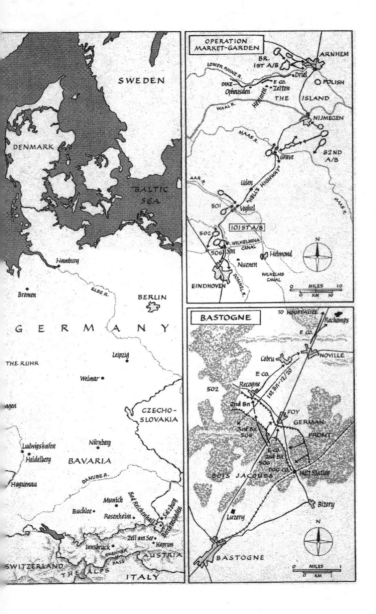

OPERATION MARKET-GARDEN

BR. 1ST A/B
ARNHEM
LOWER RHINE R.
DIKE
Ophusden
E CO.
Zetten
Driel
POLISH
THE
ISLAND
WAAL R.
NIJMEGEN
MAAS R.
Grave
82 ND
A/B
AAR R.
Uden
HELLS HIGHWAY
MAAS R.
501
Veghel
101ST A/B
502
WILHELMINA CANAL
Helmond
506
Son
WILHELMS CANAL
Nuenen
DOMMEL R.
EINDHOVEN
N
0   MILES   10
0   KM   10

SWEDEN

DENMARK

BALTIC SEA

Hamburg

Bremen
ELBE R.
BERLIN

G E R M A N Y

THE RUHR
Leipzig

Weimar

agen
CZECHO-SLOVAKIA

Ludwigshafen
Heidelberg
Nürnberg

Haguenau
BAVARIA
DANUBE R.

Buchloe
Munich
Bad Reichenhall

Rosenheim
Salzburg

Zell am See
Kaprun

Innsbruck
BRENNER PASS
AUSTRIA

SWITZERLAND
THE ALPS
ITALY

BASTOGNE

TO HOUFFALIZE
Rachamps
E CO.
Cobru
NOVILLE
Recogne
502
1st Bn 12/20
2nd Bn
FOY
GERMAN FRONT
3rd Bn 506
E CO.
2nd Bn 506
DOG CO.
Halt Station
BOIS JACQUES
Luzery
Bizory
BASTOGNE
N
0   MILES   1
0   KM   1

Army Signal Corps

In England in the winter of 1943–44 the training intensified. When Ike and Churchill inspected Easy Company in March, the men were fit and eager to go. Late in the afternoon of June 5, the company marched to the C-47 transport planes at Uppottery airfield, then loaded up for the first combat jump—the one in which "your problems begin *after* you land!"

Army Signal Corps

Army Signal Corps

Sgt. Burton Christenson of E Company drew this sketch of the moment he jumped. Lieutenant Winters is first out of the plane; Christenson is right behind him. The sky was illuminated by moonlight plus the fires and explosions. The paratroopers were getting shot at in their planes, as they descended, and on the ground.

Private Forrest Guth *(left)* and privates John Eubanks and Walter Gordon *(below)* display their first souvenirs, June 6, 1944.

Walter Gordon

Forrest Guth

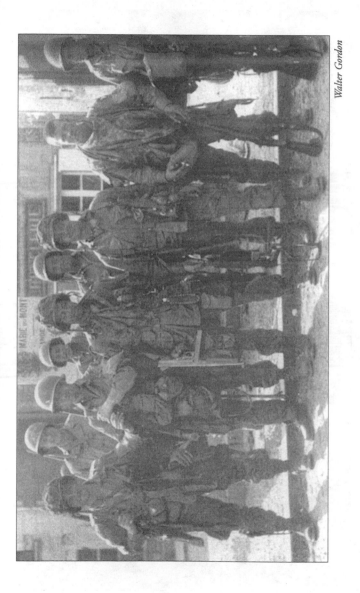

Walter Gordon

Opposite page: On June 7, in the square at Ste. Marie-du-Mont, privates Forrest Guth, Frank Mellet, David Morris, Daniel West, Floyd Talbert, and C. T. Smith of Easy Company posed with three infantrymen from the 4th Division (back row) who had come in from Utah Beach.

Below: Carentan, where Easy fought its first big battle as an intact company. Winters led the men down the road coming in from the left in a frontal assault against a German machine-gun position in the building to the right.

Al Kroachka/Army Signal Corps

Forrest Guth

Above: After taking Carentan, Easy went into a defensive position outside the town, where it held off numerous German counterattacks. Here Walter Gordon and Frank Mellet man their machine-gun position on the main line of resistance.

Opposite page: The people of Eindhoven welcome their liberators from Easy Company and the 506th, September 18, 1944.

Hans Wesenhagen

Above: Pvt. David Webster in Eindhoven. Webster was a Harvard English Lit major who wanted to be a writer and was a keen and sensitive observer of the war.

Al Kroachka/Army Signal Corps

Left: Captain Winters outside Colonel Strayer's HQ in Holland, October 1944. He was there to plan a daring rescue operation of British paratroopers on the far side of the Rhine near Arnhem, which was successfully carried out on the night of October 22–23.

Army Signal Corps

Third Platoon, Company E, loads into tenton trailers at Mourmelon on the afternoon of December 18. The Germans had broken through the American lines in the Ardennes. Short on food, ammunition, and winter clothing, Easy still had to get to Bastogne before the Germans.

1st Sgt. Carwood Lipton in his foxhole at Bastogne. E Company was in this position for nearly a month, hurling

back everything the SS Panzer divisions could throw at them, enduring the weather, prevailing.

Forrest Guth

Army Signal Corps

In mid-January, the American counterattack began. In a crisis during the attack on Foy, Capt. Ronald Speirs took command of the company and led it into the village. He was even tougher than he looks, an outstanding rifle company commander, highly respected by the men.

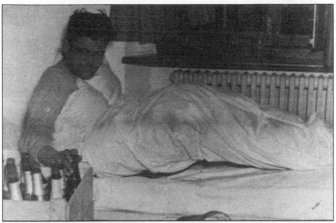

Al Kroachka/Army Signal Corps

Capt. Lewis Nixon on the morning of V-E Day.

1st Sgt. Floyd Talbert on Hitler's staff car. Ordered to turn it over to the brass, Talbert first conducted an experiment to see if the windows really were bulletproof. He found that armor-piercing ammo would do the job. Next he drained the water from the radiator. Only then did he turn it over to the regimental staff.

Al Kroachka/Army Signal Corps

Hollis Ann Hands

Major Winters under the same gate in Holland as in October 1944, forty-seven years later.

Holland, but almost none had done so. They walked around Camp Mourmelon with hand grenades hanging off their belts, clips of ammunition on their harnesses, wearing their knives and (unauthorized) side arms. To the recruits, they looked like a bunch of killers from the French Foreign Legion. To the veterans, the recruits looked "tender." Company commander Lieutenant Dike, Welsh, Shames, Foley, Compton, and the other officers worked at blending the recruits into the outfit, to bring them up to Easy's standard of teamwork and individual skills, but it was difficult as the veterans could not take field maneuvers seriously.

By the end of the second week in December, the company was back to about 65 percent of its strength in enlisted men. Officer strength was at 112.5 percent, with Dike in command, Welsh serving as X.O., and two lieutenants per platoon plus a spare. Put another way, the airborne commanders expected that casualties in the next action would be highest among the junior officer ranks. Welsh was by now the oldest serving officer in the company, and he had not been at Toccoa. Only Welsh and Compton had been in Normandy with Easy; Welsh, Compton, Dike, Shames, and Foley had spent some time in Holland.

It was the N.C.O.s who were providing continuity and holding the company together. Among the N.C.O.s who had started out at Toccoa as privates were Lipton, Talbert, Martin, Luz, Perconte, Muck, Christenson, Randleman, Rader, Gordon, Toye, Guarnere, Carson, Boyle, Guth, Taylor, Malarkey, and others. That so many of its Toccoa officers were on the 506th regimental or 2d Battalion staff helped Easy to maintain coherence. They included Major Hester and Captain Matheson (S-3 and S-4 on regimental staff) and Captains Winters and Nixon (X.O. and S-2 on battalion staff). Overall, however, after one-half year of combat, Easy had new officers and new privates. But its heart, the N.C.O. corps, was still made up of Toccoa men who had followed Captain Sobel up and down Currahee in those hot August days of 1942.

• • •

Many of the men they had run up Currahee with were in hospital in England. Some of them would never run again. Others, with flesh wounds, were on the way to recovery. In the American 110th General Hospital outside Oxford, three members of 1st platoon, Easy Company, were in the same ward. Webster, Liebgott, and Cpl. Thomas McCreary had all been wounded on October 5, Webster in the leg, Liebgott in the elbow, McCreary in the neck. Webster was practicing his writing: in his diary, he described his buddies: "120-pound Liebgott, ex–San Francisco cabby, was the skinniest and, at non-financial moments, one of the funniest men in E Company. He had the added distinction of being one of the few Jews in the paratroops. In addition, both he and McCreary, ancient men of thirty, were the company elders. McCreary was a lighthearted, good-natured little guy who, to hear him tell it, had been raised on a beer bottle and educated in the 'Motor Inn,' Pittsburgh."

According to Webster, "the gayest spot in the 110th was the amputation ward, where most of the lads, knowing that the war was over for them, laughed and joked and talked about home." Webster was right to say "most" rather than "all," as some of those with million-dollar wounds wouldn't have given a nickel for them. Leo Boyle, in another ward of the 110th, wrote Winters: "Dear Sir, Now that I've got this far, damned if I know what to write!

"After two experiences I can say it isn't all the shock of the wound that one carries away with him. It's the knowledge that you're out of the picture [fighting] for some time to come—in this, my case, a long time.

"I don't expect to be on my feet before Xmas. I do expect to be as good as new some day. There is no bone damage, just muscle and tissue damage and a large area hard to graft.

"And Sir, I hope you take care of yourself (Better care than I've seen you exercise) for the reason there are too few like you and certainly none to replace you." He added that Webster, Liebgott, Leo Matz, Paul Rogers, George Luz, and Bill Guarnere, all also residents for varying periods of time of the 110th, had been in to see him.

Forty-four years later, Boyle wrote, "I never became fully resigned to the separation from the life as a 'trooper'—separated from my buddies, and never jumping again. I was 'hooked' or addicted to the life. I felt cheated and was often mean and surly about it during my yearlong recuperation in the hospitals."

Liebgott requested, and got, a discharge and a return to duty. So did McCreary, Guarnere, and others. As noted, this was not because they craved combat, but because they knew they were going to have to fight with somebody and wanted it to be with Easy Company. "If I had my choice," Webster wrote his parents, "I'd never fight again. Having no choice, I'll go back to E Company and prepare for another jump. If I die, I hope it'll be fast." In another letter, he wrote, "The realization that there is no escape, that we shall jump on Germany, then ride transports straight to the Pacific for the battle in China, does not leave much room for optimism. Like the infantry, our only way out is to be wounded and evacuated."

Webster went to a rehabilitation ward, then toward the end of December to the 12th Replacement Depot in Tidworth, England. This Repo Depo, like its mate the 10th, was notorious throughout ETO for the sadism of its commander, its inefficiency, chickenshit ways, filth, bad food, and general conditions that were not much of a step up from an Army prison. Evidently the Army wanted to make it so bad that veterans recovered from their wounds, or partly recovered, or at least able to walk without support, would regard getting back to the front lines as an improvement. Jim Alley, wounded in Holland, recovered in hospital in England, went AWOL from the 12th Replacement Depot and hitched a ride to Le Havre, then on to Mourmelon, where he arrived on December 15. Guarnere and others did the same.

Webster did not. He had long ago made it a rule of his Army life never to do anything voluntarily. He was an intellectual, as much an observer and chronicler of the phenomenon of soldiering as a practitioner. He was almost the only original Toccoa man who never became an N.C.O. Various officers wanted to make him a squad leader, but he refused. He was there to do his duty, and he did it—he never let a buddy down in combat, in France, Holland, or Germany—but he never volunteered for anything and he spurned promotion.

•   •   •

Excitement ran high in Mourmelon. Now that Easy was in a more-or-less permanent camp, the men could expect more mail, and could hope that Christmas packages would catch up with them. There was the company furlough to Paris to anticipate; with a lot of luck, Easy might be in Paris for New Year's Eve. And there was the Champagne Bowl coming on Christmas Day, with a turkey dinner to follow. Betting was already heavy on the football game, the practice sessions were getting longer and tougher.

The future after Christmas looked pretty good, from the perspective of a rifle company in the middle of the greatest war ever fought. There would be no fighting for Easy until at least mid-March. Then would come the jump into Germany, and after that the move to the Pacific for fighting in China or a jump into Japan. But all that was a long way off. Easy got ready to enjoy Christmas.

The sergeants had their own barracks at Mourmelon. On the night of December 16, Martin, Guarnere, and some others got hold of a case of champagne and brought it back to the sergeants' barracks. They were unaccustomed to the bubbly wine. Martin popped a few corks; the other sergeants held out their canteen cups; he filled them to the brim.

"Well, hell, Johnny," Christenson said, "that's nothing but soda pop, for Christ's sake!"

They drank some of the world's finest champagne as if it were soda pop, with inevitable results. A fight broke out, "and I have to say I was in it," Martin admitted, "and we tore every one of those bunks down, and nails sticking out, I ran nails into my foot, hell it was just a battle in there."

First Sgt. Carwood Lipton came into the barracks, took one look, and started shouting: "You guys are supposed to be leaders. A bunch of sergeants doing all this crap." He made them clean up the mess before allowing them to sleep it off.

That same night, Winters and Nixon were the only two battalion staff officers at HQ. The others had taken off for Paris. Pvt. Joe Lesniewski went to the movies at one of the Mourmelon theaters. He saw a film featuring Marlene Dietrich. Gordon Carson went to bed early, to be ready for football practice in the morning.

Winters and Nixon got word by radio that all passes were canceled. At the theater, the lights went on and an officer strode onto the stage to announce a German breakthrough in the Ardennes. In the barracks, Carson, Gordon, and others were awakened by the charge of quarters, who turned on the lights and reported the breakthrough. "Shut up!" men called back at him. "Get the hell out of here!" That was VIII Corps's problem, First Army's problem. They went back to sleep.

But in the morning, when the company fell in after reveille, Lieutenant Dike told them, "After chow, just stand fast." He was not taking them out on a training exercise, as was customary. "Just stand by" were the orders. Dike told them to kill the time by cleaning the barracks. Evidently what was going on up in the Ardennes was going to be of concern to the 82d and 101st Airborne after all.

• • •

Hitler launched his last offensive on December 16, in the Ardennes, on a scale much greater than his 1940 offensive in the same place against the French Army. He achieved complete surprise. American intelligence in the Ardennes estimated the German forces facing the VIII Corps at four divisions. In fact by December 15 the Wehrmacht had twenty-five divisions in the

Eifel, across from the Ardennes. The Germans managed to achieve surprise on a scale comparable with Barbarossa in June 1941 or Pearl Harbor.

The surprise was achieved, like most surprises in war, because the offensive made no sense. For Hitler to use up his armor in an offensive that had no genuine strategic aim, and one that he could not sustain unless his tankers were lucky enough to capture major American fuel dumps intact, was foolish.

The surprise was achieved, like most surprises in war, because the defenders were guilty of gross over-confidence. Even after the failure of MARKET-GARDEN, the Allies believed the Germans were on their last legs. At Ike's HQ, people thought about what the Allied armies could do to the Germans, not about what the Germans might do to them. The feeling was, If we can just get them from out behind the West Wall, we can finish the job. That attitude went right down to the enlisted-man level. Sgt. George Koskimaki of the 101st wrote in his diary on December 17: "It has been another quiet Sunday. . . . The radio announced a big German attack on the First Army front. This should break the back of the German armies."[1]

The surprise was achieved, like most surprises in war, because the attackers did a good job of concealment and deception. They gathered two armies in the Eifel without Allied intelligence ever seeing them. By a judicious use of radio traffic, they got Ike's G-2 looking to the north of the Ardennes for any German counterattack (no one in the Allied world thought for one minute that a German counter*offensive* was conceivable). Six months earlier, on the eve of D-Day, Ike

---

[1]Rapport and Northwood, *Rendezvous with Destiny,* 422.

and his officers had an almost perfect read on the German order of battle in Normandy. In December, on the eve of the German attack, Ike and his officers had a grossly inaccurate read on the German order of battle.

The Allies were also badly deceived about the German will to fight, the German matériel situation, Hitler's boldness, and the skill of German officers in offensive maneuvers (the American generals in the Allied camp had no experience of defending against a German offensive).

The result of all this was the biggest single battle on the Western front in World War II and the largest engagement ever fought by the U.S. Army. The human losses were staggering: of the 600,000 American soldiers involved, almost 20,000 were killed, another 20,000 captured, and 40,000 wounded. Two infantry divisions were annihilated; in one of them, the 106th, 7,500 men surrendered, the largest mass surrender in the war against Germany. Nearly 800 American Sherman tanks and other armored vehicles were destroyed.

The battle began on a cold, foggy dawn of December 16. The Germans achieved a breakthrough at many points in the thinly held VIII Corps lines. Hitler had counted on bad weather to negate the Allies' biggest single advantage, air power (on the ground, in both men and armor, the Germans outnumbered the Americans). Hitler had also counted on surprise, which was achieved, and on a slow American response. He figured that it would take Ike two or three days to recognize the magnitude of the effort the Germans were making, another two or three days to persuade his superiors to call off the Allied offensives north and south of the Ardennes, and then another two or three days to start moving significant reinforcements into the battle. By then, the German armor would be in Antwerp, he hoped.

It was his last assumptions that were wrong. On the morning of December 17, Eisenhower made the critical decisions of the entire battle, and did so without consulting anyone outside his own staff. He declared the crossroads city of Bastogne as the place that had to be held no matter what. (Bastogne is in a relatively flat area in the otherwise rugged hills of the Ardennes, which is why the roads of the area converge there.) Because of his offensives north and south of the Ardennes, Ike had no strategic reserve available, but he did have the 82d and 101st resting and refitting and thus available. He decided to use the paratroopers to plug the holes in his lines and to hold Bastogne.

Finally, Eisenhower blasted Hitler's assumptions by bringing into play his secret weapon. At a time when much of the German Army was still horse-drawn, the Americans had thousands and thousands of trucks and trailers in France. They were being used to haul men, matériel, and gasoline from the beaches of Normandy to the front. Ike ordered them to drop whatever they were doing and start hauling his reinforcements to the Ardennes.

The response can only be called incredible. On December 17 alone, 11,000 trucks and trailers carried 60,000 men, plus ammunition, gasoline, medical supplies, and other matériel, into the Ardennes. In the first week of the battle, Eisenhower was able to move 250,000 men and 50,000 vehicles into the fray. This was mobility with a vengeance. It was an achievement unprecedented in the history of war. Not even in Vietnam, not even in the 1991 Gulf War, was the U.S.

Army capable of moving so many men and so much equipment so quickly.

·   ·   ·

Easy Company played its part in this vast drama, thanks to the Transportation Corps and the drivers, mostly black soldiers of the famous Red Ball express. At 2030, December 17, Ike's orders to the 82d and 101st to proceed north toward Bastogne arrived at the divisions' HQ. The word went out to regiments, battalions, down to companies—get ready for combat, trucks arriving in the morning, we're moving out.

"Not me," Gordon Carson said. "I'm getting ready to play football on Christmas Day."

"No, you're not," Lieutenant Dike said. Frantic preparations began. Mourmelon did not have an ammunition dump, the men had only the ammunition they had taken out of Holland, there was none to be found. Easy did not have its full complement of men yet or of equipment. Some men did not have helmets (they did have football helmets, but not steel ones). The company was missing a couple of machine-guns and crews. The men had not received a winter issue of clothes. Their boots were not lined or weatherproof. They had no long winter underwear or long wool socks. They scrounged what they could, but it was not much. Even K rations were short. When Easy set out to meet the Wehrmacht on the last, greatest German offensive, the company was under strength, inadequately clothed, and insufficiently armed.

It was also going out blind. As not even General McAuliffe knew the destination of the 101st as yet, obviously Colonel Sink could not brief Captain

Winters who thus could not brief Lieutenant Dike. All anyone knew was that the Germans had blasted a big hole in the line, that American forces were in full retreat, that someone had to plug the gap, and that the someone was the Airborne Corps.

Weather precluded an airdrop, and in any case it was doubtful if enough C-47s could have been gathered quickly enough to meet the need. Instead, Transportation Corps, acting with utmost dispatch, gathered in its trucks from throughout France but especially in the area between Le Havre and Paris. M.P.s stopped the trucks, Services of Supply forces unloaded them, and the drivers—many of whom had already been long on the road and badly needed some rest—were told to get to Camp Mourmelon without pausing for anything.

The process began as darkness fell on December 17. By 0900 on December 18, the first trucks and trailers began arriving in Mourmelon. The last of the 380 trucks needed for the movement of the 11,000 men of the 101st arrived at the camp at 1720. By 2000 the last man was outloaded.

Just before Easy moved out, Malarkey went into a panic. He remembered he had $3,600 in his money belt. He asked Lieutenant Compton for help; Compton put him in touch with a division fiscal officer, who said he would deposit the money, but if he did, Malarkey could not get at it until he was discharged. That was fine with Malarkey; he handed over the money and took the receipt. He climbed into his trailer with the happy thought that after the war he could return to the University of Oregon and not have to wash dishes to pay his way.

• • • •

"We were packed in like sardines," Private Freeman remembered. Captain Winters used a different image: "You were just like an animal in there, you were just packed into that trailer like a cattle car." As the trucks pulled out, Carson thought about the football practice he had been anticipating with relish, contrasted it with his actual situation, and began singing "What a Difference a Day Makes."

The trucks had no benches, and damn little in the way of springs. Every curve sent men crashing around, every bump bounced them up into the air. It was hard on the kidneys—relief came only when the trucks stopped to close up the convoy—and on the legs. The trucks drove with lights blazing until they reached the Belgium border, a calculated risk taken for the sake of speed.

As the truckborne troopers were on the road, VIII Corps command decided where to use them. The 82d would go to the north shoulder of the penetration, near St. Vith. The 101st would go to Bastogne.

The trucks carrying Easy stopped a few kilometers outside Bastogne. The men jumped out—a tailgate jump, they called it—relieved themselves, stretched, grumbled, and formed up into columns for the march into Bastogne. They could hear a firefight going on. "Here we go again," said Private Freeman.

The columns marched on both sides of the road, toward the front; down the middle of the road came the defeated American troops, fleeing the front in disarray, moblike. Many had thrown away their rifles, their coats, all encumbrances. Some were in a panic, staggering, exhausted, shouting, "Run! Run! They'll murder you! They'll kill you! They've got everything, tanks, machine-guns, air power, everything!"

"They were just babbling," Winters recalled. "It was pathetic. We felt ashamed."

As Easy and the other companies in 2d Battalion marched into Bastogne and out again (residents had hot coffee for them, but not much else), uppermost in every man's mind was ammunition. "Where's the ammo? We can't fight without ammo." The retreating horde supplied some. "Got any ammo?" the paratroopers would ask those who were not victims of total panic. "Sure, buddy, glad to let you have it." (Gordon noted sardonically that by giving away their ammo, the retreating men relieved themselves of any further obligation to stand and fight.) Still, Easy marched toward the sound of battle without sufficient ammunition.

Outside Bastogne, headed northeast, the sound of the artillery fire increased. Soon it was punctuated by small arms fire. "Where the hell's the ammo?"

Second Lt. George C. Rice, S-4 of Team Desobry of Combat Command B, 10th Armored Division (which had fallen back under heavy pressure from Noville through Foy), learned of the shortage. He jumped in his jeep and drove to Foy, where he loaded the vehicle with cases of hand grenades and M-1 ammunition, turned around, and met the column coming out of Bastogne. He passed out the stuff as the troopers marched by, realized the need was much greater, returned to the supply dump at Foy, found a truck, overloaded it and the jeep with weapons and ammunition, drove back to the oncoming column, and had his men throw it out by the handfuls. Officers and men scrambled on hands and knees for the clips of M-1 ammo. The firefight noise coupled with the panic in the faces of the retreating American troops made it clear that they were going to need every bullet they could get. Lieutenant Rice kept it coming until every man had all he could carry.[2]

As Easy moved toward Foy, the sounds of battle became intense. The 1st Battalion of the 506th was up ahead, in Noville, involved in a furious fight, taking a beating. Colonel Sink decided to push 3d Battalion to Foy and to use 2d Battalion to protect his right flank. Easy went into an area of woods and open fields, its left on the east side of the road Bastogne-Foy-Noville. Fox Company was to its right, Dog in reserve.

Sounds of battle were coming closer. To the rear, south of Bastogne, the Germans were about to cut the highway and complete the encirclement of the Bastogne area. Easy had no artillery or air support. It was short on food, mortar ammunition, and other necessary equipment, and completely lacked winter clothing even as the temperature began to plunge below the freezing mark. But thanks to 2d Lieutenant Rice, it had grenades and M-1 ammunition.

The *Currahee* scrapbook spoke for Easy, for 2d Battalion, for the 506th: "We weren't particularly elated at being here. Rumors are that Krauts are everywhere and hitting hard. Farthest from your mind is the thought of falling back. In fact it isn't there at all. And so you dig your hole carefully and deep, and wait, not for that mythical super man, but for the enemy you had beaten twice before and will again. You look first to the left, then right, at your buddies also preparing. You feel confident with Bill over there. You know you can depend on him."

---

[2]Rapport and Northwood, *Rendezvous with Destiny*, 462.

11

"They Got Us Surrounded— the Poor Bastards"

BASTOGNE

December 19–31, 1944

O N DECEMBER 19 Easy went into the line south of Foy as one part of the ring defense of Bastogne. It was, in effect, one of the wagons in the circle. Inside were the 101st Airborne, Combat Command B of the 10th Armored, plus the 463d Field Artillery Battalion. Against this force the Germans launched as many as fifteen divisions, four of them armored, supported by heavy artillery.

The fighting was furious and costly. During the nineteenth and twentieth, the 1st Battalion of the 506th, supported by Team Desobry of the 10th Armored, engaged the 2d Panzer Division at Noville, northeast of Foy. When the battalion pulled back beyond Foy on the twentieth, it had lost thirteen officers and 199 enlisted men (out of about 600). Together with Team Desrobry, it had destroyed at least thirty enemy tanks and inflicted casualties of between 500 and 1,000. Most important, it had held for forty-eight hours while the defense was being set up around Bastogne.

Easy and the other companies badly needed the time, as the situation in the defensive perimeter was fluid and confused. Easy's left was on the Bastogne-Noville road, linked to 3d Battalion on the other side. Dog Company, on the right flank of 2d Battalion, extended to the railroad station at Halt, but it was not linked to the 501st PIR. Winters worried that the battalion was not in the right position; he sent Nixon back to regimental HQ to check; Nixon returned to say the battalion was where it was supposed to be.

Easy's position was in a wood looking out on a grazing field that sloped down to the village of Foy, about a kilometer away. The trees were pines, 8 to 10 inches in diameter, planted in rows. The men dug foxholes to form a Main Line of Resistance a few meters inside the woods, with outposts on the edge. Winters set up battalion HQ just behind the company at the south edge of the woods. The first night on the MLR was quiet, even peaceful; the fighting was to the north, in Noville, 4 kilometers away.

At dawn on December 20, a heavy mist hung over the woods and fields. Winters rose and looked around. To his left he saw a German soldier in his long winter overcoat emerge from the woods. He had no rifle, no pack. He walked to the middle of a clearing. Two men with Winters instinctively brought their rifles to their shoulders, but he gave them a hand signal to hold their fire. The Americans watched as the German took off his overcoat, pulled down his pants, squatted, and relieved himself. When he was finished, Winters hollered in his best German, *"Kommen sie hier!"* The soldier put up his hands and walked over to surrender. Winters went through his pockets; all he had were a few pictures and the end of a loaf of hard black bread.

"Think of this," Winters commented. "Here is a German soldier, in the light of early dawn, who went to take a crap, got turned around in the woods, walked through our lines, past the company CP and ended up behind the Battalion CP! That sure was some line of defense we had that first night!"

German soldiers were not the only ones who got lost that day. Medic Ralph Spina and Pvt. Ed "Babe" Heffron went back into Bastogne to scrounge up some medical supplies. At the aid station Spina got some of what he needed (the 101st was already running low on medical supplies, a major problem). The two E Company men grabbed a hot meal, and although they hated to leave the stove, with darkness coming on, they set out for the line.

Heffron suggested a shortcut across a wooded area. Spina agreed. Heffron led the way. Suddenly he fell into a hole. There was a shout of surprise. Then a voice called out from under Heffron, "Hinkle, Hinkle, *ist das du?"*

Heffron came barreling out of the foxhole and took off in the opposite direction, yelling, *"Hinkle Your Ass, Kraut!"* He and Spina got reoriented and finally found the E Company CP.

(Spina, who recalled the incident, concluded: "To this day every time I see Babe, I ask him how Hinkle is feeling or if he has seen Hinkle lately.")

The medics were the most popular, respected, and appreciated men in the company. Their weapons were first-aid kits, their place on the line was wherever a man called out that he was wounded. Lieutenant Foley had special praise for Pvt. Eugene Roe. "He was there when he was needed, and how he got 'there' you often wondered. He never received recognition for his bravery, his heroic servicing of the wounded. I recommended him for a Silver Star after a devastating firefight when his exploits were typically outstanding. Maybe I didn't use the proper words and phrases, perhaps Lieutenant Dike didn't approve, or somewhere along the line it was cast aside. I don't know. I never knew except that if any man who struggled in the snow and the cold, in the many attacks through the open and through the woods, ever deserved such a medal, it was our medic, Gene Roe."

• • •

On December 20 what was left of the 1st Battalion of the 506th and Team Desobry pulled back from Noville and went into reserve. Easy awaited an attack that did not come; the damage inflicted by 1st Battalion was so great that the Germans made their assaults on other sectors of the defensive perimeter. Easy underwent artillery and mortar bombardments, but no infantry attack.

On December 21, it snowed, a soft, dry snow. It kept coming, 6 inches, 12 inches. The temperature fell to well below freezing, the wind came up, even in the woods. The men were colder than they had ever been in their lives. They had only their jump boots and battle dress with trench coats. No wool socks, no long underwear. Runners went into Bastogne and returned with flour sacks and bed sheets, which provided some warmth and camouflage. In the foxholes and on the outposts, men wrapped their bodies in blankets and their boots in burlap. The burlap soaked up the snow, boots became soggy, socks got wet, the cold penetrated right into the bones. Shivering was as normal as breathing. The men looked like George Washington's army at Valley Forge, except that they were getting fired upon, had no huts, and warming fires were out of the question.

Col. Ralph Ingersoll, an intelligence officer with First Army, described the penetrating cold: "Riding through the Ardennes, I wore woolen underwear, a woolen uniform, armored force combat overalls, a sweater, an armored force field jacket with elastic cuffs, a muffler, a heavy lined trenchcoat, two pairs of heavy woolen socks, and combat boots with galoshes over them—and I cannot remember ever being warm."[1]

For the men of Easy, without decent socks and no galoshes, feet always cold and always wet, trench foot quickly became a problem. Corporal Carson remembered being taught that the way to prevent trench foot was to massage the feet. So he took off his boots and massaged his feet. A German shell came in and hit a tree over his foxhole. Splinters tore up his foot and penetrated his thigh. He was evacuated back to Bastogne.

At the hospital set up in the town, "I looked around and never saw so many wounded men. I called a medic over and said, 'Hey, how come you got so many wounded people around here? Aren't we evacuating anybody?'"

"Haven't you heard?" the medic replied.

"I haven't heard a damn thing."

"They've got us surrounded—the poor bastards."

---

[1]Ralph Ingersoll, *Top Secret* (New York: Harcourt Brace, 1946).

General McAuliffe saw to it the wounded had booze for comfort. A medic gave Carson a bottle of crème de menthe. "I didn't even know what it was, but to this day I have liked crème de menthe." The Luftwaffe bombed the town that night. Carson remembered to get on his hands and knees for the concussion. He got sick. "Thank God for that helmet. I had already had about half that crème de menthe. It was all green in my helmet."

For the most part, all the men of Easy had to eat was K rations, and not enough of those had been distributed back at Mourmelon. The company cooks tried to bring a hot meal up after darkness, but by the time they reached the men in the foxholes, the food was cold. Mainly it consisted of white navy beans which, according to Sergeant Rader, "caused gastronomical outbursts that were something to behold." Cook Joe Domingus found some shortening and cornmeal, which he turned into corn fritters, also stone cold by the time they arrived. The men mixed the lemonade packet in their K rations with snow to make a dessert.

On the line, the days were miserable, the nights worse. The shelling was not continuous, the machine-gun fire directed at the Americans was sporadic, but snipers were active through the day. At night, the ominous silence would be broken by the nerve-racking hammering of enemy mortars, followed by cries from the wounded and calls to man the positions in preparation for an attack. Then another ominous silence.

Every two hours, the platoon sergeants would wake two men in a foxhole and lead them to the outpost (OP) position, to relieve the men on duty. "The trip out to the OP was always eerie," Christenson remembered. "You eyed all silhouettes suspiciously, skeptical of any sound. Reluctantly, you approach the OP. The silhouettes of the men in their positions are not clear. . . . Are they Germans? The suspense is always the same . . . then finally you recognize an American helmet. Feeling a little ridiculous, yet also relieved, you turn around and return to the main line, only to repeat the entire process in another two hours."

In the foxholes, the men tried to get some sleep, difficult to impossible given the cramped conditions (usually 6 feet by 2 feet by 3 or 4 feet deep, for two men). At least lying together allowed the men to exchange body heat. Heffron and Pvt. Al Vittore did manage to get to sleep the second night out. Heffron woke when Vittore threw his heavy leg over his body. When Vittore started to rub Heffron's chest, Heffron gave him a shot with his elbow in his belly. Vittore woke and demanded to know what the hell was going on. Heffron started to give him hell in return; Vittore grinned and said he had been dreaming about his wife.

"Al," Heffron said, "I can't help you, as I got combat boots, jump pants, and my trench coat on, and they are not coming off."

In other foxholes, men talked to relieve the tension. Sergeant Rader and Pvt. Don Hoobler came from the same town on the banks of the Ohio River. "Don and I would talk all night about home, our families, people and places, and what the hell were we doing in a predicament like this?" Spina recalled discussing with his foxhole mate "politics, the world's problems, plus our own. Wishing we had a drink or a hot meal, preferably in that order. We talked about what we were going to do when we got home, about a trip to Paris in a couple of weeks, go to the Follies. Mainly we talked about going home."

Sergeant Toye, back from hospital, didn't like the silence at night between mortar attacks. To break it, he would sing. "I'll Be Seeing You" was his favorite. Heffron told him to cut it, that the Krauts would surely hear him. Toye sang anyway. According to Heffron, "Joe was a hellu'va better soldier than singer."

•   •   •

Sitting in front-line foxholes was bad, being an OP was worse, going on combat patrol looking for a fight was the worst. But it had to be done. It was the inability of VIII Corps to patrol aggressively, due to insufficient manpower, that had led to the December 16 surprise when the Germans attacked in far greater force than anyone anticipated.

On December 21 Lieutenant Peacock sent Sergeant Martin to the various foxholes of 1st platoon. At each one holding a sergeant or a corporal, Martin announced, "I want all N.C.O.s back at the platoon CP—now."

The men gathered. Lieutenant Peacock, the platoon leader, as tense as ever, stopped the grumbling: "At ease. Battalion wants a platoon to go on a combat patrol, and we have been elected to be that platoon." He paused. No one spoke. Peacock went on, "We know the Krauts are in the woods in front of our MLR, but we don't know how many, or where their MLR or OPs are located. It's our job to acquire that information, and to capture some prisoners, if possible."

Questions came in a torrent. "What's the plan of attack?" Sergeant Christenson, leader of 1st squad, wanted to know.

"How will the squads be positioned?" asked Sergeant Muck of the mortar squad.

"What happens when we lost contact in those

woods?" wondered 2d squad leader Sergeant Randleman.

Peacock did not have any ready answers. "You'll know more of what you're going to do when we reach the woods," was all he could think to say. Son of a bitch, Christenson thought to himself. This is going to be another SNAFU operation, with not enough information to fill a peapod.

"We move out at 1300 hours," Peacock concluded.

Damn, was Christenson's thought. We are being led by Mister Indecision himself, to infiltrate into the German lines without a good plan is a tremendous, bungling, tactical error. But when he met with his squad, he kept his thoughts to himself. He told the men to draw ammunition and be ready to jump off at 1300.

At 1200, 1st platoon fell back a few meters from the MLR and gathered around Father Maloney, who had his Communion set out. He announced that he was giving a general absolution. After the men who wanted one received their Communion wafer, he wished them "Good luck."

Just before 1300, the platoon assembled in the woods behind the MLR. Peacock looked to Christenson "like a frightened rabbit." He had no special orders to give, offered no clarification about a plan. He just announced, "All right, men, let's move out."

The platoon moved to the extreme right flank of the battalion, along the railroad tracks. It moved through D Company's position and began advancing toward the Germans, the tracks to the right, the woods to the left. It proceeded slowly, moving in column, stopping frequently. Some 200 meters beyond the MLR, Peacock called the N.C.O.s forward. He gave his orders: each squad would form a column of twos, abreast of one another, send out two scouts on point, and proceed into the woods until contact was made.

The platoon plunged into the woods. Immediately, the columns lost touch with each other, the squads lost touch with their scouts. The snow was soft, not crunchy, and the silence complete. It was broken by a short burst from a German machine-gun. Pvt. John Julian, a scout for 2d squad, was hit in the neck and Pvt. James Welling, scouting for 3d squad, was also hit.

The machine-gunners from Easy set up their weapons and prepared to return fire. Pvt. Robert Burr Smith of 1st squad opened up with a long burst in the direction of the German fire base. When he paused, the Germans let loose another burst of their own. Christenson shouted for Martin. No answer. For Randleman. No answer. For Peacock. No answer. Only more German fire.

The 1st platoon's being decimated! Christenson thought. He shouted again. Bull Randleman came through the woods to answer. "Have you seen Martin or Peacock?" Randleman had not. Another burst of machine-gun fire cut through the trees.

"We have got to make a move," Randleman said. He joined Chris in calling for Martin. No answer. "Let's get the hell out of here," Chris suggested. Bull agreed. They called out the orders to their men and fell back to the railroad. There they met Martin, Peacock, and the remainder of the platoon.

The patrol had not been a great success. 1st platoon had uncovered the German MLR and discovered that the German OPs were thinly manned and stretched out, but it had lost one man killed (Julian) and one wounded and failed to bring in a prisoner. It spent the night shivering in the foxholes, eating cold beans and fritters, wondering if the weather would ever clear so that the 101st could be resupplied by air.

• • •

The next couple of days were about the same. Easy sent out patrols, the Germans sent out patrols. Occasional mortar attacks. Sporadic machine-gun fire. Bitter cold. Inadequate medical supplies. No hot food. Not enough food. Constant shivering was burning off energy that was not being replaced. For the privates, not enough sleep. For the N.C.O.s, almost no sleep. This was survival time, and reactions were slow due to the near-frozen limbs.

Shell bursts in the trees sent splinters, limbs, trunks, and metal showering down on the foxholes. To protect themselves, the men tried to cover their holes with logs, but not having axes made it a difficult task. One man solved the problem by putting two or three German "stiffs" over the top.

Most maddening was the inability of the American artillery to respond to German shelling or to disrupt German activity. Easy's OP men would watch with envy as German trucks and tanks moved back and forth behind the German line, bringing in the shells and food that the Americans so badly missed. Back in Bastogne, the Americans had plenty of guns, including 105 and 155 mm howitzers. They had been active the first few days of the siege, firing in a complete circle at all German attempts to break through the MLR. But by the twenty-third they were almost out of ammunition. Winters recalled being told that the single artillery piece covering the Foy-Bastogne road—his left flank—was down to three rounds. They were being saved for antitank purposes in the event of a German panzer attack down that road. In other words, no artillery support for Easy or 2d Battalion. This at a time when the men of the company were down to six rounds per mortar, one bandolier for each rifleman, and one box of machine-gun ammo per gun.

That day, however, the snow stopped, and the sky cleared. C-47s dropped supplies, medicine, food, ammunition. American artillery got back into action, curtailing German daytime activity, boosting morale on the MLR. K rations were distributed, along with ammo. But the 30-caliber for the light machine-guns and M-1s was insufficient to the need, and the 24,406 K rations were enough for only a day or so. Not enough blankets had been dropped to insure that every man had one.

• • •

Officers watched for signs of breaking. When Winters sensed that Private Liebgott was on the edge, he brought him back to battalion CP to be his runner. This gave Liebgott a chance to rest up and get away from the tension of the MLR. "Just being back 50 yards off the front line made a tremendous difference in the tension," Winters wrote.

The temptation to stay put when a patrol went out was very strong; even stronger was the temptation to report back at the aid station with trench foot or frozen feet and hands or an extreme case of diarrhea. "If all the men who had a legitimate reason to leave the MLR and go back to the aid station in Bastogne had taken advantage of their situation," Winters wrote, "there just would not have been a front line. It would have been a line of outposts."

The temptation to get out altogether via a self-inflicted wound was also strong. It did not get light until 0800. It got dark at 1600. During the sixteen hours of night, out in those frozen foxholes (which actually shrank as the night went on and the ground froze and expanded), it was impossible to keep out of the mind the thought of how easy it would be to shoot a round into a foot. A little pain—not much in a foot so cold it could not be felt anyway—and then transport back to Bastogne, a warm aid station, a hot meal, a bed, escape.

No man from Easy gave in to that temptation that every one of them felt. One man did take off his boots and socks to get frostbite and thus a ticket out of there. But for the others, they would take a legitimate way out or none. Winters recalled, "When a man was hit hard enough for evacuation, he was usually very happy, and we were happy for him—he had a ticket out to the hospital, or even a ticket home—alive.

"When a man was killed—he looked 'so peaceful.' His suffering was over."

• • • •

At first light on Christmas Eve morning, Winters inspected his MLR. He walked past Corporal Gordon, "his head wrapped up in a big towel, with his helmet sitting on top. Walter sat on the edge of his foxhole behind his light machine-gun. He looked like he was frozen stiff, staring blankly straight ahead at the woods. I stopped and looked back at him, and it suddenly struck me, 'Damn! Gordon's matured! He's a man!'"

A half hour later, at 0830, Gordon brewed himself a cup of coffee. He kept coffee grounds in his hand grenade canister, "and I'd melted the snow with my little gas stove, and I'd brewed up this lovely cup of coffee." As he started to sip it, the outposts came in with word that a German force was attempting to infiltrate Easy's lines. His squad leader, Sgt. Buck Taylor, told him to "get on that machine-gun."

Gordon brushed snow from his weapon and the ammo box adjacent to the gun, telling his assistant, Pvt. Stephen Grodzki, to look sharp, pay attention to detail. A shot from a German rifleman rang out. The bullet his Gordon in the left shoulder and exited from the right shoulder. It had brushed his spinal column; he was paralyzed from the neck down.

He slid to the bottom of his foxhole. "The canteen cup followed me and the hot liquid spilled in my lap. I can see the stream rising upward to this very day."

Taylor and Earl McClung went looking for the sniper who had shot Gordon. They found and killed him. Shifty Powers was in the next foxhole. As Shames had hoped would happen, he had recovered completely. Shifty was from Virginia, a mountain man, part Indian. He had spent countless hours as a youth hunting squirrels. He could sense the least little movement in a woods. He spotted a German in a tree, raised his M-1, and killed the man.

Paul Rogers, Gordon's best friend, Jim Alley, and another member of the 3rd platoon rushed over to Gordon. They hauled him out of the hole and dragged him back into the woods, in Gordon's words, "as a gladiator was dragged from the arena." In a sheltered area, they stretched him out to examine him. Medic Roe came up, took a quick look, and declared that it was serious. Roe gave Gordon morphine and prepared to give plasma.

Sergeant Lipton came over to see what he could do. "Walter's face was ashen and his eyes closed," Lipton recalled. "He looked more dead than alive." In the extreme cold, it seemed to Lipton that the plasma was flowing too slowly, so he took the bottle from Roe and put it under his arm inside his clothes to warm it up.

"As I looked down at Walter's face he suddenly opened his eyes. 'Walter, how do you feel?' I asked. 'Lipton,' he said in a surprisingly strong voice, 'you're standing on my hand.' I jumped back, looking down, and he was right. I had been standing on his hand." A jeep, summoned by radio, came up and evacuated Gordon to the aid station.

The German attack continued, intensified, was finally thrown back with heavy losses, thanks to a combination of Easy's rifle and machine-gun fire, mortars, and grenades, ably assisted by artillery. Lipton later counted thirty-eight dead German bodies in front of the woods. Lieutenant Welsh was hit and evacuated.

• • •

On the afternoon of Christmas Eve, the men received General McAuliffe's Christmas greetings. "What's merry about all this, you ask?" was the opening line. "Just this: We have stopped cold everything that has been thrown at us from the North, East, South and West. We have identifications from four German Panzer Divisions, two German Infantry Divisions and one German Parachute Division. . . . The Germans surround us, their radios blare our doom. Their Commander demanded our surrender in the following impudent arrogance." (There followed the four paragraph message "to the U.S.A. Commander of the encircled town of Bastogne" from "the German Commander," demanding an "honorable surrender to save the encircled U.S.A. troops from total annihilation," dated December 22.)

McAuliffe's message continued: "The German

Commander received the following reply: '22 December 1944. To the German Commander: NUTS! The American Commander.'

"We are giving our country and our loved ones at home a worthy Christmas present and being privileged to take part in this gallant feat of arms are truly making for ourselves a Merry Christmas. A. C. McAuliffe, Commanding."[2]

The men at the front were not as upbeat as General McAuliffe. They had cold white beans for their Christmas Eve dinner, while the division staff had a turkey dinner, served on a table with a tablecloth, a small Christmas tree, knives and forks and plates.[3]

Out on the MLR, Sergeant Rader was feeling terrible about having to put men out on OP duty on Christmas Eve. His childhood buddy, Cpl. Don Hoobler, suggested, "Why don't we take that post tonight and just allow the men to sleep. We can lay it off as a kind of Christmas present to the men." Rader agreed.

When darkness fell, they moved out to the OP. It was miserably cold, a biting wind taking the wind-chill factor well below zero. "As the night wore on, we talked of

---

[2]Rapport and Northwood, *Rendezvous with Destiny*, 545.

[3]There is a photograph on p. 549 of *Rendezvous with Destiny* of that dinner. The officers are looking appropriately glum, but what the men of Easy bring to my attention is the luxurious (everything is relative, they admit) surroundings. One of those staff officers was Lt. Col. (later Lt. Gen.) Harry W. O. Kinnard. Twenty years later, in an interview about the Battle of the Bulge, Kinnard said, "We never felt we would be overrun. We were beating back everything they threw at us. We had the houses, and were warm. They were outside the town, in the snow and cold." Every surviving member of E Company has sent me a copy of that newspaper story, with caustic comments, the mildest of which was, "What battle was he in?"

Winters's dinner that night consisted of "five white beans and a cup of cold broth."

our homes," Rader remembered, "our families, and how they were spending their Christmas Eve. Don felt sure all of them were in church praying for us."

On Christmas Day, the Germans attacked again, but fortunately for E Company on the other side of Bastogne. The following day, Patton's Third Army, spearheaded by Lt. Col. Creighton Abrams of the 37th Tank Battalion, broke through the German lines. The 101st was no longer surrounded; it now had ground communications with the American supply dumps. Soon trucks were bringing in adequate supplies of food, medicine, and ammunition. The wounded were evacuated to the rear.

General Taylor returned. He inspected the front lines, according to Winters, "very briskly. His instructions before leaving us were, 'Watch those woods in front of you!' What the hell did he think we had been doing while he was in Washington?"

(Winters has a thing about Taylor. In one interview he remarked, "And now you have General Taylor coming back from his Christmas vacation in Washington. . . . " I interrupted to say, "That's not quite fair." "Isn't it?" "Well, he was ordered back to testify. . . . " Winters cut me off: "I don't want to be fair.")

The breaking of the siege brought the first newspapers from the outside world. The men of the 101st learned that they had become a legend even as the battle continued. As the division history put it, the legend "was aided by the universality of the press and radio, of ten thousand daily maps showing one spot holding out inside the rolling tide of the worst American military debacle of modern times. It was aided by a worried nation's grasping for encouragement and hope; for days it was the one encouraging sight that met their eyes each morning. And the War Department, earlier than was its practice, identified the division inside the town, so even before their bloody month in the town was up, to the world the 101st became the Battered Bastards of the Bastion of Bastogne. The elements of drama were there—courage in the midst of surrounding panic and defeat; courage and grim humor in the midst of physical suffering, cold, and near-fatal shortages; a surrender demand and a four-letter-word rebuttal; and a real comradeship. . . . Courage and comradeship combined to develop a team that the Germans couldn't whip."[4]

Of course, Combat Command B of the 10th Armored Division was also in Bastogne, but it was not identified in the press. And of course the 82d Airborne fought as costly and desperate a fight on the northern shoulder of the Bulge, a fight that was at least as significant as the one at Bastogne. But it was not surrounded and never got the publicity the 101st received.

The 101st still had a complaint. As the story of the Battle of the Bulge is told today, it is one of George Patton and his Third Army coming to the rescue of the encircled 101st, like the cavalry come to save the settlers in their wagon circle. No member of the 101st has ever agreed that the division needed to be rescued!

• • •

With the encirclement broken, the men of the 101st expected to return to Mourmelon to bask in the Allied world's adulation and perhaps to celebrate the New Year in Paris. But the heroic stand at Bastogne had been a defensive action; to win the war the Allies were going

---

[4]Rapport and Northwood, *Rendezvous with Destiny*, 586.

to have to resume their offensive; the Germans had
come out of their fixed positions in the West Wall and
made themselves vulnerable; Eisenhower wanted to
seize the opportunity. But his problem at the end of
December was the same as it had been in the middle of
the month, a manpower shortage. The stark truth was
that the Germans outnumbered the Allies on the
Western Front. The United States had not raised
enough infantry divisions to fight a two-front war. This
was a consequence of the prewar decision by the
Government to be lavish with deferments for industrial
and farm labor, and to refrain from drafting fathers.
There was also a shortage of artillery shells, brought on
by a decision in September—when it seemed the war in
Europe would be over in a matter of weeks—to lower
production of shells on the industrial priority list. To go
over to a general offensive, as he had decided to do, Ike
needed the 101st and 82d in the line.

It was a question of timing. Eisenhower wanted to
attack even before New Year's Eve, but Monty, commanding the forces (all American) on the northern
shoulder of the Bulge, stalled and shivered and made
excuses, so it did not happen.

For Easy, that meant staying in the line. Conditions
improved, somewhat—the men got overshoes and
long underwear and sometimes hot food. But the cold
continued, the snow did not go away, the Germans hit
the company with mortar and artillery fire daily,
patrols had to be mounted, German patrols had to be
turned back.

• • •

On December 29, Easy was in the same woods it had
occupied for nine days. With the clear weather, the

men on OP duty could see Foy below them and Noville across open fields and along the road about 2 kilometers to the north.

Shifty Powers came in from an OP to report to 1st Sergeant Lipton. "Sergeant," he said, "there's a tree up there toward Noville that wasn't there yesterday." Powers had no binoculars, but Lipton did. Looking through them, Lipton could not see anything unusual, even after Powers pinpointed the spot for him.

One reason Lipton had trouble was that the object was not an isolated tree; there were a number of trees along the road in that area. Lipton expressed some doubts, but Powers insisted it had not been there the previous day. Lipton studied the spot with his binoculars. He saw some movement near the tree and then more movement under other trees around it. Then he saw gun barrels—88s by their appearance, as they were elevated and 88s were the basic German antiaircraft weapon as well as ground artillery piece. Lipton realized that the Germans were putting an antiaircraft battery in among the trees, and had put up the tree Powers spotted as part of their camouflage.

Lipton put in a call for a forward artillery observer. When he arrived, he saw what Powers and Lipton had seen. He got on the radio, talking to a battery of 105 mm back in Bastogne. When he described the target he had no trouble getting approval for full battery fire, despite the short supply of artillery ammunition.

To zero in on the target, the observer called for a round on a position he could locate on his map, about 300 meters to the right of the trees. One gun fired and hit the target. Then he shifted the aim 300 meters to the left and called for all the battery's guns to lay in on the same azimuth and range. When he got a report that all was ready, he had his guns fire for effect, several rounds from each gun.

Shells started exploding all around the German position. Lipton watched through his binoculars as the Germans scrambled to get out of there, salvaging what they could of their guns, helping wounded to the rear. Within an hour the place was deserted.

"It all happened," Lipton summed up, "because Shifty saw a tree almost a mile away that hadn't been there the day before."

•   •   •

The German 88 battery had been going into place as a part of renewed pressure the Germans were putting on Bastogne. Having failed in their original plan to get across the Meuse River, the Germans needed Bastogne and its road net to hold their position in the Bulge and to be prepared for withdrawal. They launched furious attacks against the narrow corridor leading into the town from the south, and increased the pressure all around. By the end of the year eight German divisions, including three SS Panzer Divisions, were fighting in the Bastogne area. Patton's Third Army was attacking north, toward Bastogne; U.S. First Army, under Gen. Courtney Hodges (who was under Monty at this time) was scheduled to begin an attack south "sometime soon." If they linked up in time, they would cut off the Germans in the Bulge salient. If the Germans could stop Patton's thrust, and take Bastogne, they would have the road net that would enable them to escape.

That was the situation on New Year's Eve. At midnight, to celebrate the coming of the year of victory and to demonstrate how much things had changed in Bastogne in the past few days, every gun in Bastogne and every mortar piece on the MLR joined in a sere-nade of high explosives hurled at the Germans.

• • •

Corporal Gordon, along with more than a dozen other wounded Easy men, was evacuated to the rear. Another seven men from the company lay buried in shallow graves in the woods. Easy had put 121 officers and men on the trucks back in Mourmelon twelve days earlier. Its fighting strength was down to less than 100.

Gordon was taken by ambulance to Sedan, then flown to England and on to a hospital in Wales. He was heavily sedated, paralyzed, hallucinating. He was placed in a plaster cast from his waist to the top of his head, only his face was left unplastered. But the cast that kept him immobile also prevented treatment of the wounds made by the bullet entering and exiting his back, so it was removed and replaced by the device known as the Crutchfield tongs. The apparatus was applied by boring two holes in the crown of his head, then inserting steel tongs into the holes and clamping them into place. A line attached through pulleys pro-vided traction while preventing any movement without the need for a cast. He stayed in that position, flat on his back gazing up at the ceiling, for six weeks. Slowly he began to have some feeling in his extremities.

The doctor, Maj. M. L. Stadium, told him that had the bullet varied one-half inch in one direction, it would have missed him; had it varied that much in the other direction, the wound would have been fatal. Gordon considered himself to be "fortunate, very for-tunate. A million dollar wound." Only a man who had been in the front line at Bastogne could describe such a wound in such words.

12

The Breaking Point

BASTOGNE

January 1–13, 1945

URING THE SIEGE Easy had been on the defensive, taking it. The greatest disadvantage to being on the defensive in the woods was that the pines gave an optimum tree burst to artillery shells. But in other ways being on the defensive had some decided advantages. By New Year's Day, the snow was a foot deep in some places, frozen on top, slippery. Even the shortest infantry movements were made under the most trying conditions. To advance, a man had to flounder through the snow, bending and squirming to avoid knocking the snow off the branches and revealing his position. Visibility on the ground was limited to a few meters. An attacker had little contact with the men on his left and right, and he could not see a machine-gun position or a foxhole until he was almost on top of it. There were no roads, houses, or landmarks in the woods, so an advancing force would report its position by radio only by approximation. Squads on the attack had to move on compass bearings until they bumped into somebody, friend or enemy. Ammunition boxes for resupply were hand-carried to the foxholes, as always, but in this case by men who had no clear idea of direction.

Attacking in the cleared grazing fields was equally daunting. There was only one road, Noville-Foy-Bastogne, and it was ice-coated on top, with black ice under the snow. German 88s were zeroed in on the road, which was also mined. But the alternative to attacking down the road was to come cross-country over the fields, which offered no concealment.

• • •

The cultivated woods that had been home to Easy for twelve days were called the Bois Jacques. They extended to Easy's right (east) a couple of kilometers, to the railroad track and beyond. To its front (north) an open field sloped down to the village of Foy. The Germans held the Bois Jacques to the northeast. Their position was a wedge into the 101st lines; it was the closest they were anywhere to Bastogne, only 3 kilometers away. Before the 101st could launch any general offensive, the Germans had to be driven from the Bois Jacques and Foy taken. The next objective would be the high ground around Noville.

New Year's Day was quiet, but that evening Division assigned 2d Battalion of the 506th the task of attacking and clearing out the Bois Jacques. That night, a few German planes dropped bombs on E Company. Sergeant Toye was hit by a piece of shrapnel on his wrist. This was his third wound; he had been hit in Normandy and then again in Holland. He was a walking wounded; the medic sent him back to the aid station to get patched up. Before leaving, Toye checked in with Sergeant Malarkey, who said in parting, "You lucky S.O.B.!"

To carry out the attack, at first light on January 2 the battalion shifted to its right, to the railroad track; 1st Battalion, in regimental reserve, moved into 2d Battalion's old position. Second Battalion formed skirmish lines on the Foy-Bizory road, looking to the northeast into the dense woods, waiting for the order to move out. (This was the same place from which 1st platoon had moved out on patrol on December 22.) A battalion of the 501st was on 2d Battalion's right. It would be attacking in support.

Winters called out the command, "Move out!" The men began the advance. Moving in those dense woods was an exhausting process under the best of circumstances, completely so when carrying rifles, machineguns, mortars, grenades, knives, ammunition, and rations. The struggle to get through caused the body to sweat profusely, which was not a problem until one stopped; after a few minutes the wet underclothing could chill the body to the bone.

Immediately upon plunging into the woods, contact between platoons, even squads, sometimes even man to man, was lost. The snow and trees absorbed the noise so that even the clank of equipment, a sign that the men on each side were advancing with you, was absent. The sense of isolation coupled with the feeling of tension to create a fearful anticipation of the inevitable enemy response.

Machine-gun fire from directly in front hit E Company. Simultaneously, supporting American artillery began to whine over the heads of the men.

Immediately German artillery fired back, but not as counterbattery; the German shells were landing in and on the paratroopers. As quickly as it started, the firing ceased. In Sergeant Christenson's analysis, "The denseness of the woods was a bewilderment and confusion to the Krauts, whose visibility was no better than ours. Had they known that two battalions were moving toward their position in giant skirmish lines, the shelling and machine-gun fire would have been much more intense."

The advance resumed. Again machine-gun fire broke out, as the lead elements began to encounter the German OPs. American artillery resumed firing, salvo after salvo. German counterfire became intense. Cries of "I'm hit!" and shouts for medics could be heard all along the line. Still the advance continued. Men threw grenades and fired their rifles at Germans retreating through the woods.

After covering between 800 and 900 meters (Easy Company men refer to this as the "1,000 yard attack"), the attackers came to a logging road through the woods. There most of them halted, but some men penetrated a few meters into the woods on the other side to make certain no Germans were hiding there. Christenson was standing on the road with a few of his 1st platoon men when suddenly, to the right, there was the most improbable sight. A German soldier on horseback came galloping into view.

As the Americans saw him, he saw them. He whirled the horse around and began to retreat. Corporal Hoobler quickly got off three shots, smiled and jumped into the air, shouting, "I got him! I got him!" Christenson found himself having the odd thought that he had been hoping the horseman would make his getaway.

From over to the left, in the woods across the road, Pvt. Ralph Trapazano called out, "Hey, Chris, I've got a Kraut." Christenson moved down in his direction, went 5 meters past his position, and cut into the woods, holding his M-1 ready to fire with safety off. He approached the German from his right side. "There stood a very strong-looking SS trooper, camouflage jacket on, submachine-gun in his left hand, his arms hanging straight down his sides. But his weapon was pointed at Trap. Trap was down in a prone position with his M-1 pointed at the Kraut's chest. There wasn't a hint of fear on the SS trooper's face."

Christenson pointed his M-1 at the German's chest and told him, in his high school German, to drop his weapon. The German looked in Christenson's eyes and saw he meant to shoot, looked at his rifle and sensed that Christenson was taking up the slack on the trigger. He dropped his submachine-gun and raised his hands.

Christenson told Trapazano, "The next time you are confronted with an arrogant son-of-a-bitch like this, shoot the bastard."

• • •

So far Easy had been lucky. To its right the 501st had been attacked while it was attacking. The 26th SS Panzer Grenadier Regiment of the 12th SS Division (*Hitlerjugend*) hit with tanks, artillery, and infantry, inflicting heavy loss. On Easy's left flank, tanks and infantry from the 9th SS Division hit the other companies of the 502d. But in Easy's sector, things were relatively quiet.

Darkness was coming on. The word went down the line to dig in. The men were harassed by sporadic machine-gun fire and occasional artillery bursts, which prompted them to cut branches from the nearest source to cover their foxholes. This was dangerous and difficult, because it meant exposure. When machine-gun fire or shell fire came in, it was a desperate mad dash for the foxhole, with adrenaline racing through the body. When the foxhole sanctuary was complete, a man was exhausted, his clothes and body drenched with sweat. Now he sat, got cold, then colder, then began uncontrollable shivering. "When you were convinced that your body could stand no more," Christenson commented, "you found out that it could."

Hoobler was in a state of exhilaration after shooting a man on horseback. He moved from one position to another, hands in his pockets, batting the breeze with anyone who would talk. In his right-hand pocket he had a Luger he had picked up on the battlefield. A shot rang out. He had accidentally fired the Luger. The bullet went through his right thigh, severing the main artery. In great pain, Hoobler rolled about the ground, crying out for help. Private Holland, the 1st platoon medic, tried to bandage the wound. Two men carried Hoobler back to the aid station, but he died shortly after arrival.

• • •

It was a severely cold night that never seemed to end. Dawn came slowly. There was no firing. Sergeant Martin came walking down 1st platoon lines. Although his reputation was that he seldom raised his voice and never gave orders in a harsh tone, this time he said gruffly, biting off the words, "I want all the 1st platoon noncoms at the platoon CP in ten minutes."

Sergeants Rader, Randleman, Muck, and Christenson, and Cpls. Robert Marsh and Thomas McCreary gathered at the CP. Martin suggested that they sit down. Lts. Stirling Horner, Peacock, and Foley were there. Horner spoke first: "Your platoon commander, Lieutenant Peacock, has been awarded a thirty-day furlough to the States and he leaves today." He explained that the PR man at Division HQ thought it would be a great idea to send one officer from each regiment involved in the heroic defense of Bastogne to the States for a war bond drive and other publicity purposes. Colonel Sink decided to make the selection by drawing lots. Captain Nixon won, Peacock came in second in the 506th. Nixon said he had already seen the States and didn't want to go, so Peacock got the assignment.

Everyone looked at Peacock, who stammered, "I have been awarded this furlough, I feel certain, because of the great job you men did in Holland and here, and the only thing I can say is thanks."

Sergeant McCreary jumped up, ran to Peacock, and started pumping his hand, saying, "Boy, am I glad to hear you're going home, Lieutenant! That's the best news we've had since we left Mourmelon."

Peacock, completely misunderstanding, blushed. He said he felt overwhelmed, that praise from one of the men was the highest praise. The sergeants smiled at each other. They were feeling as happy to see Peacock going as he was to be going. The noncoms felt they had carried his load throughout Holland and the Ardennes. "No one tried harder than Peacock," Christenson declared, "but it was a job he was not cut out for."

Peacock announced that Lieutenant Foley was taking command of the platoon. Then with a cheery "Good luck to you all," he was gone.

• • •

As Peacock left, Father John Maloney brought Joe Toye back from the aid station in Bastogne in his jeep. He dropped Toye off by the road. Toye started walking across the field toward the front line. Winters saw him, his arm in a sling, heading back toward the front.

"Where are you going?" Winters asked. "You don't have to go back to the line."

"I want to go back with the fellows," Toye replied, and kept walking.

That afternoon, January 3, Winters pulled 2d and 3d platoons, plus an attached bazooka team from the 10th Armored, out of the advanced position. He left 1st platoon, temporarily attached to D Company, which like most of the companies in the 101st was down to 50 percent or less of authorized strength and needed help to maintain the MLR. Second and 3d platoons began hiking back to their old position in the section of the woods overlooking Foy.

It was about 1530. The lead units decided to take a shortcut across the open field to get to the foxholes before dark. The other units followed. The Germans saw them.

When the men ducked into the woods, they noticed immediately that the Germans had zeroed artillery in on the position. There were shell holes and branches from tree bursts all around the foxholes. The shell holes were big, indicating heavy artillery, probably 170 mm. No one had to give an order; every man went to work at once to strengthen the cover of his foxhole.

Sergeant Lipton grabbed an ax and ran over to the nearest small trees, about 50 meters beyond his foxhole. He heard German guns open in the distance. There was not enough time to get back to his foxhole, so he jumped into a small open hole someone had started to dig and then abandoned. It was so shallow that even when lying flat in it, Lipton's head from his nose up was above ground. So he saw the first shells bursting in the trees.

The sound was deafening and terrifying. The ground rocked and pitched as in an earthquake. The men from the bazooka team had no foxholes; two of them were killed immediately, a number of others wounded.

Sgt. Joe Toye was in the open, shouting orders to his men to take cover. "They always said if you can hear the shells, you'll be O.K.," he recalled. "I did not hear the shell." It exploded just above him. Shrapnel all but tore off his right leg and hit him in the stomach, chest, and both arms. (The shrapnel in his chest area was later removed by two separate operations, taking it out from the back.)

As suddenly as it began, the shelling stopped. It had been the worst shelling Easy had endured in the war. All through the woods men were calling out for a medic. Lipton ran back to his foxhole to get his rifle, expecting an infantry attack. He heard someone moaning in the next foxhole; a tree 16 inches in diameter had fallen over it. Lipton tried to move the tree, but could not. Help arrived. The men dug around the tree, and Pvt. Shep Howell came out grinning.

Toye yelled for help; he wanted someone to drag him into his foxhole. Sergeant Guarnere got to him first and began dragging him over the ground.

The shelling resumed. The Germans had planned well. As they anticipated, the pause had brought men out of the foxholes to help the wounded. A shell burst over Guarnere's head. Shrapnel tore into his right leg, mangling it. After a few minutes, the shelling ceased.

Lipton came out of his foxhole. Lieutenant Dike

called out to him. "I can still hear him with that deep voice of his," Lipton recalled. "He was about 25 yards away, without his helmet or a weapon. 'Sergeant Lipton,' he yelled to me, 'you get things organized here, and I'll go for help.' And with that he left."

Lipton began rounding up the men who had not been hit. "Some of them were close to breaking, some were amazingly calm." He sent some to tend to the wounded, others to organize to receive the infantry attack he was sure was coming. Then he went to check on Guarnere and Toye.

Lipton looked down at Guarnere. Guarnere looked up and said, "Lip, they got ol' Guarnere this time." Malarkey joined them. Guarnere and Toye, as he recalled, were conscious and calm, no screaming or yelling. "Joe says, 'Give me a cigarette, Malark.' And I lit the cigarette for him."

There was a pause in our interview. I urged him to go on. "I don't want to talk about it," Malarkey said. Another pause, and then he continued: "Joe smoked, looked at me, and asked, 'Jesus, Malark, what does a man have to do to get killed around here?'"

Stretcher bearers got to Guarnere first. As he was being carried away he called out to Toye, "I told you I'd get back to the States before you!"

Lt. Buck Compton commanded 2d platoon. He was very close to his men, too close in the opinion of the officers. "Compton was a close friend of mine," Malarkey said. "He didn't like the status symbol in the Army. He was more friendly with enlisted men than he ever was with officers." He was especially close to Guarnere and Toye.

When he came out of his foxhole, Compton saw carnage all around him. The nearest wounded were his friends Guarnere and Toye, their legs dangling from their bodies, their blood turning the snow bright red all around them.

Compton started running to the rear, shouting for medics, or help of some kind. He finally calmed down at the aid station; it was found he had a severe case of trench foot. He was evacuated.

Compton had won a Silver Star at Brécourt Manor on June 6, 1944. He had been wounded later in Normandy, and again in Holland. He had stood up to everything the Germans had thrown at him from December 17 to January 3. But the sight of his platoon being decimated, of his two friends torn into pieces, unnerved him.

•   •   •

Peacock gone, Dike taking a walk, Compton gone, one replacement lieutenant who had turned himself in to the aid station with trench foot (which by this time almost every member of the company had) and another who was suspected of shooting himself in the hand—the battalion commander had to be concerned with the problem of the breaking point. Winters related his feelings in an interview: "I had reached that stage in Bastogne where I knew I was going to get it. Sooner or later, I'm gonna get it. I just hope the hell it isn't too bad. But there never was a fear in me that I was gonna break. I just felt that I was going to be hit sooner or later. But as far as the breaking point, no."

After a reflective pause, he went on, "But you don't see people getting hit around you every day, every day, every day, continuing on and on, and—not knowing how long this was going to go on. Is this going to go on forever? Am I ever going to see home again?"

For the officer, he continued, with the additional burden of making decisions constantly, under pressure, when there had been a deprivation of sleep and inadequate food, it was no wonder men broke.

It was the policy of the U.S. Army to keep its rifle companies on the line for long periods, continuously in the case of the companies in infantry divisions, making up losses by individual replacement. This meant that replacements went into combat not with the men they had trained and shipped overseas with, but with strangers. It also meant the veteran could look forward to a release from the dangers threatening him only through death or serious wound. This created a situation of endlessness and hopelessness, as Winters indicated.

Combat is a topsy-turvy world. Perfect strangers are going to great lengths to kill you; if they succeed, far from being punished for taking life, they will be rewarded, honored, celebrated. In combat, men stay underground in daylight and do their work in the dark. Good health is a curse; trench foot, pneumonia, severe uncontrollable diarrhea, a broken leg are priceless gifts.

There is a limit to how long a man can function effectively in this topsy-turvy world. For some, mental breakdown comes early; Army psychiatrists found that in Normandy between 10 and 20 percent of the men in rifle companies suffered some form of mental disorder during the first week, and either fled or had to be taken out of the line (many, of course, returned to their units later). For others, visible breakdown never occurs, but nevertheless effectiveness breaks down. The experiences of men in combat produces emotions stronger than civilians can know, emotions of terror, panic, anger, sorrow, bewilderment, helplessness, uselessness, and each of these feelings drained energy and mental stability.

"There is no such thing as 'getting used to combat,'" the Army psychiatrists stated in an official report on Combat Exhaustion. "Each moment of combat imposes a strain so great that men will break down in direct relation to the intensity and duration of their exposure . . . psychiatric casualties are as inevitable as gunshot and shrapnel wounds in warfare. . . . Most men were ineffective after 180 or even 140 days. The general consensus was that a man reached his peak of effectiveness in the first 90 days of combat, that after that his efficiency began to fall off, and that he became steadily less valuable thereafter until he was completely useless."[1]

By January 3, 1945, Easy Company had spent twenty-three days on the front line in Normandy, seventy-eight in Holland, fifteen in Belgium, a total of 116. Statistically, the whole company was in danger of breaking down at any time.

• • •

There was no German infantry follow-up attack that night, nor in the morning. The medics cleared out the wounded. The bodies of the dead stayed out there, frozen, for several more days. Lieutenant Dike reappeared. Things got back to normal.

On January 5, E Company was pulled back to regimental reserve south of Foy. There two men, the acting battalion commander and the 1st sergeant of E Company, thought about the same problem, the officers of that company.

---

[1]Quoted in John Keegan, *The Face of Battle* (New York: Penguin Books, 1976), 335–36.

As Winters put it, "I look at the junior officers and my company commanders and I grind my teeth. Basically we had weak lieutenants. I didn't have faith in them. What the hell can I do about this?" He knew that if he were lucky enough to get some additional officers, they would be replacements just over from the States, after completing a hurry-up training program. As to the company commander, Winters stated flatly: "Dike was sent to us as a favorite protégé of somebody from division HQ, and our hands were tied." Winters saw no quick solution. In the meantime, he decided, "In a pinch, talk to your sergeants."

His 1st sergeant wanted to talk. Lipton asked for a private conversation. Winters said to meet him in the woods behind battalion CP that night.

They met, and Lipton expressed his concern about the company commander. He described Dike's actions, or lack of them, with damning detail. He ended by saying, "Lieutenant Dike is going to get a lot of E Company men killed."

Winters listened intently, asked a few questions, kept his own counsel.

Replacements came in. "I could not believe it," John Martin confessed. "I could not believe that they were going to give us replacements and put us on the attack. I figured, Jesus, they'll take us out of here and give us some clothes or something. But, no, they get you some replacements, and 'Come on boys, let's go.' And then that's when we start attacking."

He was right. The woods form a U around Foy, with the village smack in the middle. In the attack of January 3, the Americans had taken control of the right-hand portion of the U. Next would come an attack on the left-hand portion.

On January 9 the company participated in the clearing operation in the woods west of Foy. Resistance was light. The company reached its objective and dug in.

Suddenly a shell burst in the trees, then another and another. They kept coming. Cpl. George Luz was caught out in the open. He began racing toward his foxhole. Sergeant Muck and Pvt. Alex Penkala called out to him to jump in with them, but he decided to get to his own and with shell bursts all around, splinters and branches and whole trees coming down, made it and dived in.

Lipton was sharing a foxhole with Sgt. Bob Mann, the Company HQ radio man. The Germans sent over some mail. A shell that was a dud hit just outside their foxhole. Lipton looked at it. Mann lighted a cigarette. Lipton had never smoked, but he asked for one, and that night had his first cigarette.

Luz went to check on Muck and Penkala, the men who had offered to share their foxhole with him. The hole had taken a direct hit. Luz started digging frantically. He found some pieces of bodies and a part of a sleeping bag.

• • •

The 101st now held all the woods that encircled Foy from the east, west, and south. But Foy, down in its little valley, was not the objective; Noville and the high ground was. General Taylor had wanted to carry on the January 9 attack right into Noville, but for that he needed tank support, and as the tanks could only operate on the road, he had to have Foy. The village had already changed hands four times.

The 2d Battalion of the 506th got selected to take Foy. It was pulled out of the line west of Foy and put back in south of the village. Winters picked Easy to lead the assault. It was a simple, brutal operation. Charge across an open, snow-covered field of some 200 meters in length down into the village, where every window could be a machine-gun post, where every German had brick-and-mortar protection, that was all there was to it. No subtlety, no maneuvers, just charge and get close enough to the enemy to use grenades to root them out of rooms. The key was to get across the field quickly. If the men pressed the attack, if the cover fire was heavy enough, it should be simple. If they paused, it could be costly.

Division ordered the attack to kick off at 0900. Winters did not like the timing. He argued for a first-light start, to reduce exposure, but was turned down.

Winters was watching as Easy formed up for the attack. Standing behind him was a platoon leader from Dog Company, 1st Lt. Ronald C. Speirs.

• • •

Speirs was an officer with a reputation. Slim, fairly tall, dark hair, stern, ruggedly handsome, he cultivated the look of a leader, and acted it. One of his fellow D Company junior officers, Lt. Tom Gibson, described him as "a tough, aggressive, brave, and resourceful rifle platoon leader." His nicknames were "Sparky" (among his fellow officers) and "Bloody" (with the enlisted). He had led a bayonet attack and won the Silver Star in Normandy.

There were stories. The rumor mill swirled around Lieutenant Speirs. No one ever saw "it" happen with his own eyes, but he knew someone who did. They may be just stories, but they were believed, or half-believed, by the men of E Company.

One story was about the time in Normandy when Speirs had a major problem with drinking in his platoon. He put out a blanket order. No more wine. None. The next day he ran into a drunken noncom. He gave an order, the noncom back-talked him, and he took out his pistol and shot the man between the eyes.

The conclusion to the story goes like this: "And he never had any trouble with drinking after that."

Then there was the day in Normandy when Speirs was walking down a road by himself and passed a group of ten German P.O.W.s. They were under guard and were digging a roadside ditch. Speirs stopped, broke out a pack of cigarettes, and gave one to each P.O.W. They were so appreciative he jumped into the ditch and gave them the whole pack. Then he took out his lighter and gave each one a light. He stepped back up on the road and watched them inhale and chat.

Suddenly and without warning he unslung the Thompson .45-caliber submachine-gun he always carried and fired into the group. He continued raking back and forth until all the P.O.W.s were dead. The guard was stunned. Speirs turned and walked away.

Tom Gibson, who related this story to me (I heard it from many other sources, although no one saw it happen), commented, "I firmly believe that only a combat soldier has the right to judge another combat soldier. Only a rifle company combat soldier knows how hard it is to return his sanity, to do his duty and to survive with some semblance of honor. You have to learn to forgive others, and yourself, for some of the things that are done."

Gibson said he had told the story often over the years, never naming names, but using it as an example of what can happen in war. He continued, "We all know war stories seem to have a life of their own. They have a way of growing, of being embellished. Whether the details are precise or not there must be a kernel of truth for such a story to ever have been told the first time."

•   •   •

Winters was not thinking about Speirs and his reputation. He was watching Easy Company attack. Speirs and other officers from the unengaged companies stood behind him. Winters had placed the two machine-guns of HQ section to provide covering fire over the open fields sloping away in front of them, about 200 meters across from the tree line to the town line.[2] There were some scattered trees and haystacks in the field.

Lieutenant Foley, who led 1st platoon on the attack, described the situation: "We knew that Foy had not been tested the previous day or scouted last evening. In the days before we were well aware of the coming and going of trucks and tanks. We were witness to the many attacks and counterattacks that had taken place. We had seen F Company get chopped up in their efforts to hold this spot. Now they were commanded by a 2d lieutenant. So the unknown was ahead."

The company moved out, line abreast. The covering fire opened up. There were only a few random rifle shots from the village. Still, as Winters put it, "It was tough going for the men through that snow in a skir-

---

[2]Standing on the spot in 1991 with Winters, Lipton, and Malarkey, when Winters indicated that he had set up one machine-gun just there, pointing at my wife Moira's feet, she looked down, bent over, and picked up a 30-caliber shell casing to hand to him. (The field had recently been plowed.)

misher formation, but the line was keeping a good formation and moving at a good pace."

First platoon, on the left flank, came on an area with some cow pens and small outbuildings. Foley had the shacks checked out. As the men from the platoon (only twenty-two of them) went to work, three Germans were seen scrambling into a shack. Foley had it surrounded, kicked the door in, then said in his best German, "Come out with hands up!" No reply.

Foley pulled the pin on a fragmentation grenade and tossed it in. After the explosion, the Germans emerged, shaken and bleeding. One was a 1st lieutenant, the other two were sergeants. Foley started questioning them about the whereabouts of other German troops. One of the sergeants reached his hand into his opened coat. Another made a similar move. The third cried out, *"Dummkopf!"*

One of Foley's men cut the Germans down with a burst from his submachine-gun. "We had no prisoners," Foley commented, "but we had the concealed pistols." The platoon hurried to rejoin the others.

•   •   •

Dike looked left and could not see his 1st platoon. His other two platoons were moving forward steadily. They were being fired on but had not taken any casualties. But Dike was naked on his left, or so he thought. He made a disastrous decision, the kind of decision that gets men killed. He signaled for the 2d and 3d platoons to join Company HQ section behind two haystacks.

From Winters's point of view: "Suddenly the line stopped about 75 yards from the edge of the village. Everybody hunkered down in the snow behind those stacks and stayed there for no apparent reason. I could not get any response from Lieutenant Dike on the radio. The company was a bunch of sitting ducks out there in the snow." He worried about how long he could keep up the suppressing fire.

• • •

First platoon caught up with the company, grouped behind the haystacks. Foley came to Dike for orders. Dike didn't know what to do. Foley insisted he had to do something; Lipton and the other sergeants supported him strongly.

Dike came up with a plan. It consisted of sending 1st platoon on a wide flanking movement to the left, to circle the village and launch an attack from the far side. Meanwhile he would direct machine-gun and mortar fire from the haystacks. For that purpose, Dike said he was keeping the platoon's mortar and machine-gun men with him, to participate in the suppressing fire. So eighteen riflemen of 1st platoon went out into the snow, to try to get into Foy from the far side.

Lieutenant Foley and Sergeant Martin had only a few minutes to plan the route that would get them to an assault position. They picked a path that provided, every 10 meters or so, a tree to hide behind. The line of trees went on into the distance.

One by one they took off. Within minutes, snipers began to fire, cries for "Medic!" went up and down the line. The platoon returned the fire, but without noticeable effect. Foley went to the nearest wounded man. "This was Smith from California. He moaned and groaned as I ripped open the aid kit and before I found his wound he began 'confessing.' Imagine! And what he 'confessed' was that he and two other buddies had come across a PX ration and taken it. This consisted of Hershey bars and cigarettes! I told him that he wasn't dying as I cut open his pants leg, sprinkled on the sulfa and wrapped his leg."

Martin told Pvt. Frank Perconte to move behind another tree and start shooting into the buildings from there. "So Frank goes over and gets behind a tree a little bigger than his head, but it wasn't quite big enough for his ass. And they shot him in the ass."

(When Lipton saw Perconte later in the day, he was lying in the snow in a pool of blood but was still conscious and strong. Lipton asked, "Perconte, how bad are you hit?" He grinned and replied, "Lip, a beautiful wound, a beautiful wound.")

Martin directed Pvt. Harold Webb to a tree and told him where to fire. Foley got on the radio. "We're held up by sniper fire. We can't spot the location. We've lost five men. Can you locate? Advise."

Someone from company CP called back to say that the first haystack to Foley's right could be the spot. Foley came back, "Rake that g——d——stack," even as his platoon began firing at it.

• • •

Lieutenant Dike, in Lipton's judgment, had "fallen apart." He was frozen behind the haystacks, he had no plan, he didn't know what to do.

To the watching Winters, that was obvious. "Here he had everybody hunkered down in the snow and staying there for no apparent reason." Winters was frustrated by his inability to raise Dike on the radio. "Get going!" he would call out. "Keep going." No response. Easy Company was taking needless casualties. All it needed was the leadership push to get across the last open space and into town. But the leadership wasn't there.

Winters grabbed an M-1 and started to run across the field, headed for the stationary company and its pinned-down 1st platoon. He intended to take command, get those men moving. But as he ran down, he thought, Geeze, I can't do this. I'm running this battalion. I can't commit myself. He turned and raced back.

"And as I was coming up, there was Speirs standing right in front of me. 'Speirs! Take over that company and relieve Dike and take that attack on in.'"

Speirs took off running. Winters turned his attention to his job. Lieutenant Foley described the results: "Winters commanded the machine-gunners to lay down a base of protective fire so that we [1st platoon] could finish off what we had started, and for the mortars to concentrate on those two haystacks. A grenade launcher let go with several rounds, and when that stack began to burn, the two snipers became casualties."

Regiment put I Company (twenty-five men strong) on the right, into the attack. But success or failure rested with E Company. This was an ultimate test of the company. It had reached a low point. Neither the officers nor the men were, on the average, up to the standards of the company that had jumped into Normandy. None of the officers who led on D-Day were with the company in 1945. More than half the enlisted men were new. The core of the old company left was the N.C.O.s. They were Toccoa men, and they had held the company together since Dike took over in Holland.

They lived in a state of high alert and sharp tension. They lived and soldiered and tried to suppress feelings, always there, feelings that John Keegan points out are the products "of some of man's deepest fears: fear of wounds, fear of death, fear of putting into danger the lives of those for whose well-being one is responsible. They touch too upon some of man's most violent passions; hatred, rage and the urge to kill."[3]

In this torrent of passion uncontrollable thoughts raced through their minds. They had seen their officers take a walk or break or just cower, or go mute (as Lieutenant Dike was at this moment of crisis). If they did not have the option of walking away, they did have the option of not leading. No one could force them to do so.

Just as they could not force Dike to act. These N.C.O.s were Toccoa men, all that was left in Easy from that hot summer of 1942 and Captain Sobel. They had held the company together through a long stretch of inept command at the top and heavy losses among the enlisted ranks.

So this was the test. Back in '42 the question was, Can a citizen army be trained and prepared well enough to fight Germans in a protracted campaign in Northwest Europe? Hitler was not the only one who had answered no. But the answer that counted would come on the snow-filled fields of Belgium in January 1945; for Easy Company the test was now being given.

The sergeants had it ready to be tested. The Toccoa core of the company was ready to be led, and to lead. At this moment, Speirs arrived, breathless. He managed to blurt out to Dike, "I'm taking over."

Sergeant Lipton and the others filled him in. He barked out orders, 2d platoon this way, 3d platoon that way, get those mortars humping, all-out with those machine-guns, let's go. And he took off, not looking back, depending on the men to follow. They did.

---

[3]Keegan, *The Face of Battle*, 16.

"I remember the broad, open fields outside Foy," Speirs wrote in a 1991 letter, "where any movement brought fire. A German 88 artillery piece was fired at me when I crossed the open area alone. That impressed me."

Standing at the site in 1991 with Winters and Malarkey, Lipton remembered Speirs's dash. He also recalled that when they got to the outbuildings of Foy, Speirs wanted to know where I Company was. "So he just kept on running right through the German line, came out the other side, conferred with the I Company C.O., and ran back. Damn, that was impressive."

• • •

As the platoons with Speirs moved out, 1st platoon started to move toward them. Sergeant Martin made a last-minute check. He noticed Private Webb, in firing position behind a tree, not moving. "Come on, Webb, let's go, get out, come on!" No response. "Well, hell, they were still shooting, so I made a dash over to the tree, which is just a little bigger than your hand. And I jumped right on top of him, because it's hard to lay down beside. I turned him around and they'd shot him right between the eyes."

• • •

The company surged into Foy. The men fired the full range of weapons available to a rifle company: M-1s, tommy guns, bazookas, light machine-guns, mortars, and grenades. They had artillery support. They created a tremendous uproar with bullets zinging off buildings, explosions in the rooms from American grenades, the thump of the mortars taking off, the boom when they hit, scattering bricks and dust through the air.

Resistance was strong, even so. German snipers, bypassed in the first rush, began to inflict casualties. No one could locate one guy especially, who had stopped movement at a corner with two hits. Then Shifty Powers, the man who had spent so much of his youth spotting for squirrels in the upper tree trunks of the Virginia mountains, called out, "I see 'em" and fired. "We weren't pinned down anymore," Lipton remembered, "so we continued the attack."

Everyone resumed firing and advancing. Strong as the opposition had been, the Germans—the 6th Company of the 10th Panzergrenadier Regiment of the 9th Panzer Division—were only fighting a rear-guard action to cover a withdrawal to Noville. Still they fought tenaciously, skillfully, and without panic to keep the escape route open. But as Speirs moved his men forward, and threatened to cut the road behind the German position, three Tiger tanks lumbered off, all that was left of the panzer company. A platoon or so of infantry got out with them. Some 100 Germans, mostly wounded, surrendered. Easy Company had won the test of will. It had taken Foy.

Lipton and Popeye Wynn looked at the place where the sniper had held them up, the one Powers shot at. They found the sniper with a bullet right in the middle of the forehead.

"You know," Wynn commented, "it just doesn't pay to be shootin' at Shifty when he's got a rifle."

•   •   •

It was early afternoon. A movie camera team moved in to take film of the victory. Back on the ridge line at the edge of the woods, Winters noticed two photographers taking pictures of the stretcher bearers bringing in the wounded from 1st platoon. "When the detail reached about 25 yards from the woods, well out of danger, one photographer put down his camera and dashed out to grab hold of the soldier to help carry him. He grabbed him in such a way that he got as much blood on the sleeve and front of his nice new, clean, heavily fleeced jacket as possible. Then this guy turned toward his buddy, who was still taking pictures, and put on a big act of being utterly exhausted as he struggled across those final few yards to the woods. At that point he immediately dropped out."

That evening, Colonel Sink called for a meeting at regimental HQ for all the principal parties involved in the attack. Sink opened with a question for Winters: "What are you going to do about Company E?"

"Relieve Lieutenant Dike and put Lieutenant Speirs in command," Winters replied.

Sink agreed with the decision, and the meeting ended. Lieutenant Foley also agreed. He wrote, "We were glad to see Dike leave, not only because he failed the 1st platoon but even back in the woods when the 2d platoon was hit with those tree bursts, it was evident that 'Foxhole Norman' wasn't meant to be our C.O."

It quickly became clear that Speirs was; indeed, he had already demonstrated that, in the rush on Foy.

13

Attack

NOVILLE

January 14–17, 1945

"WHEN WORD CAME DOWN for this attack, it pissed me off," Winters remembered. "I could not believe that after what we had gone through and done, after all the casualties we had suffered, they were putting us into an attack. It just had the flavor of an ego trip for General Taylor, a play to show Eisenhower that now that Taylor's back his troops will get off their asses and go into the attack."

That is not fair to General Taylor. The attack was part of a general offensive designed to cut through to the north and link up with the U.S. First Army, thereby trapping the German tanks in the tip of the salient. Or as many as were left, after Monty's shilly-shallying about getting going on the counteroffensive. The Germans had begun to pull their tanks back. They could be expected to fight with all they had to keep that escape route open.

As to putting a company as badly mauled as Easy into a frontal attack over a snowfield in bright daylight, this didn't come about because Taylor wanted glory but because Eisenhower needed men. He had no reserves available to throw into the attack, this was the moment to attack, he had to attack with what was there on the front lines. In other words, Easy was paying the price for the policy of limited mobilization. There simply were not enough troops for the job.

• • •

After Foy fell, Easy and the other companies in 2d Battalion were put into regimental reserve, south of the village. At 0415 the following day, January 14, the Germans launched a counterattack on Foy with six tanks and a company of infantry. It was repulsed, but then another attack with fourteen tanks and a battalion forced the 3d Battalion of the 506th out of Foy. Easy was alerted, but with the help of artillery the 3d Battalion was able to mount its own successful counterattack and by 0930 was back in the village.

These actions were carried out under horrid conditions. Another cold front had passed through the area. Daytime temperatures were about 20 degrees F; at night the mercury plunged to below zero. There was almost daily snow. It was difficult for Division to move supplies up the Bastogne-Foy road because of drifts and demands elsewhere. As a result, the men of Easy were almost as badly off as during the first week of the siege. There was not enough food. There were insufficient overshoes, blankets, and sleeping bags. Bed sheets were used for snow suits.

The terrain in front of Easy was also difficult. There was open ground to cross to get to Noville, dense woods still to be cleared. The Germans held the high ground and the solid Belgian buildings in Noville offered sniper and machine-gun positions while providing the Germans with hiding places for tanks.

Colonel Sink told Winters that 2d Battalion would have the honor of leading the attack on Noville. He would jump off at 1200, January 14, moving from the woods south of Foy around to the left (west), occupy the tiny village of Recogne, then attack over an open, snow-covered field toward Cobru, another tiny village a kilometer or so east of Noville. On Winters's left, 1st Battalion would move north through the woods to clear them out.

Winters was unhappy with the orders. He had 2 kilometers of snow-covered open fields to cross to get to Cobru. It was a bright sunny day. Why attack at high noon? Winters would have preferred to wait through the night, then set out at first light to cross the field. But Eisenhower wanted action, Monty wanted action, Taylor wanted action, Sink wanted action, so 2d Battalion's HQ, Dog, Easy, and Fox Companies would have to provide it.

There was a fairly deep shoulder running southwest out of Noville to near Recogne. Winters saw that by sending his men straight for it, he could pick up more and more cover as they got closer to Noville. He put the battalion in single file to cut through the snow, dangerous but quick.

As Easy and the rest of 2d Battalion moved out, so did the 1st Battalion on the left. German tanks in Noville got 1st Battalion in their sights and let loose with some 88s. They did not see 2d Battalion marching toward Noville in the shelter of that shoulder.

Winters glanced to his left. The 88s were tearing up the 1st Battalion. "Men were flying through the air," Winters recalled. "Years later, in the movie *Doctor Zhivago*, I saw troops crossing snow-covered fields, being shot into by cannon from the edge of the woods, and men flying through the air. Those scenes seemed very real to me."

Easy was having its own problems. German machine-guns in Noville opened on the company, at a draw and stream that slowed the Americans while they were exposed. Speirs set up two of his machine-guns to answer the fire. As the American machine-gunners let loose with a burst, a group of eight or ten would dash across the small stream.

The stream was narrow enough for most of the men to jump across. But Pvt. Tony Garcia, carrying an ammo bag with six rounds of mortar ammunition, fell into the stream. He was soaked. By the time his group reached Noville, "my clothing had frozen, causing a crackling sound as I walked. This, however, saved me from going on an all-night patrol which was to have made contact with one of our own units. The platoon sergeant said I could be heard all the way to Berlin and for me to stay put."[1]

By 1530 2d Battalion had crossed the field and was snuggled up to the underside of the shoulder. By dark

---

[1]Garcia has another memory of that day: "One of the more disturbing incidents that affected me was seeing a horse standing in the snow helpless with one of its front legs shattered by a shell fragment. One of the noncoms mercifully put it out of its misery with a couple of bullets to the head. Though man's brutality to one another is tragic enough, to see helpless animals suffer by his actions is even more tragic."

it had worked its way around to a draw on the southeast corner of Cobru.

Speirs held a meeting of the officers and 1st Sergeant Lipton. He outlined the plan of attack for the morning, up the draw to Noville, with 2d platoon on the left, 3d on the right. Friendly tanks were supposed to be coming up on the right in support on the Foy-Noville road. After the meeting Speirs told Lipton to lead the 2d platoon in the attack.

Lipton pulled 2d platoon together to brief the men. Winters stood to the side, listening. Lipton told them the distance to the town was about 800 meters, that they should move quickly to get down the road and into the shelter of the buildings, that they should clear out the buildings working together as teams with rifles and grenades, that the mortar men should be ready to drop rounds on German strong points, that the machine-gunners should set up and lay down a base of fire in support, that they should not bunch up, and so on. Winters's sole comment was that the distance was more like 1,000 meters.

As the meeting broke up, the men could hear tank motors starting up and tanks moving around. It was not possible to determine if it was Germans pulling out or Americans coming along the Foy-Noville road.

Winters remembers the night as the coldest of his life. There was little shelter, only hastily dug foxholes. The men had worked up a sweat getting to Cobru. They shivered through the night. They would lie down and drift off, only to be awakened by intense shivering in their now-frozen clothes. Most gave up on trying to sleep. It got so bad that at one point Winters though about ordering a night attack, but decided against it because of the danger of shooting each other in the confusion.

Lipton was uneasy about leading 2d platoon on an attack without knowing what was up ahead, so he decided to go forward with a radio man to scout the situation in Noville. The two men came to a barn on the outskirts of the village, entered it by a door in the back and felt their way through to a door that opened into a courtyard near the main road through Noville. Everything was quiet. Lipton called Speirs on the radio to tell the C.O. where he was and to request permission to scout the town. He said he could see some Sherman tanks up ahead and asked if Speirs knew if American armor had already taken the town. Speirs did not know and told Lipton to look around.

Lipton moved silently forward to the tanks. They were knocked out. American bodies lay frozen and strewn around them. They had been left there when Team Desobry had withdrawn from Noville on December 20, almost a month earlier. The Germans still held the town. Lipton and his radio man withdrew.

* * *

The attack jumped off at dawn, January 15. There was resistance, strongest on the right hand side of the road against 3d platoon. The 2d platoon quickly got into the center of Noville and up to the burned-out Shermans. The 3d platoon got into a burned-out building and set up a CP. Over the radio came a message, "Friendly armor on the right."

As Lieutenant Shames and Sergeant Alley got that message, they heard tanks outside the building. Anxious to get the show on the road, Alley told

Shames he was going to link up with those tanks. Shames decided to join him. They moved by several burned-out buildings and rounded a corner into the main road. Up ahead, between two buildings, partway out, was the tank they sought.

Alley moved up to the side of the tank. The tank commander was standing in the turret looking the other way, so Alley shouted to him over the roar of the engine to "Come this way." The tank commander turned, and Alley realized he had mistaken a German tank for an American. The German swore, dropped into his tank, and began traversing his turret toward Alley and Shames.

They said not a word to each other. They took off so fast they were kicking snow in the German's face. The tank followed. The Americans ran around a corner. Shames saw an open window and dived in head first. Alley ran 3 meters or so past him and jumped into a doorway with his rifle ready for the infantry he was sure would be with the German tank.

The tank turned the corner and drove right past Shames and Alley. It came to the place where 2d platoon was clearing out buildings, near the burned-out Shermans. Lipton and his men dived under the Shermans or ducked behind walls for protection. The German tank stopped and, swiveling its turret, put a shell into each one of the knocked-out Shermans to prevent anyone from using their guns to put a shell into his tank as he drove past. Lipton recalled, "When those shells hit the Shermans, it felt to us under them that they jumped a foot in the air."

The tank roared out of town, headed north toward safety. A P-47 fighter plane spotted it, strafed it, and dropped a bomb on it, destroying the tank.

Alley went to look for Shames. He heard moaning and cries for help. When he got to the window Shames had dived through, he looked and burst into laughter. He saw his lieutenant tangled up in bedsteads, springs, and furniture in a basement Shames had not realized was there.

By noon, 2d Battalion held Noville and had set up a perimeter defense. The little village and its surrounding hills had been an objective of the 101st since December 20. Finally it was in American hands.

•   •   •

"We had looked northward at Noville from our positions outside Foy since shortly after we had arrived at Bastogne," Lipton wrote, "and we had convinced ourselves it would be our final objective in the Bastogne campaign." But there was one more attack to make; General Taylor wanted 2d Battalion to move farther north, in the direction of Houffalize, to clear the village of Rachamps.

Rachamps was off the highway, over to the right (east). It was in a valley. The snow-covered ground sloped gently down to it from all sides, giving an effect similar to attacking from the rim of a saucer toward its center. The 2d Battalion attacked from the south and southwest, while 1st Battalion on the left came down from north of the village. The men were well-spread and advanced steadily. The Germans put up some resistance, mainly artillery using white phosphorus shells. But as the men of the 506th got to the outskirts of the village, most of the German defenders fled. As the Americans moved in, the Germans began bombarding the village.

Sgt. Earl Hale was one of the first into Rachamps.

He and Liebgott ducked into a barn, where they surprised and made prisoner six SS officers. Hale lined them up nose to nose and told them that if he and Liebgott got killed they were going to take the Germans with them. Hale covered them with his tommy-gun to make the point.

A shell exploded outside. Hale was standing by the door. He got hit by a piece of shrapnel and went down. An SS officer pulled his knife from his boot and slashed Hale's throat. He failed to cut an artery or sever the windpipe, but did cut the esophagus. Blood gushed out. Liebgott shot the officer who did the cutting, then the others. Medic Roe got sulfa powder on Hale's wound. A jeep evacuated him to Luxembourg, where an amazed doctor patched him up, leaving a crooked esophagus. Because of Hale's condition, the doctor gave him a medical order stating that he did not have to wear a necktie. (Later, Hale was stopped by an irate General Patton who chewed him out for not wearing his necktie. Hale triumphantly produced his slip of paper, leaving Patton for once speechless.)

•   •   •

The easy victory at Rachamps showed how completely the 101st Airborne had won its head-to-head battles with a dozen crack German armored and infantry divisions. The Americans had gone through a much more miserable month than the Germans, who had an open and bountiful supply line. For the 101st, surrounded, there were no supplies in the first week and insufficient supplies thereafter. Those were the weeks that tried the souls of men who were inadequately fed, clothed, and armed. This was war at its harshest, horrible to experience. The 101st, hungry, cold, underarmed, fought the finest units Nazi Germany could produce at this stage of the war. Those Wehrmacht and SS troops were well fed, warm, and fully armed, and they heavily outnumbered the 101st.

It was a test of arms, will, and national systems, matching the best the Nazis had against the best the Americans had, with all the advantages on the German side. The 101st not only endured, it prevailed. It is an epic tale as much for what it revealed as what happened. The defeat of the Germans in their biggest offensive in the West in World War II, and the turning of that defeat into a major opportunity "to kill Germans west of the Rhine," as Eisenhower put it, was a superb feat of arms. The Americans established a moral superiority over the Germans. It was based not on equipment or quantity of arms, but on teamwork, coordination, leadership, and mutual trust in a line that ran straight from Ike's HQ right on down to E Company. The Germans had little in the way of such qualities. The moral superiority was based on better training methods, better selection methods for command positions, ultimately on a more open army reflecting a more open society. Democracy proved better able to produce young men who could be made into superb soldiers than Nazi Germany.

What veterans of far-flung campaigns these German soldiers were was revealed in a little incident in Rachamps. Sergeant Rader related it: "I almost killed a Kraut prisoner for laughing at me after I got to the town, only to have someone grab my M-1 and shout, 'Sarge, he has no lips or eyelids!' He had lost them on the Russian front, frozen off."

The battle made the 101st into a legend. The legend that began in Normandy and grew in Holland reached its climax in Bastogne. The 101st Airborne was the most famous and admired of all the eighty-nine divisions the United States Army put into the Second World War. Ever since, men have worn that Screaming Eagle on their left shoulders with the greatest of pride.

•　•　•

In Rachamps, Speirs set up company CP in a convent. It was the first time the CP had been in a building since Easy left Mourmelon a month earlier. That night the nuns brought into the large hall of the convent a group of twelve- and thirteen-year-old girls to sing a serenade for E Company. The program included French and Belgian songs, several in English, and the German marching song, "Lili Marlene."

The next morning, January 17, the 17th Airborne Division relieved the 101st on the line. Easy Company got into trucks to begin a move to Alsace. The trucks took the men back down the highway they had sat astride for four weeks, through Bastogne. It was only the second time most of the men had seen Bastogne—first on December 19 when they marched through the town while frightened American soldiers fled to escape the German onslaught, second on January 17, the town secured.

Although the men had seen little of Bastogne, that name—and the experience it represented—would stay with them forever. Whenever thereafter a man from Easy experienced cold or hunger or sleep deprivation, he would remind himself of Bastogne and recall that he had been through much worse.

Easy's losses were heavy. Exact figures are impossible to come by; in the hurry-up movement out of Mourmelon the company roster was not completed;

replacements came in as individuals or in small groups and were not properly accounted for on the roster; wounded men dropped out of the line only to come back a few days later. An estimate is that Easy went into Belgium with 121 officers and men, received about two dozen replacements, and came out with 63. The Easy men killed in action in Belgium were Sgt. Warren Muck, Cpl. Francis Mellett, and Pvts. A. P. Herron, Kenneth Webb, Harold Webb, Carl Sowosko, John Shindell, Don Hoobler, Harold Hayes, Alex Penkala, and John Julian.

The best description of the cost of the Battle of the Bulge to Easy Company comes from Private Webster, who rejoined the company during the truck ride to Alsace. He had been wounded in early October; it was mid-January. He wrote, "When I saw what remained of the 1st platoon, I could have cried; eleven men were left out of forty. Nine of them were old soldiers who had jumped in either Holland or Normandy or both: McCreary, Liebgott, Marsh, Cobb, Wiseman, Lyall, Martin, Rader, and Sholty. Although the other two platoons were more heavily stocked than the 1st, they were so understrength that, added to the 1st, they wouldn't have made a normal platoon, much less a company."

Beyond the wounded and killed, every man at Bastogne suffered. Men unhit by shrapnel or bullets were nevertheless casualties. There were no unwounded men at Bastogne. As Winters put it, "I'm not sure that anybody who lived through that one hasn't carried with him, in some hidden ways, the scars. Perhaps that is the factor that helps keep Easy men bonded so unusually close together."

They knew each other at a level only those who

have fought together in a variety of tactical situations can achieve, as only those who endured together the extreme suffering of combined cold, not enough food, and little sleep while living in constant tension could attain.

They knew fear together. Not only the fear of death or wound, but the fear that all this was for nothing. Glenn Gray wrote, "The deepest fear of my war years, one still with me, is that these happenings had no real purpose. . . . How often I wrote in my war journals that unless that day had some positive significance for my future life, it could not possibly be worth the pain it cost."[2]

They got through the Bulge because they had become a band of brothers. The company had held together at that critical moment in the snow outside Foy because 1st Sergeant Lipton and his fellow N.C.O.s, nearly all Toccoa men, provided leadership, continuity, and cohesiveness. Despite a new C.O. and new officers and enlisted recruits, the spirit of E Company was alive, thanks to the sergeants. Having Winters as 2d Battalion X.O. and usually as acting battalion C.O. (Lieutenant Colonel Strayer spent most of the month at regimental HQ, working on an acting basis for Colonel Sink as S-3) was a great help. And Speirs was proving to be an excellent company commander, able to draw out of the company its best.

That spirit was well described by Webster. By this time Webster had been wounded twice and returned to combat after each occasion. He would not allow his parents to use their influence to get him out of the front lines. He would not accept any position of

---

[2]Gray, *The Warriors,* 24.

responsibility within E Company. He was a Harvard intellectual who had made his decision on what his point of view of World War II would be, and stuck to it.

He was a man of books and libraries, a reader and a writer, sensitive, level-headed, keenly observant, thoughtful, well-educated. Here he was thrown in the most intimate contact (pressed together on an open truck on icy roads in hilly country, sleeping in a foxhole with other enlisted men) with ill-educated hillbillies, Southern farmers, coal miners, lumbermen, fishermen, and so on among most of the enlisted men in the company. Of those who had been to college, most were business or education majors. In short, Webster was thrown in with a group of men with whom he had nothing in common. He would not have particularly liked or disliked them in civilian life, he just would not have known them.

Yet it was among this unlikely group of men that Webster found his closest friendships and enjoyed most thoroughly the sense of identification with others.

His description of his truck ride with his platoon to Alsace deserves to be quoted at length:

"We squished through the mud to our trucks and climbed in. McCreary and Marsh lit cigarettes. Martin made a wisecrack about a passing officer. I asked what had happened to Hoobler. Killed at Bastogne. Poor Hoobler, who got such a kick out of war, dead in the snow. And the others? Muck and his buddy Penkala, who had the deepest hole in one position, had been killed by a direct hit. Sowosko was shot through the head attacking Foy. And so on. Some replacements who had come in after Holland had also died. A lot of men had been evacuated for trench foot, too many, McCreary thought. The platoon wasn't what it used to be."

Webster thought that it was. He had followed a long and complicated route through the Replacement Depots to rejoin the company, a time of frustration and loneliness for him among that host of khaki-clad look-alike soldiers. Now he was home, back with 1st platoon, back with Easy Company.

"It was good to be back with fellows I knew and could trust," he wrote. "Listening to the chatter in the truck, I felt warm and relaxed inside, like a lost child who has returned to a bright home full of love after wandering in a cold black forest."

There were missing chairs at home. They belonged to the men who had been killed, badly wounded, or had broken. But as Webster's reaction indicates, although Easy had lost many members, and gained others, thanks to the former E Company officers now on battalion or regimental staff and to the noncoms, it remained an organic whole.

14

The Patrol

HAGUENAU

January 18–February 23, 1945

IN MID-JANUARY, desperate to save what they could of their men and equipment in the Bulge, the Germans launched a diversionary operation in Alsace, code name Nordwind (Northwind), in an attempt to draw American troops from the Ardennes area. As in the mid-December attack in the Ardennes, they struck a thinly held sector of the front. (When Patton's Third Army left Alsace to go to the Ardennes, U.S. Seventh Army had slid to its left to take over his position, as well as holding its own.) When Nordwind began, Eisenhower sent the 101st to Alsace to bolster the line.

When word reached the paratroopers that they were to be taken by truck to Alsace, it was accompanied by a rumor that turned out to be exaggerated: the Germans had broken through. Winters's thought was,

My God, don't they have anybody else in this army to plug these gaps?

It was a long trip. Alsace was 160 miles south and slightly east of Bastogne. The weather was cold and miserable, with falling snow. The roads were slippery and dangerous. The trucks proceeded at a walking pace; men could jump off, relieve themselves, and catch up to reboard without difficulty. Watching the process was often comical, however, because from outside to inside the men were wearing baggy pants, OD pants, long underwear, and OD-colored undershorts. All had buttons—no zippers. Men tried to get everything open while still wearing their gloves. Sometimes it seemed to take forever.

The convoy went from Bastogne to Bellefontaine, Virton, Etain, Toul, Nancy, Drulingen, arriving on January 20. The 506th PIR went into regimental reserve.

While on the road, Sergeant Lipton became ill, with chills and a high fever. At Drulingen he went to see the medical officer, who examined him and declared that he had pneumonia and had to be evacuated to a hospital. Lipton said he was 1st sergeant of E Company and could not possibly leave. As the doctor could not evacuate him that night anyway, he told Lipton to come back in the morning.

Lieutenant Speirs and Sergeant Lipton had a room in a German house for the night. (Alsace, on the border between France and Germany, changes hands after every war. In 1871 it became German territory; the French got it back in 1919; in 1940 it became German again, in 1945, French.) The room had only a single bed. Speirs said Lipton should sleep on it. Lipton replied that wasn't right; as the enlisted man, he would sleep in his sleeping bag on the floor. Speirs simply replied, "You're sick," which settled it.

Lipton got into the bed. The elderly German couple who lived in the home brought him some schnapps and *Apfelstrudel*. Lipton had never drunk anything alcoholic, but he sipped at the schnapps until he had finished a large glass, and ate the strudel. He fell into a deep sleep. In the morning, his fever had broken, his energy had returned. He went to the medical officer, who could not believe the improvement. The doctor called it a miracle.

Speirs, delighted by the recovery, said that he and Winters had recommended Lipton for battlefield promotion and that Colonel Sink wanted to talk to him. Lipton went to regiment, where Sink gave him a one-hour grilling on his combat experiences.

Easy stayed in reserve for nearly two weeks, moving almost daily from one village to another. The weather warmed. The sun shone, and the snow began to melt. The ground got mushy. A supply truck arrived carrying an issue of shoepacs complete with arctic socks and felt insoles. "Where were you six weeks ago in Bastogne, when we needed you?" the men shouted at the drivers. Dirty clothes, blankets, and sleeping bags were picked up by the Quartermaster Company and sent to a G.I. laundry. Portable showers capable of handling 215 men an hour were brought in; Easy moved through them as a company. The water wasn't hot, but at least it wasn't ice cold either. Soap and lather, scrub and scrub—it took a major effort to remove six weeks of dirt and sweat.

Movies arrived, including *Rhapsody in Blue, Buffalo Bill*, and *Our Hearts Were Young and Gay. Stars and Stripes, Yank*, and *Kangaroo Khronicle* brought news of the outside world (not as welcome as one would have supposed, because the news from the Pacific showed that the war there had a long way to go; this ignited rumors that the 101st was going to be shipped to the Pacific for "the big jump" on Japan).

• • •

On February 5, Easy moved into the line as the 506th relieved the 313th Infantry of the 79th Division in the city of Haguenau. The population was nearly 20,000, which was big-time for the paratroopers in Europe. Carentan had about 4,000 residents, Mourmelon about 4,500, and Bastogne maybe 5,500. Haguenau lay astride the Moder River, a tributary of the Rhine. Easy's position was on the far right flank of the 506th, at the junction of the Moder and a canal that ran through town to cut off the loop in the Moder.

"Our position was somewhat like a point into the German lines," Lieutenant Foley recalled. Easy occupied the buildings on the south bank, the Germans held the buildings on the north bank. The river was high, out of its banks, the current swift. It varied from about 30 to as much as 100 meters wide, it was too far to throw grenades across but close enough for machine-gun, rifle, and mortar fire. Both sides had artillery support. A few kilometers behind their lines the Germans had a huge railway gun (probably a 205 mm) from World War I. It fired shells as big as the 16-inch naval guns that had supported the Americans at Utah Beach.

The paratroopers moved into buildings that had been occupied by the 79th Division. Webster and five other members of 1st platoon took over a building at the juncture of the Moder and the canal. "In keeping with the best airborne tradition of relying on madmen instead of firepower," Webster wrote, "six of us with

one B.A.R. relieved eighteen 79th Division doggies
with a water-cooled 50 and an air-cooled 30-caliber
machine gun." The 79th Division men told 1st platoon that this was a quiet sector, no offensives by
either side, but Webster noted that they left in a hurry
after the briefest of briefings.

The building the 1st squad of 1st platoon occupied
was a wreck. Sections of walls had been blasted away,
the roof partially removed by mortar shells, all the
windows broken, the floors ankle deep in plaster,
bricks, and broken glass, the banisters ripped off for
firewood, the toilets choked with excreta, the basement a cesspool of ashes, ordure, and ration cans.

Looking the place over, Cpl. Tom McCreary expressed the general sentiment of his squad: "We got it
made."

This was the first time anyone in the squad had
lived indoors on the firing line. The men set out to
improve their quarters. They rearranged the cellar,
putting the bunks and C rations in one room, throwing the trash in another. They found some gas-burning
lamps and a working stove. They spliced into a
German field telephone system and established communications with the 1st platoon CP. When they
needed to relieve themselves, they went to the third
floor, "where the toilet bowl was only half full."

George Luz, radio man for the 1st platoon CP, paid a
visit. McCreary's squad showed off their accommodations with pride. "If you think this is good," Luz
responded, "you should see Company HQ. They're living like kings." He looked around again, and added,
"Them bastards."

(Webster shared Luz's feelings. He went back to the
company CP as seldom as possible because "there was

altogether too much rank in that place and a private didn't stand a chance.")

As on the Island, movement by day was impossible. Snipers were always ready to blast anyone caught in the open. The least movement would bring down mortars; two or three men outside would justify a couple of rounds of 88s. So, Webster recorded, "our major recreation was eating. We spent more time preparing, cooking, and consuming food than in any other pursuit."

The company's task was to hold the line, send out enough patrols to keep contact with the Germans, and serve as forward artillery observers. McCreary's squad held observation post No. 2. Two men, one at the third-floor window, the other in the basement with the telephone, were on duty for an hour at a time. From the window, the men had a beautiful view of the German section of town. They could call for artillery fire just about whenever they wanted, a luxury previously unknown. The Germans would reply in kind.

It was hard to say which was more dangerous, mortars, aimed sniper fire, machine-gun bursts, 88s, or that big railway gun. One thing about the monster cannon, although it was so far to the rear the men could not hear it fire, they could hear the low-velocity shell coming from a long way off. It sounded like a train. Shifty Powers recalled that he was an observer in a third-floor window. When he heard the shell, he had time to dash downstairs into the basement before it landed.

Although the men lived in constant danger—a direct hit from the railway gun would destroy whole buildings—they were in a sense spectators of war. Glenn Gray writes that the "secret attractions of war" are "the delight in seeing, the delight in comradeship, the delight in destruction." He continues, "War as a spectacle, as something to see, ought never to be underestimated."[1] Gray reminds us that the human eye is lustful; it craves the novel, the unusual, the spectacular.

War provides more meat to satisfy that lust than any other human activity. The fireworks displays are far longer lasting, and far more sensational, than the most elaborate Fourth of July display. From OP 2 Webster could see "the shells bursting in both friendly and hostile zones of Haguenau and watch the P-47s strafing right and left." At night, the antiaircraft batteries miles behind the line turned their searchlights straight into the sky, so that the reflections from the clouds would illuminate the front. Both sides fired flares whenever an observer called for them; a man caught outside when one went off had to stand motionless until it burned out. Every machine-gun burst sent out tracers that added to the spectacle.

The big artillery shells would set off fires that crackled and flamed and lighted up the countryside. "There's something eerie about a fire in combat," Webster noted. "The huge, bold flames seem so alien and strident in a situation where neither side dares show the tiniest match flame."

War satisfies not only the eye's lust; it can create, even more than the shared rigors of training, a feeling of comradeship. On February 9, Webster wrote his parents, "I am home again." His account of life in OP 2 mentions the dangers endured but concentrates on his feelings toward his fellow squad members. "How does danger break down the barriers of the self and give man an experience of community?" Gray asks. His

[1] Gray, *The Warriors*, 28–29.

answer is the "power of union with our fellows. In moments [of danger] many have a vague awareness of how isolated and separate their lives have hitherto been and how much they have missed. . . . With the boundaries of the self expanded, they sense a kinship never known before."[2]

(Webster and Pvt. Bob Marsh had orders one night to set up the machine-gun on the porch of his building, to provide covering fire for a patrol if needed. They were exposed in such a way that if they fired, a German self-propelled gun directly across the river would spot them without the aid of observers. But they decided that if the patrol was fired upon, they would open up with everything they had, "because the lives of some twenty men might depend on us." Webster, who never volunteered for anything, commented, "This was one of those times where I could see playing the hero even if it meant our death.")

Gray's third "delight" provided by war is delight in destruction. There is no gainsaying that men enjoy watching buildings, vehicles, equipment being destroyed. The crowds that gather in any city when a building is about to be demolished illustrates the point. For the soldier, seeing a building that might be providing shelter to the enemy get blasted out of existence by friendly artillery is a joyous sight. In his World War I diary German soldier Ernst Juenger wrote of "the monstrous desire for annihilation which hovered over the battlefield. . . . A neutral observer might have perhaps believed that we were seized by an excess of happiness."[3]

---

[2]Gray, *The Warriors*, 43–46.

[3]Quoted in Gray, *The Warriors*, 52.

The soldier's concern is with death, not life, with destruction, not construction. The ultimate destruction is killing another human being. When snipers hit a German on the other side, they would shout, "I got him! I got him!" and dance for joy. Pvt. Roy Cobb spotted a German walking impudently to and fro before a cottage a couple of hundred meters away. He hit him with his first shot. Pvt. Clarence Lyall, looking through his binoculars, said the hurt, perplexed expression on the German's face was something to see. As the soldier tried to crawl back to the cottage, Cobb hit him twice more. There were whoops and shouts each time he got hit.

As always on the front line, there was no past or future, only the present, made tense by the ever-present threat that violent death could come at any instant. "Life has become strictly a day to day and hour to hour affair," Webster wrote his parents.

* * *

Replacements came in. This was distressing, because when an airborne division, which was usually brought up to strength in base camp in preparation for the next jump, received reinforcements while on the front line, it meant that the division was going to continue fighting. At OP 2, "four very scared, very young boys fresh from jump school" joined the squad. Webster commented: "My heart sank. Why did the army, with all its mature huskies in rear echelon and the Air Corps slobs in England, choose to send its youngest, most inexperienced members straight from basic training to the nastiest job in the world, front line infantry?"

One of the replacements was 2d Lt. Hank Jones, a West Point graduate (June 6, 1944, John Eisenhower's class) who had completed jump school at Benning in late December. He left New York in mid-January, landed at Le Havre, and arrived in Haguenau in mid-February. As Lieutenant Foley commented, "Teach them how to say 'Follow me' and ship them overseas was the quickest way to replace the casualties." Jones was cocky, clean-cut, likable. He was eager for a chance to prove himself.

He would quickly get his opportunity, because the regimental S-2, Captain Nixon, needed some live prisoners for interrogation. On February 12 he asked Winters to arrange to grab a couple of Germans. Winters was still a captain, a distinct disadvantage in dealing with the other two battalion commanders, who were lieutenant colonels. But he had friends on the regimental staff, where Colonel Strayer was X.O. and Nixon and the S-4 (Matheson) were old E Company men. Matheson scrounged up some German rubber boats for Winters to use to get a patrol over the river. Winters picked E Company for the patrol.

It would be a big one, twenty men strong, drawn from each platoon plus Company HQ section, plus two German-speaking men from regimental S-2. Lieutenant Foley picked Cobb, McCreary, Wynn, and Sholty from 1st platoon. Once across the river, the patrol would divide into two parts, one led by Sgt. Ken Mercier, the other by Lieutenant Jones.

The men selected for the patrol spent two days outside Haguenau practicing the handling of the rubber boats. On February 14, Winters and Speirs visited OP 2, much to the dismay of the 1st squad, because they stood in front of the OP studying the German position with binoculars, gesturing with their hands, waving a map. "We inside cursed heartily," Webster recalled, "fearing that a German observer would spot them and call down artillery fire on our cozy home."

The plan Winters and Speirs worked out would call on Easy to display many of its hard-earned skills. The lead scout would be Cpl. Earl McClung, a part Indian who had a reputation for being able to "smell Krauts." The patrol would rendezvous at a D Company OP, where the men would drink coffee and eat sandwiches until 2200. They would come to the river under cover of darkness and launch the first rubber boat. It would carry a rope across the river to fasten to a telephone pole on the north side so that the others could pull their boats across. Once in the German lines the patrol would split into two sections, the one under Lieutenant Jones going into town, the other under Sergeant Mercier to a house on the bank of the river suspected of being a German outpost.

Whether or not the patrol succeeded in capturing prisoners, it would have plenty of support for its retreat back across the river. If either section ran into trouble, or got its hands on prisoners, the section leader would blow a whistle to indicate that the withdrawal was under way. That would be the signal for both sections to gather at the boats, and for Lieutenant Speirs and Sergeant Malarkey to start the covering fire.

The covering fire had been worked out down to the smallest details. Every known or anticipated German position was covered by designated rifle fire, machine-gun, artillery, and mortar fire. A 57 mm antitank gun was borrowed from Division and emplaced to shoot into the basement of a house that could not be hit by indirect artillery fire. D Company had a 50-caliber machine-gun (stolen from the 10th Armored at Bastogne) set up to rake the German positions. The 1st platoon would have its 30-caliber machine-gun set up on the balcony of OP 2, ready to spray the German dwelling across the river, if necessary (the crossing would be made right in front of OP 2).

The night of February 15 was still and dark. The German mortars shot only a couple of flares and one or two 88s fired. The American artillery was silent, waiting for the whistle. The searchlights were out, as Speirs had requested. The Americans shot no flares. There was no small arms firing, there was no moon, there were no stars.

The first boat got across successfully. Two others made it. The fourth boat, with McCreary and Cobb in it, capsized. They drifted a hundred meters or so downstream, managed to get out, tried again, only to capsize once more. They gave it up as a bad job and returned to OP 2.

Jones and Mercier gathered the men who had made it over, divided them, and set out on their tasks. With Mercier was a just-arrived replacement from Company F. Without Speirs or Winters knowing it, the young officer—gung-ho and eager to prove himself—had attached himself to the patrol. As he followed Mercier up the north bank of the river, he stepped on a Schu mine and was killed. He had been on the front line barely twenty-four hours.

Mercier continued toward his target, eight men following him. When he got close enough to the German outpost, he fired a rifle grenade into the cellar window. As it exploded, the men rushed the building and threw hand grenades into the cellar. As those grenades exploded, Mercier led the men into the cellar, so close behind the blast that Pvt. Eugene Jackson, a replacement who had joined up in Holland, was hit in the face and head by fragments of shrapnel. In the cellar, the Americans found the still-living Germans in a state of shock. They grabbed one wounded and two uninjured men and dashed back outside. Mercier blew his whistle.

The signal unleashed a tremendous barrage. It shook the ground. Heavy artillery from the rear was supplemented by mortars and the antitank gun. Webster, watching from the balcony of OP 2, described the scene: "We saw a sheet of flame, then a red ball shoot into the basement of a dwelling across the creek. The artillery shells flashed orange on the German roads and strong points. Half a mile away to our direct front a house started to burn. D Company's 50-caliber opened up behind us in a steady bark. A solid stream of tracers shot up the creek, provoking a duel with a German burp gun which hosed just as steady a stream of tracers back at D Company from the protection of an undamaged cellar."

Mercier and his men dashed back to the boats, where they met Jones and his section. As they started to cross, they decided that the wounded German soldier was too far gone to be of any use, so they abandoned him by the river bank. One of the replacements, Pvt. Allen Vest, drew a pistol to kill the man, but was told to hold his fire. The wounded German was not going to do them any harm, and there was no point to revealing their position. Some men swam, using the rope to pull themselves back across; others used boats.

Once across, the patrol members ran to the cellar at OP 2, pushing the two prisoners in front of them. As they reached the cellar, German artillery shells exploded in the backyard, the beginning of a barrage by the Germans all across E Company's line.

Down in the cellar, the patrol members crowded around the prisoners. The Americans were excited, many of the men chattering—or rather shouting over the tremendous noise—trying to describe individual experiences. Their blood was up.

"Lemme kill 'em, lemme kill 'em!" shouted Vest, rushing toward the prisoners with his pistol drawn. Somebody stopped him.

"Get outta here, Vest. They want these bastards back at battalion," someone else yelled.

The prisoners, according to Webster, "were a pair of very self-possessed noncoms, an *Unteroffizier* (buck sergeant) and a *Feldwebel*, or staff sergeant. They stood calm, like rocks, in a hot, smelly room full of men who wanted to kill them, and they never moved a finger or twisted their expressions. They were the most poised individuals I've ever seen."

As the explosions outside increased, Private Jackson, who had been wounded on the patrol, began screaming, "Kill me! Kill me! Somebody kill me! I can't stand it, Christ I can't stand it. Kill me, for God's sake kill me!" His face was covered with blood from a grenade fragment that had pierced his skull and lodged in his brain.

Sergeant Martin related, "Of course no one was going to kill him, because there is always hope, and that goddamn prisoner made me so goddamn mad I started kicking that goddamn sonofabitch, and I mean I kicked that bastard every way I could." He concluded lamely, "Emotions were running real high."

Someone telephoned for a medic with a stretcher, quick. Roe said he would be there in a flash.

Jackson continued to call out. "Kill me! Kill me! I want Mercier! Where's Mercier?" He was sobbing.

Mercier went to him and held his hand. "That's O.K., buddy, that's O.K. You'll be all right."

Someone stuck a morphine Syrette in Jackson's arm. He was by then so crazed with pain he had to be held down on the bunk. Roe arrived with another medic and a stretcher. As they carried the patient back toward the aid station, Mercier walked beside the stretcher, holding Jackson's hand. Jackson died before reaching the aid station.

"He wasn't twenty years old," Webster wrote. "He hadn't begun to live. Shrieking and moaning, he gave up his life on a stretcher. Back in America the standard of living continued to rise. Back in America the race tracks were booming, the night clubs were making their greatest profits in history, Miami Beach was so crowded you couldn't get a room anywhere. Few people seemed to care. Hell, this was a boom, this was prosperity, this was the way to fight a war. We read of black-market restaurants, of a manufacturer's plea for gradual reconversion to peacetime goods, beginning immediately, and we wondered if the people would ever know what it cost the soldiers in terror, bloodshed, and hideous, agonizing deaths to win the war."

During a pause in the German barrage, guards escorted the prisoners back to Captain Winters at battalion HQ. Mercier was smiling from ear to ear as he handed over the two live prisoners. The buck sergeant talked a lot, the staff sergeant remained silent.

• • •

The night was no longer peaceful. Both sides fired everything they had. Fires blazed up and down the river. Tracers crisscrossed over the water.

Whenever there was a lull, the men at OP 2 could hear a wheezing, choking, gurgling sound from across the river. The wounded German soldier abandoned by the patrol had been shot in the lungs. Webster and his buddies debated what to do, kill him and put him out of his misery or let him die in peace. Webster favored killing him, because if he were left alone the Germans would send a patrol to fetch him, and he could report on all the activity around OP 2. "Then they will shell us even more," Webster predicted.

Webster decided to haul himself across the river, using the rope, and knife the man. McCreary vetoed the idea. He said the Germans would use the wounded man as bait for a trap. Webster decided that he was right. A hand grenade would be better.

Accompanied by Pvt. Bob Marsh, Webster moved cautiously down to the river bank. He could hear the German gasping and slobbering in ghastly wheezes. "I pitied him," Webster wrote, "dying all alone in a country far from home, dying slowly without hope or love on the bank of a dirty little river, helpless."

Marsh and Webster pulled the pins on the grenades and threw them beside the German. One exploded, the other was a dud. The wheezing continued. The Americans returned to their outpost, got more grenades, and tried again. The wheezing continued. They gave it up; let him die in his own time.

When the shelling finally ceased, just before dawn, the wheezing went on, getting on everyone's nerves. Cobb decided he could take it no more. He grabbed a grenade, went to the river bank, heaved it over, and finally killed the German.

• • •

During the night Sergeant Lipton had been hit by a mortar shell, one fragment on his right cheek close to his ear and the other in the back of his neck. He went to the aid station and got patched up. (Thirty-four years later he had the metal in his neck removed when it started giving him trouble.)

The following day, February 16, Winters called Lipton to battalion HQ, to present him with his Honorable Discharge as an enlisted man, effective February 15, and a copy of the orders awarding him a battlefield commission as a 2d lieutenant, effective February 16. "When I was wounded I was a civilian!" Lipton remarked. "I had already been discharged, and my commission had not yet been effective. I've often wondered how it would have been handled if I had been killed by that mortar shell." He added, "I have always felt that the battlefield commission was the greatest honor that I have ever had."

•   •   •

Lieutenant Jones, by all accounts, performed well on his first patrol—meaning, apparently, he wisely let Mercier make the decisions. Within a week, Jones was gone, having been promoted to 1st lieutenant. "After one patrol!" Lieutenant Foley commented. "Jones was a West Pointer, a member of the WPPA, the West Point Protective Association, known by the ring they all wore. 'It don't mean a thing if you don't have that ring!'" Jones moved on to a staff job at regiment. Malarkey wrote, "It was rumored that the conclusion of the war was fast approaching and that West Pointers, who would staff the peacetime army, were being protected."

•   •   •

Colonel Sink was so delighted with the successful patrol, he ordered another one for the next night. In the meantime, however, it had snowed, then turned colder. The snow was frozen on top, crunchy, noisy. The cold air had cleared out the sky and the moon was shining. Winters thought a patrol under such circumstances was suicidal, so he decided to disobey orders.

Sink and a couple of staff officers came to 2d Battalion CP to observe. They had a bottle of whiskey with them. Winters said he was going down to the river bank to supervise the patrol. When he got to the outpost, he told the men to just stay still. With the whiskey working on him, Sink would soon be ready for bed. The patrol could report in the morning that it had gotten across the river and into German lines but had been unable to get a live prisoner.[4]

Some of the men wanted liquor too. Cobb and Wiseman went out on a daytime scrounging mission, even though orders were never to show yourself in daylight. They found a cellar filled with schnapps. They grabbed two bottles each and, shot at by German snipers, ran down the street like schoolboys with stolen apples.

Wiseman got hit in the knee. He stumbled and fell, breaking his bottles. Cobb saved his. The two men ducked into a cellar and started enjoying the schnapps. "You take a bunch of G.I.s," Martin pointed out,

---

[4]Glenn Gray writes, "To be required to carry out orders in which he does not believe, given by men who are frequently far removed from the realities with which the orders deal . . . is the familiar lot of the combat soldier. . . . It is a great boon of front-line positions that disobedience is frequently possible, since supervision is not very exact where danger of death is present. Many a conscientious soldier has discovered he could reinterpret military orders in his own spirit before obeying them." *The Warriors*, 189.

"there is no such thing as just taking a shot of schnapps. You have to drink the whole goddamn thing before you quit." Wiseman and Cobb drank a bottle each. When they got back to 1st platoon HQ, roaring drunk, Cobb got into a fight with Marsh.

Lieutenant Foley separated the men. He chewed out Cobb for being off-limits, disobeying orders, being drunk and disorderly, and so on. Cobb became enraged and began mouthing off. He ignored Foley's direct order to shut up. Instead, he charged Foley. Two men grabbed him and threw him down. Sergeant Martin pulled his .45 pistol. Foley told him to holster his weapon, ordered Cobb arrested, and had him taken back to regiment for lockup.

Wiseman, meanwhile, loudly rejected Medic Roe's order to evacuate. He said he was staying with his friends.

Foley got his platoon settled down, then went to regimental HQ to write up court-martial papers for Cobb. It took him several hours. He took the papers to Colonel Sink and told him the details. As Foley was leaving, Sink said to him, "Foley, you could have saved us all a lot of trouble. You should have shot him."

Wiseman, still drunk, refused any aid for his wound. He said he would talk to Sergeant Rader, no one else. Rader tried to talk some sense into him, without success. He too was court-martialed. "This ordeal was another blow to my mind," said Rader, "after Hoobler died and Howell was injured at Bastogne."

• • •

On February 20, Easy went into reserve, as the 3d Battalion, 506th, took over its position. Within hours of Easy's departure, the Germans scored a direct hit on OP 2. Winters got his promotion to major that day. On February 23, the 36th Division relieved the 101st. The airborne division moved to Saverne, in the rear, in preparation for a return to Mourmelon.

The 101st had seldom been in a rear area. What the men saw there made them wonder how any supplies ever reached the front line. Twice in Haguenau they had received a beer ration of three bottles each. The cigarettes they got were Chelseas or Raleighs, much despised. No soap, an occasional package of gum, once some toothpaste—except for C and K rations and ammunition, that was all that reached the front lines. Being near a supply depot in the rear, the men learned why. The port battalions unloading the ships coming from America got their cut, the railroad battalions helped themselves to Milky Way candy bars and cases of Schlitz beer, chalking it up to "breakage," the truck drivers took the cartons of Lucky Strikes (by far the favorite brand), and by the time division quartermaster and regimental and battalion S-4 skimmed off the best of what was left, the riflemen on the front line were fortunate to get C rations and Raleigh cigarettes.

• • •

Shifty Powers got a new M-1. That was a mixed blessing. He had been using one issued to him in the States. He loved that old rifle. "It seemed like I could just point it, and it would hit what I'd pointed it at. The best shooting rifle I ever owned. But every time we'd have an inspection, I'd get gigged because it had a pit in it, in the barrel. You can't get those pits out of those barrels, you know. It's pitted in there." He got tired of being gigged, turned it in and got a new M-1. "And I declare, I couldn't hit a barn with that rifle. Awfulest shooting thing there ever was." But at least he wasn't being gigged any longer.

Colonel Silk sent down orders to follow a rigorous training schedule while in reserve. Speirs thought this an idiotic proposal and made no effort to conceal his sentiments. He told the men of Easy that he believed in training hard and sensibly back in base camp and in taking it easy in a reserve area.

Speirs could not get the company out of two compulsory formations. The first was to hold a drawing for rotation back to the States. One man from every company would go home for a thirty-day leave; he would be chosen in a company lottery. The winner had to have been in Normandy, Holland, Bastogne, and a total absence of black marks on his service record. No VD, no AWOL, no court-martial. Only twenty-three men in Easy were eligible. Speirs shook up the names in a steel helmet and drew out Forrest Guth's slip. There was a polite cheer. Speirs said he hated to lose Guth but wished him luck. A couple of men shook his hand. The remainder walked sadly away, according to Webster, "like men who had glimpsed Paradise on their way to hell."

The second formation was a battalion review. Speirs's philosophy was to avoid the unnecessary but to do properly and with snap the required. He told the men he wanted them to look sharp. Rifles would be clean. Combat suits had to be washed. A huge boiler was set up; the men cooked their clothing with chunks of soap. It took a long time; Private Hudson decided he would skip it. When he showed up for the formation in his filthy combat suit, Speirs berated him furiously. Foley, his platoon commander, jumped on him. Sergeant Marsh, his acting squad leader, tried to make him feel the incredible magnitude of his offense. Hudson grinned sheepishly and said, "Gosh, gee whiz, why is everybody picking on me?"

General Taylor came for the battalion review, trailed by a division PR photographer. As luck would have it, he stopped before Hudson and talked with him. The photographer took their picture together, got Hudson's name and home-town address, and sent the photo to the local newspaper with a copy to Hudson's parents. Of course the general looked great talking to a battle-hardened soldier just off the front lines rather than a bunch of rear echelon parade-ground troopers. "So," Webster commented, "the only man in E Company with a dirty combat suit was the only man who had his picture taken with the general."

• • •

"We didn't realize it yet," Winters said, "but we all started walking with more care, with eyes in the backs of our heads, making sure we didn't get knocked off." After Haguenau, he explained, "you suddenly had a gut feeling, 'By God, I believe I am going to make it!'"

15

"The Best Feeling in the World"

MOURMELON

February 25–April 2, 1945

O N FEBRUARY 25 the men of Easy Company had a unique experience for them but commonplace for their fathers, riding through France on "40-and-8s," French railway boxcars that held either forty men or eight horses. It was the company's first train ride during the war, and it was properly appreciated. The weather was warm and sunny, the 40-and-8s were knee-deep in straw, there was plenty to eat, and no one shot at them.

"As we jolted through France," Webster wrote, "swinging our feet out the door, waving to the farmers, and taking a pull on the schnapps bottle, I thought there was nothing like going away from the front. It was the best feeling in the world."

They were returning to Mourmelon, but not to the barracks. This time they were billeted in large green twelve-man wall tents, about a mile outside what

Webster called "the pathetically shabby garrison village of Mourmelon, abused by soldiers since Caesar's day, consisting of six bars, two whorehouses, and a small Red Cross club." In Webster's scathing judgment, "Mourmelon was worse than Fayetteville, North Carolina."

The first task was to get clean. There were showers, although the water was lukewarm at best. But for men who had not had a proper shower since leaving Mourmelon ten weeks ago, the chance to soap and scrub, scrub and soap, lather, rinse, and repeat was pure joy. Then they got clean clothes and new Class A uniforms. But when they got to their barracks bags, left behind when the company went to Bastogne, their joy turned to fury. The rear echelon "guards" had opened the storage area to the 17th Airborne as that division moved into the Bulge, and the boys from the 17th had pillaged as if there were no tomorrow. Missing were jumpsuits, shirts, regimental insignia, jump boots, British airborne smocks, panels from Normandy and Holland parachutes, Lugers, and other priceless souvenirs.

The regime imposed by Major Winters added to their discontent. New recruits had come in, and to integrate them into the companies, Winters instituted a rigorous training program. It was like basic all over again, and hated. Webster was so fed up "that I sometimes, in forgetful moments, wished to return to the relative freedom of combat."

• • •

One of the recruits was Pvt. Patrick S. O'Keefe. He had joined the Army when he was seventeen, gone through jump school, and shipped out from New York on the *Queen Elizabeth* in late January. "I was sound asleep when we passed Ireland," O'Keefe recalled, which disappointed him as both his parents were born in County Kerry, the first landfall for cross-Atlantic traffic. He arrived in Mourmelon shortly after the company returned there. His first impression of the men was that "they were all tough, old and grizzled. I thought, 'You have bitten off more than you can chew, O'Keefe.'" He was assigned to 1st platoon, under Lieutenant Foley and Sergeant Christenson.

His third night in Mourmelon, O'Keefe went out on a night problem, starting at midnight. Walking in the dark in single file, he lost sight of the man in front of him and drew a sharp breath. He tensed, looking around.

A quiet voice from behind said, "You're O.K., son. Just kneel down and look up and you can catch sight of them against the sky." O'Keefe did, saw them, muttered, "Thanks," and moved on. Later he discovered that the advice had come from Major Winters. So here was Winters, his battalion staff cavorting in Paris, leading an all-night exercise for recruits.

O'Keefe took the lead scout position just before dawn. At first light there was to be a simulated attack against a fixed enemy position on the other side of an open field. O'Keefe got to the last ridge before the target. He signaled with his hand for the battalion to stop. He was nervous at the thought of an eighteen-year-old kid leading a group of combat-wise veterans. He signaled for the second scout behind him to come forward, with the idea he would ask to trade places. Private Hickman came up with a rush and before O'Keefe could say a word blurted out, "Boy, am I glad you are up here. I only joined this outfit three weeks ago."

Realizing the battalion was full of replacements restored O'Keefe's gift of gab. "That's O.K., kid," he said to Hickman. "I'm going over the ridge to see what's on the other side. You go back and be ready to pass my signal when I give it."

In a couple of minutes O'Keefe was back on the ridge line, holding his rifle up with both hands as a signal, "Enemy in sight." Foley moved his platoon up to the starting line, shouted, "Lay down a field of fire!" and the attack began. After a few minutes of blasting away, Joe Liebgott jumped up, gave an Indian war whoop, rushed toward the objective, and attacked the machine-gun pit with his fixed bayonet, ripping open the sandbags, playing the hero. O'Keefe and the other replacements were mightily impressed.

• • •

On March 8, Colonel Sink got around to making permanent assignments to officers who had been serving in an acting capacity for as long as two months. Lieutenant Colonel Strayer became regimental X.O. Major Winters became 2d Battalion C.O. There was some realignment, as Major Matheson shifted from regimental S-4 to S-3, replacing Captain Nixon, who went from regimental S-3 to S-3 for 2d Battalion. Lieutenant Welsh, recovered from his Christmas Eve wound, became 2d Battalion S-2. Captain Sobel replaced Matheson as regimental S-4.

Nixon's demotion from regimental to battalion staff came about because of his drinking. Like everyone else who knew him, Sink recognized that Nixon was a genius in addition to being a brave, common-sense soldier, but Sink—an uninhibited drinker himself ("Bourbon Bob" was his behind-his-back nickname)—could not put up with Nixon's nightly drunks. He asked Winters if Winters could handle Nixon. Winters was sure he could as they were the closest of friends.

Former Easy Company officers were by March occupying key positions in regiment (S-3 and S-4) and battalion (the C.O. of 1st Battalion was Lieutenant Colonel Hester; Winters was C.O. of 2d Battalion, where the S-2 and S-3 were from Easy). One of their number, Matheson, eventually became a major general and C.O. of the 101st Airborne in Vietnam. One is bound to say, one last time, that Captain Sobel must have been doing something right back in the summer of '42 at Toccoa.

You could never prove it with Winters, whose feelings for Sobel never softened. Indeed, Sobel's return provided Winters with one of the most satisfactory moments of his life. Walking down the street at Mourmelon, Major Winters saw Captain Sobel coming from the opposite direction. Sobel saw Winters, dropped his head, and walked past without saluting. When he had gone a further step or two, Winters called out, "Captain Sobel, we salute the rank, not the man."

"Yes, sir," Sobel answered as he snapped off a salute.

Webster and Martin, standing nearby, were delighted ("I like to see officers pull rank on each other," Webster commented), but not half so much as Winters.

(Winters had another pleasure in Mourmelon, this one on a daily basis. German P.O.W.s were working in the hospital; at dusk each evening they would march back to their stockade. As they marched, they sang their marching songs. "They sang and marched with pride and vigor," Winters wrote, "and it was beautiful. By God, they were soldiers!")

The man who had replaced Sobel and Winters as C.O. of Easy, Captain Speirs, continued to impress both officers and enlisted men. "Captain Speirs promises to be as good an officer as Winters," Webster thought. He realized that many disagreed with him, men "who loathed Speirs on the ground that he had killed one of his own men in Normandy, that he was bull-headed and suspicious, that he believed there was no such thing as Combat Exhaustion." But to Webster, "He was a brave man in combat, in fact a wild man, who had gotten his Silver Star, Bronze Star, and three Purple Hearts legitimately. Speirs swears by common sense, combat noncoms, and training with the emphasis on battle, rather than the book. I like Speirs."

There were shake-ups among the noncoms. Sergeant Talbert replaced Lieutenant Lipton as 1st sergeant. A genial man, Talbert was appreciated by the enlisted men because he ignored red tape and did things by common sense rather than the book. Carson became company clerk; Luz became a platoon runner; the platoon sergeants, all original Toccoa privates, all wounded at least once, were Charles Grant (2d), Amos Taylor (3d), and Earl Hale (1st).

Hale's promotion caused some mumble-mumble in 1st platoon. The men had nothing against him except that he was an outsider (he had been in Company HQ section as a radio man). The men of the platoon circulated a rumor to the effect that Hale had complained to Winters that his wife was after him to get another stripe, and Winters had given him the platoon as a result. What made the men of the platoon unhappy was the way Johnny Martin got passed over. "I guess the officers didn't like his flip attitude," Webster commented, "yet he was the quickest thinker, the best leader among us, and a natural for a platoon sergeant."

Martin thought so, too. Having survived three campaigns without a wound, he decided to let the medics know that he had a trick cartilage in his knee that incapacitated him for combat. He was soon on his way back to the States.

"The Toccoa men were thinning out like maple leaves in November," Webster wrote. "A sense of hopelessness and exasperation filled the old men in Mourmelon. Here we were, still hiking over meadow and marsh, still trampling the rutabagas and breaking the fences, still in the field on training exercises."

The veterans tried goldbricking to get out of field exercises. They would report on sick call in the morning. Speirs would ask the trouble, grunt, and send them to the aid station. There they could get admitted to the hospital for a day. A day of just lying around, reading magazines. It was easy to pull. They all did it, but never more than twice. Even Webster preferred pretend war to reading or doing nothing.

•   •   •

The Ides of March brought a well-deserved reward to the men of the 101st Airborne. There was a division parade before the most brass the men had ever seen. General Eisenhower was there, along with General Taylor, Lt. Gen. Sir Frederick Morgan, Lt. Gen. Lewis Brereton, President Roosevelt's secretary Stephen Early, Maj. Gen. Matthew Ridgway, and others.

In preparation, "everybody scrubbed and washed, polished and shined, disassembled, cleaned and reassembled all weapons," as Lieutenant Foley recalled. "Ribbons were dug up and positioned precisely on the blouse." The men painted their helmets, stenciled the insignia of the 506th on the side, and when they were dry, oiled them until they glistened in the sun. There was a practice parade in anticipation. Of course, the officers got the men on the parade ground three hours before Ike and his party arrived; of course the men cursed the Army and its ways.

Eisenhower finally arrived. He drove past the whole division, then climbed up on a reviewing stand to give a speech. He announced that the division had received a Presidential Distinguished Unit Citation, the first time in the history of the Army that an entire division had been so cited, for its performance at Bastogne. In a short speech, Ike was effusive in his praise: "You were given a marvelous opportunity [in Bastogne], and you met every test. . . . I am awfully proud of you."

He concluded with a mixture of praise and exhortation: "With this great honor goes also a certain responsibility. Just as you are the beginning of a new tradition, you must realize, each of you, that from now on, the spotlight will beat on you with particular brilliance. Whenever you say you are a soldier of the 101st Division, everybody, whether it's on the street, in the city, or in the front line, will expect unusual conduct of you. I know that you will meet every test of the future like you met it at Bastogne."[1]

Webster, who was becoming ever more the cynic about the Army and who was exercising vigorously the soldier's right to grouse, was impressed in spite of himself. Private O'Keefe commented, "Even the new

---

[1]Rapport and Northwood, *Rendezvous with Destiny*, 697–99.

replacements like myself felt enormous pride in marching in that review."

For Lieutenant Foley, there was "the surprise to end all surprises." Standing behind General Taylor was his senior aide, none other than Capt. Norman Dike.

Sergeant Hale, who had had his throat slashed in the Ardennes and who had medical permission to go without a tie, had his Bronze Star presented to him by General Eisenhower. Ike wanted to know why he was not wearing a tie. Hale explained. When General Taylor confirmed Hale's story, Ike gave his big laugh and said Hale was the only man in the entire European Theater of Operations to pull this one off.

• • •

There were furloughs and leaves, to England, the Riviera, Paris, Brussels, and evening passes to Reims. Captain Speirs got to go to England, where he had married a British woman who believed her husband had been killed in North Africa. Foley got to Paris and on return confessed he could not remember a thing. There were some USO shows, with big-name performers, including Marlene Dietrich.

Garrison life was soft, but it had its price. To bring discipline and appearance up to a proper rear echelon standard, the Army had to have some method of enforcing rules and regulations. Threatening members of a rifle company that had just come off the line and was about to go back in with a visit to the stockade was less a threat than a promise. Taking hard cash out of the hands of men who were anticipating a pass to Paris, however, caught their attention.

A private in the 101st received $50 per month base pay, a $50 bonus for hazardous duty, and an additional

$10 for being in a combat zone. General Taylor set up a summary court in Mourmelon, and it began imposing heavy fines for violations. A man found in improper uniform was fined $5. Carrying a Luger in one's pocket cost $25. Speeding in a jeep or truck cost $20. Disorderly conduct was a $25 offense.

Training continued. It progressed through squad and platoon to company and then to battalion level. The division was preparing for a daylight airborne mission, Operation Eclipse, a drop on and around Berlin.

No one was going to drop on Berlin until the Allied armies had gotten across the Rhine. For months, the men of Easy had been anticipating a jump on the far side of the river, but when it came, Easy did not participate. Eisenhower decided to give the 17th Airborne a chance at a combat jump and assigned it to Operation Varsity, the largest airborne operation of all time (the 17th plus the British 1st and 6th Airborne Divisions) and to save the 82d and 101st for Berlin.

Nonparticipation in Operation Varsity was a disappointment to many of the replacements, who had gone through the rigors of jump school, joined the most famous airborne division in the world in Belgium or Germany, and never taken part in a combat jump. At Mourmelon a unit of Troop Carrier Command made it possible for men who wished to do so to make a few jumps, to qualify for their paratrooper bonus or just for the fun of it. Lieutenant Foley made two. But that wasn't like the real thing.

So on March 24 the members of E Company watched with mixed feelings as one C-47 after another roared down the runway at the nearby airfield, circled, formed up into a V of Vs, nine abreast, and headed northeast. "It was a beautiful sight," Foley recalled.

"It made your heart pump faster and for a guy like me, having been integrated into a company that had been on two combat jumps, I did feel that I had missed the last opportunity."

Some of the old soldiers felt the same way. To his amazement, Webster found himself wishing that he was jumping with the 17th. "It would have been fun." Instead, he stood on the ground with his buddies, cheering, giving the V-for-Victory sign, shouting, "Go get 'em, boys! Give 'em hell!" Then, Webster wrote, "I watched them fade in the distance with a dull drone and I suddenly felt lonely and abandoned, as though I had been left behind."

One 506th man who was not left behind was Captain Nixon. General Taylor selected him to jump with the 17th as an observer for the 101st. Fortunately for Nixon, he was assigned to be jumpmaster of his plane. The plane was hit; only Nixon and three others made it out before it crashed. Nixon was attached to the 17th for only one night; on March 25 he was sent back over the Rhine and flown by a special small plane back to the 2d Battalion in Mourmelon. The jump qualified Nixon to be one of two men in the 506th eligible to wear three stars on his jump wings— Normandy, Holland, and Operation Varsity. The other was Sergeant Wright of the Pathfinders, who had been in Easy Company back at Toccoa.

German resistance to Operation Varsity was fierce. Meanwhile infantry and armored divisions of the U.S. First Army were pouring across the Rhine via the recently captured Ludendorff Bridge at Remagen, then swinging north to encircle the German army defending Germany's industrial heartland in the Ruhr.

Eisenhower needed to bolster the ring around the

Ruhr. The 82d and 101st were available. The orders came at the end of March. The company was moving out, back to the front, this time on the Rhine River.

The veterans resolved not to take any chances. The end of the war was in sight, and they now believed what they could not believe at Bastogne, that they were going to make it. Safe. More or less intact. They wanted to escape the boredom of garrison, they knew how to take care of themselves, they were ready to do their job, but not to be heroes.

In contrast to the veterans, the replacements thought Mourmelon was a super place. They trained with veterans, day and night, in realistic problems, all under the watchful eye of a man who was a legend in E Company, Major Winters. They had learned lifesaving lessons. They had gotten to know and be accepted by the veterans. They were proud to be in the company, the regiment, the division, and were eager to show that they were qualified to be there.

So Easy was ready at the end of March, when orders came to prepare to move out. It would be by truck, to the Rhine. Webster was delighted to be getting out of Mourmelon, apprehensive and excited about going back into combat, and disappointed that he was not jumping into battle. "I had hoped to make another jump," he wrote, "rather than ride to the front in trucks, for there is an element of chance in an airborne mission—it may be rough; it may be easy; perhaps there will be no enemy at all—which appeals to me more than a prosaic infantry attack against an enemy who knows where you are and when you're coming."

Private O'Keefe was about to enter combat for the first time. He has a vivid memory of the occasion. "We wore light sweaters under field jackets, trousers bloused over combat boots, trench knife strapped on right leg, pistol belts with attached musette bags, one phosphorus grenade and one regular hand grenade taped onto our chest harness, canteens, first aid kit, K rations stuffed into our pockets, steel helmet and rifle. We carried cloth bandoliers for our rifle clips in place of the old-fashioned cartridge belts. Our musette bags carried a minimum of shorts, socks, shaving gear, sewing kit, cigarettes, etc." After hearing Mass celebrated by Father John Maloney and receiving a general absolution, O'Keefe pulled himself into a truck and was off for Germany.

• • •

Easy Company was about to enter its fifth country. The men had liked Britain and the English people enormously. They did not like the French, who seemed to them ungrateful, sullen, lazy, and dirty. They had a special relationship with the Belgians because of their intimate association with the civilians of Bastogne, who had done whatever they could to support the Americans.

They loved the Dutch. Brave, resourceful, overwhelmingly grateful, the best organized underground in Europe, cellars full of food hidden from the Germans but given to the Americans, clean, hard-working, honest were only some of the compliments the men showered on the Dutch.

Now they were going to meet the Germans. For the first time they would be on front lines inside enemy territory, living with enemy civilians. And if the rumor proved true, the one that said instead of living in foxholes they were going to be billeted in German houses, they would be getting to know the Germans in an intimate fashion. This would be especially true once the Ruhr pocket was eliminated and the advance across central Germany began. Then they would be staying in a different house every night, under conditions in which the occupants would have only a few minutes notice of their arrival.

They would be coming as conquerors who had been told to distrust all Germans and who had been forbidden by the nonfraternization policy to have any contact with German civilians. But except for Liebgott and a few others, they had no undying hatred of the Germans. Many of them admired the German soldiers they had fought. Webster was not alone in feeling that most of the atrocities they had heard about were propaganda. Anyway they would soon see for themselves whether all the Germans were Nazis, and if the Nazis were as bad as the Allied press and radio said they were.

16

Getting to Know the Enemy

GERMANY

April 2–30, 1945

Tᴏᴇ ʀᴇᴀᴄᴛɪᴏɴꜱ ᴏꜰ ᴛʜᴇ ᴍᴇɴ ᴏꜰ Eᴀꜱʏ to the German people depended on their different preconceptions and experiences. Some found reasons to reinforce their hatred; others loved the country and the people; nearly every one ended up changing his mind; all of them were fascinated.

The standard story of how the American G.I. reacted to the foreign people he met during the course of WWII runs like this: He felt the Arabs were despicable, liars, thieves, dirty, awful, without a redeeming feature. The Italians were liars, thieves, dirty, wonderful, with many redeeming features, but never to be trusted. The rural French were sullen, slow, and ungrateful while the Parisians were rapacious, cunning, indifferent to whether they were cheating Germans or Americans. The British people were brave, resourceful, quaint, reserved, dull. The Dutch were, as noted, regarded as simply wonderful in every way (but the average G.I. never was in Holland, only the airborne).

The story ends up thus: wonder of wonders, the average G.I. found that the people he liked best, identified most closely with, enjoyed being with, were the Germans. Clean, hard-working, disciplined, educated, middle-class in their tastes and lifestyles (many G.I.s noted that so far as they could tell the only people in the world who regarded a flush toilet and soft white toilet paper as a necessity were the Germans and the Americans), the Germans seemed to many American soldiers as "just like us."

G.I.s noted, with approval, that the Germans began picking up the rubble the morning after the battle had passed by, and contrasted that with the French, where no one had yet bothered to clean up the mess. Obviously they noted with high approval all those young German girls and the absence of competition from young German boys. They loved the German food and beer. But most of all, they loved the German homes.

They stayed in many homes, from the Rhine through Bavaria to Austria, sometimes a different one each night. Invariably they found running hot and cold water, electric lights, a proper toilet and paper, coal for the stove.

Webster wrote of this period, "Coming off guard into your own home was a sensation unequaled in the army. We left the hostile blackness behind when we opened the outside door. Beyond the blackout curtains a light glowed and, as we hung our rifles on the hat rack and shed our raincoats, idle chatter drifted from the kitchen and gave us a warm, settled feeling. A pot of coffee would be simmering on the stove—help yourself. Reese would be telling about a shack job he had in London, while Janovek, Hickman, Collette, and Sholty played blackjack. Wash your hands at the sink. This was home. This was where we belonged. A small, sociable group, a clean, well-lighted house, a cup of coffee—paradise."

Even better, the men were not getting shot at, or shooting. No wonder so many of them liked Germany so much. But as Webster commented, "In explaining the superficial fondness of the G.I. for the Germans, it might be well to remember the physical comforts which he enjoyed nowhere else in the army but in the land of his enemies."

The experiences of the men of E Company in Germany illustrates how much better off during the war the German people were than the people of Britain, France, Belgium, and Holland. Of course in the big cities in Germany it was, by mid-April of 1945, Götter-dämmerung, but in the countryside and small villages, where, although there was usually some destruction at the main crossroads, the houses generally were intact, complete with creature comforts such as most people thought existed in 1945 only in America.

By no means was every G.I. seduced by the Germans. Webster went into Germany with a complex attitude: he didn't like Germans, he thought all Germans were Nazis, but he discounted as propaganda the stories about concentration camps and other atrocities. He found the German people "too hard-faced." He thought the French were "dead and rotting," but Germany was only "a crippled tiger, licking its wounds, resting, with a burning hatred in its breast, ready to try again. And it will."

Despite himself, Webster was drawn to the people. "The Germans I have seen so far have impressed me as clean, efficient, law-abiding people," he wrote his parents on April 14. They were churchgoers. "In Germany everybody goes out and works and, unlike the French, who do not seem inclined to lift a finger to help themselves, the Germans fill up the trenches soldiers have dug in their fields. They are cleaner, more progressive, and more ambitious than either the English or the French."[1]

Orders from on high were nonfraternization. G.I.s were not supposed to talk to *any* Germans, even small children, except on official business. This absurd order, which flew in the face of human nature in so obvious a way, was impossible to enforce. Officers, especially those who hated the Germans, tried anyway. Webster was amused by the intensity of Lieutenant Foley's feelings. He wrote that Foley "had become such a fiend on the nonfraternization policy that he ordered all butts field-stripped [i.e. torn apart and scattered] so that the Germans might derive no pleasure from American tobacco."

Webster also recalled the time he and Foley were picking out houses for the night. "As we walked around to the backyard for a closer inspection, we were greeted with a horrifying spectacle that aroused all the nonfraternization fervor in Foley: two infantry-

---

[1] Writing of the G.I.s' experience with the German people and of the effect of feeling that they were "just like us," Glenn Gray points out, "The enemy could not have changed so quickly from a beast to a likable human being. Thus, the conclusion is nearly forced upon the G.I.s that they have been previously blinded by fear and hatred and the propaganda of their own government." Gray, *The Warriors*, 152.

men sociably chatting with a couple of Fräulein. Unspeakable, outrageous, unmilitary, forbidden. Lt. Foley gave them hell and bade them be on their way. With the resigned air of men who knew the barren futility of the non-fraternization policy, the gallants sulkily departed."

It is worth pausing here to see the Americans as conquerors through the microcosm of E Company. They took what they wanted, but by no means did they rape, loot, pillage, and burn their way through Germany. If they did not respect property rights, in the sense that they commandeered their nightly billets without compensation, at least when the Germans moved back in after they left, the place was more or less intact. Of course there were some rapes, some mistreatment of individual Germans, and some looting, but it is simple fact to state that other conquering armies in WWII, perhaps most of all the Russian but including the Japanese and German, acted differently.

Webster told a story that speaks to the point. "Reese, who was more intent on finding women than in trading for eggs, and I made another expedition a mile west to a larger village where there were no G.I.s. Like McCreary, Reese tended to show an impatience with hens and a strong interest in skirts, regardless of age or appearance, he'd tell me, 'There's a nice one. Boy that's a honey. Speak to her Web, goddamn!' Since I was shy, however, and those females invariably looked about as sociable as a fresh iceberg, I ignored his panting plaints. Besides, the Fraus weren't apt to be friendly in public, where the neighbors could see them. Maybe indoors or at night. Finally we came to a farm where a buxom peasant lass greeted us. Reese smiled. After I had gotten some eggs, Reese, who kept winking at her, gave her a cigarette and a chocolate bar, and, as love bloomed in the garden of D ration [a newly issued food package] and Chelseas, I backed out the door and waited in the sun. No dice, Reese later reported. I returned home with a helmetful of eggs, Reese with a broken heart. But it was, as he said, 'good fratranizin' territory.' He tried again that night before the six o'clock curfew went into effect. No luck."

Had Reese been a Soviet, German, or Japanese soldier, this little nonincident probably would have turned out differently.

• • •

The company moved by truck from Mourmelon to the Ruhr pocket. The 101st took up positions on the west bank of the Rhine, facing Düsseldorf. The 2d Battalion's sector was from Stürzelberg on the north to Worringen on the south, with the 82d Airborne on the battalion's right flank. The 82d faced Cologne.

It was more an occupation position than front line. The platoons kept outposts down on the river bank, while the men stayed in homes in various small villages. There was some artillery shelling, back and forth, but not much. There was no small arms fire.

The men were on outpost each night. Here Private O'Keefe got his initiation. One night he was on outpost with Pvt. Harry Lager, who had also just joined the company at Mourmelon, in a ready-made foxhole beside the dike. They heard a *thump, thump, thump.* O'Keefe whispered to Lager, "Stay in the hole but make room for me to drop in in a hurry. I'm going up on that dike to see if I can make out what that is approaching."

Up on the dike, O'Keefe recalled, "I couldn't see a damn thing but the noise was almost on top of me.

Suddenly the nose of a small tank stuck out through the fog. I yelled, 'Halt, who goes there?' and ready to dive off that dike into the hole with Lager."

A voice came out of the tank: "It's just a couple of Limeys, and we're lost." O'Keefe ordered the man to come down to be inspected. A British sergeant did so, saying, "By God, Yank, are we glad to see you! We started out on that bloody dike at midnight, and we can't find our way off."

"What's making that noise?" O'Keefe asked.

"Oh, that," the Brit replied. "It's one of our treads. It broke. We can only travel about two miles an hour. The tread goes around but hits the ground on each rotation." O'Keefe suggested that the sergeant put his crewmate out in front, walking ahead, else they might get plastered at the next checkpoint. The sergeant said he would. O'Keefe rejoined Lager, glad to note that Lager had them covered with his M-1 the whole time. The little incident gave Lager and O'Keefe confidence in themselves and one another. They decided they had the hang of it.

Another night, at another place along the river, O'Keefe was on outpost with a recent recruit, Pvt. James Welling. From West Virginia, Welling was thirty years old, making him just about the oldest man in the company. O'Keefe was the youngest. Although Welling had just joined the company, he was a combat veteran who had been wounded in the Battle of the Bulge, volunteered for paratroopers after discharge from hospital in England, made all five qualifying jumps in one day, and was now a member of the 101st.

On the outpost, they were standing in a waist-deep foxhole when a ten-ton truck came barreling along the road. "Halt," O'Keefe yelled, three times. No one heard him. A convoy of nine trucks, bumper to bumper, passed him by, engines roaring.

"What do you do when you yell 'Halt!' and you realize that they'll never hear you?" O'Keefe asked Welling.

"Not much you can do," he replied.

Half an hour later the trucks came back, full speed, except now there were only eight trucks.

"Jim, what's down that road?" O'Keefe asked.

"I don't know, nobody said."

A quarter of an hour later Captain Speirs showed up, "madder than hell." He shouted at Welling, "Why didn't you stop those trucks? The bridge is out down there and one of those trucks is now hanging over the edge." Having heard various stories about Speirs's temper, O'Keefe expected the worst. But Welling shouted right back:

"How the hell were we going to stop nine trucks going fullborc? And why didn't someone tell *us* the bridge was out? Hell, we didn't even know there was a bridge there."

"Where's the other guard?" Speirs demanded.

O'Keefe stepped out of a shadow with his M-1 pointed about waist high and said as menacingly as he could, "Right here, sir." Speirs grunted and left.

A night or so later, a jeep came along, no lights. Welling called out "Halt!" The jeep contained Captain Speirs, another captain, and a major in the backseat. Welling said the password. Speirs gave the countersign in a normal conversational tone. Welling couldn't make out what he had said and repeated the challenge. Speirs answered in the same tone; Welling still didn't hear him. Tense and a bit confused, O'Keefe lined up his M-1 on the major in the back. He looked closely and realized it was Winters.

Welling gave the password for the third time. The captain who was driving finally realized Welling had not heard and yelled out the countersign. Speirs jumped out of the jeep and started to curse out Welling.

Welling cut him off: "When I say, 'Halt!' I mean 'Halt!' When I give the password, I expect to *hear* the countersign." Speirs started sputtering about what he was going to do to Welling when Winters interrupted. "Let's go, Captain," he said in a low voice. As they drove off, Winters called out to Welling, "Good job."

•   •   •

There were patrols across the Rhine, seldom dangerous except for the strong current in the flooded river, nearly 350 meters wide. When Winters got orders on April 8 to send a patrol to the other side, he decided to control the patrol from an observation post to make certain no one got hurt. Winters set the objectives and controlled the covering artillery concentration, then monitored the patrol step by step up the east bank of the river. Lieutenant Welsh, battalion S-2, accompanied him and was disgusted with the safety limits Winters insisted on. "We went through the motions of a combat patrol," Winters remembered, "and found nothing. Everyone returned safely."

Most patrols were similarly unsuccessful. Malarkey reported that a replacement officer took out a patrol, got across the river, advanced several hundred yards inland, drew fire from a single rifleman, reported over the radio that he had met stiff resistance, and withdrew to friendly territory, to the mingled relief and disgust of his men.

A couple of days later, things didn't work out so well. The patrol leader was Maj. William Leach, recently promoted and made regimental S-2 by Sink. He had been ribbed unmercifully back at Mourmelon when his gold leaves came through: "When are you going to take out a patrol, Leach?" his fellow officers asked. He had never been in combat and consequently had no decorations. Characterized by Winters as "a good staff officer who made his way up the ladder on personality and social expertise," Leach wanted to make a career out of the Army. For that, he felt he needed a decoration.

The night of April 12, Leach set out at the head of a four-man patrol from the S-2 section at regimental HQ. But he made one fatal mistake: he failed to tell anyone he was going. Easy Company men on outpost duty heard the splashing of the boat the patrol was using as it crossed the river. As far as they were concerned, unless they had been told of an American patrol at such and such a time, any boat in the river contained enemy troops. They opened up on it; quickly the machine-guns joined in. The fire ripped the boat apart and hit all the men in it, including Leach. Ignoring the pitiful cries of the wounded, drowning in the river, the machine-gunners kept firing bursts at them until their bodies drifted away. They were recovered some days later downstream. In the judgment of the company, Leach and four men had "perished in a most unnecessary, inexcusable fashion because he had made an obvious and unpardonable mistake."

• • •

That day the company got the news that President Roosevelt had died. Winters wrote in his day book, "Sgt. Malley [of F Company]—good news—made 1st Sgt. Bad news—Pres. Roosevelt died."

"I had come to take Roosevelt for granted," Webster wrote his parents, "like spring and Easter lilies, and now that he is gone, I feel a little lost."

Eisenhower ordered all unit commanders to hold a short memorial service for Roosevelt on Sunday, April 14. Easy Company did it by platoons. Lieutenant Foley, who "never was much enamored with Roosevelt," gathered his platoon. He had a St. Joseph missal in his musette bag; in it he found a prayer. He read it out to the men, and later claimed to be "the only man who ever buried Franklin D. as a Catholic."

• • •

Overall, Easy's time on the Rhine, guarding the Ruhr pocket, was boring. "Time hung so heavily," a disgusted Webster wrote, "that we began to have daily rifle inspections. Otherwise, we did nothing but stand guard on the crossroads at night and listen to a short current events lecture by Lieutenant Foley during the day." With their high energy level and the low demands on them, the men turned to sports. They found some rackets and balls and played tennis on a backyard court, or softball in a nearby field.

Webster was no athlete, but he had a high level of curiosity. One day he realized "the fulfillment of a lifetime ambition," when he and Pvt. John Janovek scaled a 250-foot-high factory smokestack. When they got to the top, they had a magnificent view across the river. To Webster, "the Ruhr seemed absolutely lifeless," even though "everywhere we looked there were factories, foundries, steel mills, sugar plants, and sheet-metal works. It looked like Chicago, Pittsburgh, and St. Louis decentralized."

• • •

On April 18, all German resistance in the Ruhr pocket came to an end. More than 325,000 German soldiers surrendered.

Easy was put to guarding a Displaced Persons' camp at Dormagen. There were Poles, Czechs, Belgians, Dutch, French, Russians, and others from different parts of Nazi-occupied Europe in the camp, tens of thousands. They lived in a common barracks, segregated by sex, crowded, all but starving in many cases, representing all ranges of age. Once liberated, their impulse was to catch up on their rest and their fun, so sadly lacking for the past few years. Webster reported that they "were contentedly doing nothing. They had worked hard under the Germans, and eaten little. Now they would rest."

Their happiness, singing, and willingness to do favors for the soldiers endeared them to the men of Easy. KP was now a thing of the past. No member of Easy ever peeled a potato after this point or swept a room or washed a mess kit or policed the area. There were always D.P.s for that, especially as the Americans were so generous in paying.

More than a few men took along a combination son and servant. Luz practically adopted a thin little boy, Muchik, who wore battered shoes much too large. His parents had died in the slave labor camp. Muchik's big dark eyes and bright energetic demeanor were irresistible to Luz. He got Muchik a uniform of sorts and brought him along for the tour of Germany, teaching him the fundamentals of Army profanity as they rode along. As the division history notes, "Though strict orders were given that no D.P.s were to be taken along, some of the personnel spoke very broken English, never appeared in formations, and seemed to do a great deal of kitchen police."[2]

In short, Easy was about to depart on a tour of Germany that would be first-class in every way. Comfortable homes each night, great food and wine, free to take almost whatever they wanted, being driven along an autobahn reserved for them, riding at a leisurely pace on big rubber tires, with wondrous sights to see, the dramatic Alps on one side, the dramatic disintegration of what had been the most feared army in the world on the other, with body servants to care for their every need.

Except one. They would have loved to have brought some of the D.P. girls along, but they did no better with them than they had with the German girls. Like G.I.s everywhere, they assumed that a D ration and a couple of Chelseas were the key to any woman's heart, only to be disappointed.

The second-generation Czechs and Poles in the company had been especially excited. They spent all their spare time, night and day, using their limited language ability to court the stocky, balloon-chested peasant girls of their fathers' native lands. But contrary to their expectations, the girls, with their Catholic upbringing and Central European background, were chaste.

For Webster, the effect of the D.P. camp was to stir up his hatred of the Germans. "Why were these people here?" he asked himself about the D.P.s. They had done nothing, had no politics, committed no crime, possessed nothing. They were there because the Nazis needed their labor.

"There was Germany and all it stood for," Webster

---

[2]Rapport and Northwood, *Rendezvous with Destiny*, 715.

concluded. "The Germans had taken these people from their homes and sentenced them to work for life in a factory in the Third Reich. Babies and old women, innocent people condemned to live in barracks behind barbed wire, to slave twelve hours a day for an employer without feeling or consideration, to eat beet soup, mouldy potatoes, and black bread. This was the Third Reich, this was the New Order: Work till you died. With cold deliberation the Germans had enslaved the populace of Europe." So far as Webster was concerned, "The German people were guilty, every one of them."

The guard duty lasted only a few days. Back on the Rhine, Winters instituted a training schedule that included reveille, inspection, calisthenics and close-order drill, squad tactics, map reading, and so forth. The day ended with retreat. It was like being back in basic training, and much resented.

As always in a rear echelon area, rank was being pulled, widening the distance between the enlisted men and the officers. Lt. Ralph D. Richey, a gung-ho replacement officer serving as battalion S-1, was particularly obnoxious. One day he had the company lined up for inspection. An old German woman rode her bicycle innocently through the ranks. Richey became so enraged that he fetched her a blow that knocked her off her bicycle. She burst into tears; he stormed at her and ordered her to move on. The men were disgusted by his behavior.

The following day the company made a forced 5-mile speed march, Lieutenant Richey leading. The men rolled up their sleeves and carried their weapons as comfortably as possible. Richey was furious. He halted the company and gave the men hell. "I have never seen such a sloppy company," he shouted. "There are 120 men in this company and I see 120 different ways of carrying a rifle. And you guys think you're soldiers!"

The incident set Webster off on a tirade. "Here was a man who had made us ashamed of our uniform railing at us for being comfortable on a speed march," he wrote. "Here was the army. Officers are gentlemen, I'll do as I damn please. No back talk. You're a private. You can't think. If you were any good, you'd be an officer. Here, carry my bedroll. Sweep my room. Clean my carbine. Yes sir. Why didn't you salute? You didn't see me! Well, by God, go back and salute properly. The looies, God bless 'em. Privileges before responsibilities."

Not all officers were like Richey. Captain Speirs, for all his bluster and reputation, cared for the men. Sensing their boredom, he arranged a sightseeing trip to Cologne. He wanted them to see the city and the effects of air bombardment (Cologne was one of the most heavily bombed cities in Germany).

Two things most impressed the men. First, the extent of the destruction. Every window was shattered, every church had been hit, every side street was blocked with rubble. The magnificent cathedral in the center of town had been damaged but had survived. The giant statue of Bismarck on a horse was still standing, but Bismarck's sword, pointing toward France, had been cut off by flying shrapnel.

A group of Easy men wandered to the Rhine, where they began pointing and laughing at the grotesque ruins of the *Hängebrücke*, or suspension bridge. An elderly German couple stood beside them. To the shame of the Americans, the Germans began to cry and shake their heads. All their beautiful bridges had been twisted and mangled, and here were American boys laughing.

The second impression was not of destruction but of people. Lieutenant Foley noted that "the residents, on their own volition, were determined to clean up and sweep out the ruins of war. Along most of the streets there were neat stacks of salvageable cobblestones. Houses were worked on to remove the debris. They were still in bad shape, yet they appeared almost ready to be rebuilt. Amazing."

• • •

April 19 was a big day for the company. The division quartermaster handed out thirty-four pairs of socks per platoon, or about one pair for each man, plus three bottles of Coca-Cola (accompanied by stern orders to turn in the bottles) and two bottles of American beer per man. The men got paid for February and March, in the form of Allied Military Marks; these were their first marks and they were ordered to turn in all their French, British, Dutch, Belgian, and American money for marks.

On April 22 the company loaded up in the German version of the 40-and-8s. The cars had been sprayed with DDT and filled with straw. Each man got five K rations.

They were off to Bavaria and the Alps. Bradley had assigned the 101st to U.S. Seventh Army. Its objectives were Munich, Innsbruck, and the Brenner Pass. The purpose was to get American troops into the Alps before the Germans could create a redoubt there from which to continue the war. Hitler's Eagle's Nest in Berchtesgaden was the presumed HQ for this combination last stand and the beginning of a guerrilla war against the occupiers. Eisenhower's biggest fear was that Hitler would get to the Eagle's Nest, where he would be well protected and have radio facilities he could use to broadcast to the German people to continue the resistance or begin guerrilla warfare.

It turned out that the Germans had neither serious plans nor sufficient resources to build a Mountain Redoubt, but remember we are only four months away from a time when everyone assumed the German Army was kaput, only to be hit by the Bulge. So the fear was there, but the reality was that in its drive to Berchtesgaden, Easy was as much as 100 miles behind the front line, in a reserve position, never threatened. The company's trip through Germany was more a grand tour than a fighting maneuver.

*   *   *

The tour began with a 200-kilometer train ride through four countries. So great was the Allied destruction of the German rail system that to get from the Ruhr to southern Germany it was necessary to go through Holland, Belgium, Luxembourg, and France. The men rode in open cars, sleeping, singing, swinging their feet out the doors, sunbathing on the roof of the 40-and-8. Popeye Wynn led them in endless choruses of the ETO theme song, "Roll Me over in the Clover."

The train passed within 25 miles of Bastogne. The division history commented, "The occasional evidence of the bitter fighting of three months before made the hair rise on the necks of many of the veterans of Bastogne. But at the same time, remembering only snow, cold, and dark and ominous forests, they were surprised at the beauty of the rolling lands under the new green of spring."[3]

They got back into Germany and then to the Rhine

---

[3]Rapport and Northwood, *Rendezvous with Destiny,* 723.

at Ludwigshafen, where they got off the train and switched to a vehicle called DUKW: D (1942), U (amphibian), K (all-wheel drive), W (dual rear axles). These DUKWs had come in with the invasion of the south of France. These were the first E Company had seen. The DUKW was outstanding in every respect, but because it was a hybrid, neither the War nor the Navy Department ever really got behind it. Only 21,000 were built in the course of the war.

The men of E Company wished it had been 210,000, or even 2,100,000. A DUKW could carry twenty fully equipped riflemen in considerable comfort. It could make 5 knots in a moderate sea, 50 miles per hour on land riding on oversized rubber tires. It was a smooth-riding vehicle, without the bounce of the deuce-and-a-half G.I. truck or the springless jarring of the jeep. Webster said the DUKW "rides softly up and down, like a sailboat in a gentle swell."

They crossed the Rhine on the Ernie Pyle Bridge, a pontoon structure built by the engineers, and headed toward Munich. They went through Heidelberg, and Webster was entranced. "When we saw all the undamaged buildings and the beautiful river promenade, where complacent civilians strolled in the sun, I was ready to stay in Heidelberg forever. The green hills, the warm sunlight, the cool, inviting river, the mellow collegiate atmosphere—Heidelberg spelled paradise in any language."

From then on the convoy traveled a circuitous route southeast, skirting mountains, on main roads and side paths. All the while, Webster wrote, "we marveled at the breathtaking beauty of Germany. As a writer said in the *New Yorker*, it seemed a pity to waste such country on the Germans."

In midafternoon, Speirs would send Sergeants Carson and Malarkey on ahead to pick out a company CP in such-and-such a village. They were to get the best house and reserve the best bedroom for Captain Speirs.

Carson had high school German. He would pick the place, knock on the door, and tell the Germans they had five minutes to get out, and they were not to take any bedding with them. Give them more than five minutes, Speirs had told them, they will take everything with them.

Once the advance party came on an apartment complex three stories high, perfect for HQ and most of the company. Carson knocked on doors and told tenants, *"Raus in funf minuten."* They came pouring out, crying, lamenting, frightened. "I knocked on this one door," Carson recalled, "and an elderly lady answered. I looked at her and she stared at me. God, it was a picture of my own grandmother. Our eyes met and I said, *'Bleib hier,'* or stay here."

Malarkey picked up the story. "Then Speirs would finally show up and you wouldn't see Speirs for about two or three hours. He was the worst looter I ever saw. He couldn't sleep at night thinking there was a necklace or something around." Whenever he got a chance, Speirs would mail his loot back to his wife in England. He needed the money it would bring; his wife had just had a baby.

Nearly all the men of Easy, like nearly all the men in ETO, participated in the looting. It was a phenomenon of war. Thousands of men who had never before in their lives taken something of value that did not belong to them began taking it for granted that whatever they wanted was theirs. The looting was profitable, fun, low-risk, and completely in accord with the practice of every conquering army since Alexander the Great's time.

Lugers, Nazi insignia, watches, jewelry, first editions of *Mein Kampf*, liquor, were among the most sought-after items. Anything any German soldier had was fair game; looting from civilians was frowned upon, but it happened anyway. Money was not highly valued. Sgt. Edward Heffron and Medic Ralph Spina caught a half-dozen German soldiers in a house. The Germans surrendered; Heffron and Spina took their watches, a beautiful set of binoculars, and so forth. They spotted a strongbox on the shelf. Spina opened it; it was a Wehrmacht payroll in marks. They took it. In Spina's words, "There we were two boys from South Philly who just pulled off a payroll caper with a carbine and a pistol."

Back at their apartment, Heffron and Spina debated what to do with the money as they knocked back a bottle of cognac. In the morning they went to Mass at the Catholic church and gave the money away to the worshipers, "with the exception of some bills of large denominations which we split up," Spina confessed. "We weren't that drunk not to keep any for ourselves."

They took vehicles, of all types, private and Army. Pvt. Norman Neitzke, who had come in at Haguenau, remembered the time his squad started to drive away in a German ambulance only to find that a German doctor with a pregnant woman was in the back trying to deliver a baby. The Americans hopped out.

One morning Lieutenant Richey grabbed the camera of a German woman photographing the convoy. But instead of taking it, he threw it on the ground and shot it with his pistol. This earned him the nickname "The Camera Killer."

* * *

Contact with the enemy picked up as the convoy moved southeast, but not in the sense of combat. The men began to see German soldiers in small groups, trying to surrender. Then larger groups. Finally, more field gray uniforms than anyone could have imagined existed.

Easy Company was in the midst of a German army in disintegration. The supply system lay in ruins. All the German soldiers wanted was a safe entry into a P.O.W. cage. "I couldn't get over the sensation of having the Germans, who only a short time ago had been so difficult to capture, come in from the hills like sheep and surrender," Webster wrote. When the convoy reached the autobahn leading east to Munich, the road was reserved for Allied military traffic, the median for Germans marching west to captivity. Gordon Carson recalled that "as far as you could see in the median were German prisoners, fully armed. No one would stop to take their surrender. We just waved."

Webster called the sight of the Germans in the median "a tingling spectacle." They came on "in huge blocks. We saw the unbelievable spectacle of two G.I.s keeping watch on some 2,500 enemy." At that moment the men of the company realized that the German collapse was complete, that there would be no recovery this spring as there had been last fall.

There was still some scattered, sporadic resistance. Every single bridge was destroyed by German engineers as the Allies approached. Occasionally a fanatic

SS unit would fire from its side of the stream. It was more an irritant than a threat or danger. The Americans would bring forward some light artillery, drive the SS troops away, and wait for the engineers to repair the old or make a new bridge.

Winters was struck by the German fanaticism, the discipline that led German engineers to blow their own bridges when the uselessness of the destruction was clear to any idiot, and "the total futility of the war. Here was a German army trying to surrender and walking north along the autobahn, while at the same time another group was blowing out the bridges to slow down the surrender."

• • •

On April 29 the company stopped for the night at Buchloe, in the foothills of the Alps, near Landsberg. Here they saw their first concentration camp. It was a work camp, not an extermination camp, one of the half-dozen or more that were a part of the Dachau complex. But although it was relatively small and designed to produce war goods, it was so horrible that it was impossible to fathom the enormity of the evil. Prisoners in their striped pajamas, three-quarters starved, by the thousands; corpses, little more than skeletons, by the hundreds.

Winters found stacks of huge wheels of cheese in the cellar of a building he was using for the battalion CP and ordered it distributed to the inmates. He radioed to regiment to describe the situation and ask for help.

The company stayed in Buchloe for two nights. Thus it was present in the morning when the people of Landsberg turned out, carrying rakes, brooms, shovels, and marched off to the camp. General Taylor, it turned out, had been so incensed by the sight that he had declared martial law and ordered everyone from fourteen to eighty years of age to be rounded up and sent to the camp, to bury the bodies and clean up the place. That evening the crew came back down the road from the camp. Some were still vomiting.

"The memory of starved, dazed men," Winters wrote, "who dropped their eyes and heads when we looked at them through the chain-link fence, in the same manner that a beaten, mistreated dog would cringe, leaves feelings that cannot be described and will never be forgotten. The impact of seeing those people behind that fence left me saying, only to myself, 'Now I know why I am here!'"

17

Drinking Hitler's Champagne

BERCHTESGADEN

May 1–8, 1945

O N THE FIRST TWO DAYS of May, the company drove south from Munich, moving slowly through streams of German soldiers walking in the opposite direction. Often there were more German soldiers with weapons going north than there were Americans going south. "We looked at each other with great curiosity," Winters remembered. "I am sure both armies shared one thought—just let me alone. All I want is to get this over with and go home."

On May 3, Colonel Sink got orders to have the 506th ready to move out at 0930 the following day, objective Berchtesgaden.

• • •

Berchtesgaden was a magnet for the troops of all the armies in southern Germany, Austria, and northern Italy. South of Salzburg, the Bavarian mountain town of Berchtesgaden was Valhalla for the Nazi gods, lords, and masters. Hitler had a home there and a mountain-top stone retreat called the Aldershorst (Eagle's Nest) 8,000 feet high. Thanks to a remarkable job of road building, cars could get to a parking place within a few hundred feet of the Aldershorst. There a shaft ran into the center of the mountain to an elevator which lifted into the Aldershorst. The walls of the elevator were gold leaf.

It was to Berchtesgaden that the leaders of Europe had come in the late 1930s to be humiliated by Hitler. Daladier of France, Mussolini of Italy, Schuschnigg of Austria, Chamberlain of Britain, and others. They had feared Hitler, as had the whole world. Now that Hitler was dead, the fear was removed, but that only high-lighted the fascination with Hitler and his favorite retreat, which seemed to hold one of the keys to his character.

It was to Berchtesgaden that the highest-ranking Nazi leadership flocked, to be near their Führer. Himmler, Goering, Goebbels, Martin Bormann had houses in the area. There was a fabulous apartment complex for the SS.

It was to the Berchtesgaden area that much of the loot collected by the Nazis from all over Europe had come. The place was stuffed with money, in gold and in currency from a dozen countries, with art treasures (Goering's collection alone contained five Rembrandts, a Van Gogh, a Renoir, and much more). It was bursting with booze, jewelry, fabulous cars.

So Berchtesgaden was really two magnets: the sym-bolic home of Hitler's mad lust for power, and the best looting possibilities in Europe. Everybody wanted to get there—French advancing side by side with the

101st, British coming up from Italy, German leaders who wanted to get their possessions, and every American in Europe.

Easy Company got there first.

• • •

On May 4, the 101st moved out by convoy down the autobahn between Munich and Salzburg, with 2d Battalion in the lead. The Americans passed Rosenheim and the Chiem See. At Siegsdorf they turned right on the direct highway to Berchtesgaden. About 14 kilometers down the road, they ran into the tail of the French 2d Armored Division, the first division to enter Paris, with its famous commander Gen. Jacques Philippe Leclerc.

The 2d Armored supposedly had been on the right flank of the 101st for the past week, but the Americans had not been able to keep in touch with it. The French were there one minute, gone the next. So far as the Americans could make out, they were looting their way through Germany. Whenever they got a truckload or two of loot, they'd send it back home to France. Now they were lusting to get into Berchtesgaden, only an hour's drive or so up into the mountains to the south. But the French were stopped by a blown bridge over a deep ravine. They did not have bridging equipment, and some SS fanatics were holding out on the south side of the ravine, using automatic weapons and mortars.

Easy Company and the remainder of 2d Battalion began mixing in with the French, everyone standing around watching a long-range, useless exchange of fire while waiting for the 101st engineers to come forward. Winters asked Sink if he wanted to send a platoon to outflank the German roadblock. "No," Sink replied, "I don't want anybody to get hurt."

That was sensible. There was no point to taking casualties at this stage of the war. But there was Berchtesgaden, just on the other side of the roadblock, almost in hand. Sink changed his mind. "Take the 2d Battalion back to the autobahn," he told Winters, "and see if you can outflank this roadblock and get to Berchtesgaden." If he succeeded, Sink wanted him to reserve the famous Berchtesgaden Hof for regimental HQ.

Winters led the battalion on a backtrack to the autobahn, then east to Bad Reichenhall, where another blown bridge stopped the Americans for the night. The following morning, May 5, with Easy Company leading the way, the 2d Battalion drove unopposed to Berchtesgaden and took the town without having to fire a shot.

It was like a fairy-tale land. The snowcapped mountains, the dark green woods, the tinkling icy creeks, the gingerbread houses, the quaint and colorful dress of the natives, provided a delight for the eye. The food, liquor, accommodations, and large number of Luftwaffe and Wehrmacht service women, plus camp followers of various types, provided a delight for the body.

Accommodations were the first order of business. Winters and Lieutenant Welsh went to the Berchtesgaden Hof. As they walked in the front door of the hotel, they could see the backs of the service personnel disappear around the corner. They went into the main dining room, where they saw a waiter putting together a large set of silverware in a 4-foot-long velvet-lined case.

There was no need for orders. Winters and Welsh simply walked toward the man, who took off. The Americans split the silverware between them. Forty-five years later, both men were still using the Berchtesgaden Hof's silverware in their homes.

After getting what he most wanted out of the place, Winters then put a double guard on the hotel "to stop further looting," as he put it—with a straight face—in one of our interviews. But, he berated himself, "What a fool I was not to open the place to the 2d Battalion," because when regimental and then divisional HQ arrived, they took everything movable.

Winters picked one of the homes of Nazi officials, perched on the hillside climbing the valley out of Berchtesgaden, for his battalion HQ. He told Lieutenant Cowing, his S-4, to go to the place and tell the people they had fifteen minutes to get out. Cowing was a replacement officer who had joined up in mid-February, back in Haguenau. He had not been hardened by battle. He returned a few minutes later to tell Winters, "The people said no, they would not move out."

"Follow me," Winters declared. He went to the front door, knocked, and when a woman answered, he announced, "We are moving in. Now!" And he and his staff did just that, as the Germans disappeared somewhere.

"Did I feel guilty about this?" Winters asked himself in the interview. "Did my conscience bother me about taking over this beautiful home? No! We had been living in foxholes in Normandy, we had been in the mud at Holland, the snow in Bastogne. Just a few days earlier we'd seen a concentration camp. These people were the reason for all this suffering. I had no sympathy for their problem, nor did I feel that I owed them an explanation."

Nor did the enlisted men have the slightest problem, physical or psychological, in taking over the SS barracks, an Alpine-style apartment house block that was the latest thing in modern design, plumbing, and interior decoration. Officers and sergeants got sumptuous homes of Nazi officials perched on the mountainsides overlooking Berchtesgaden.

Winters set up the guard around town, mainly to direct traffic and to gather up surrendering German troops to send them to P.O.W. cages in the rear. Private Heffron was thus in command at a crossroads when a convoy of thirty-one vehicles came down from the mountain. At its head was Gen. Theodor Tolsdorf, commander of the LXXXII Corps. He was quite a character, a thirty-five-year-old Prussian who had almost set the record for advancement in the Wehrmacht. He had been wounded eleven times and was known to his men as Tolsdorf the Mad because of his recklessness with their lives and his own. Of more interest to E Company men, he had been in command of the 340th Volksgrenadier Division on January 3 in the bitter fighting in the Bois Jacques and around Foy and Noville.

Tolsdorf expected to surrender with full honors, then be allowed to live in a P.O.W. camp in considerable style. His convoy was loaded with personal baggage, liquor, cigars and cigarettes, along with plenty of accompanying girlfriends. Heffron was the first American the party encountered. He stopped the convoy; Tolsdorf said he wished to surrender; Heffron summoned a nearby 2nd lieutenant; Tolsdorf sent the lieutenant off to find someone of more suitable rank;

Heffron, meanwhile, seized the opportunity to liberate General Tolsdorf's Luger and briefcase. In the briefcase he found a couple of Iron Crosses and 500 pornographic photographs. He thought to himself, A kid from South Philly has a Kraut general surrender to him, that is pretty good.

* * *

Everyone was grabbing loot at a frantic pace. German soldiers were everywhere—Wehrmacht, Waffen SS, Luftwaffe, officers, noncoms, privates—looking for someone to surrender to, and Dog, Easy, and Fox Companies of the 506th were the first to get to them. From these soldiers, Webster wrote his parents on May 13, "we obtained pistols, knives, watches, fur-lined coats, camouflaged jump jackets. Most of the Germans take it in pretty good spirit, but once in a while we get an individual who does not want to be relieved of the excess weight of his watch. A pistol flashed in his face, however, can persuade anybody. I now have a Luger, two P-38's, a Schmeissere machine pistol, two jump smocks, one camouflaged winter jacket, several Nazi flags about three feet by two, and a watch."

The Eagle's Nest had been thoroughly worked over by the Army Air Force. The elevator to it had been put out of action. But to men who had been up and down Currahee innumerable times, the climb to the top was more a stroll than a challenge. Alton More was one of the first to get there. In the rubble, he found two of Hitler's photo albums filled with pictures of the famous politicians of Europe who had been Hitler's guests. An officer from the company demanded that More turn over the albums to him. More refused. The officer threatened to court-martial him.

More was in Malarkey's platoon. Malarkey ran to battalion HQ to see Winters. He explained the situation. Winters told his jeep driver to "take Malarkey back to his quarters and return with Private More and all his gear." When More arrived, Winters made him a driver for Battalion HQ. Thus was More able to take the albums home with him to Casper, Wyoming.

• • •

With lodging taken care of, and having looted more than they could carry or could ever hope to get home, the next thing these young Americans needed was a set of wheels. No problem: in the vehicle parks in and around town there were German army trucks, sedans, Volkswagens, and more, while scattered through town and in the garages attached to the hillside homes were luxury automobiles. Sergeant Hale got a Mercedes fire engine, complete with bell, siren, and flashing blue lights. Sergeant Talbert got one of Hitler's staff cars, with bulletproof doors and windows. Sergeant Carson got Hermann Goering's car, "the most beautiful car I have ever seen. We were like kids jumping up and down. We were Kings of the Road. We found Captain Speirs. He immediately took over the wheel and off we went, through Berchtesgaden, through the mountain roads, through the country with its picture-book farms."

As more brass poured into Berchtesgaden on May 7 and 8, it was more difficult for a captain to hold on to a Mercedes. Speirs got orders to turn it over to regiment. Carson and Bill Howell were hanging around the car when Speirs delivered the sad message.

Carson asked Howell if he thought those windows really were bulletproof. Howell wondered too. So they paced off ten yards from the left rear window, aimed their M-1s and fired. The window shattered into a thousand pieces. They gathered up the broken glass and walked away just as a captain from regiment came to pick up the car.

Before Talbert turned over his Mercedes, he too did some experimenting. He was able to report to Winters that the windows were bulletproof, but that if you used armor-piercing ammo, it would get the job done. Winters thanked him for his research, agreeing that one never knew when this kind of information would come in handy.

The men tried another experiment. They drained the water from the radiator of the Mercedes, to see if it could run without it. With a third luxury car, they decided that before turning it in they would see if it could survive a 30-meter crash, so they pushed it over a cliff.

So the brass got luxury automobiles without windows or water, or wrecks (Talbert's Mercedes burned out the engine trying to climb the road to the Eagle's Nest). The men ended up with trucks, motorcycles, Volkswagens, scout cars, and the like, which were good enough, and anyway the fuel came as free as the vehicle. The Americans would just fill up and drive off.

"It was a unique feeling," Winters recalled. "You can't imagine such power as we had. Whatever we wanted, we just took."

• • •

With lodging and wheels taken care of, the next thing was liquor. Every cellar held some wine, but the greatest cache of all was discovered by one of the few non-drinkers in the battalion, Major Winters. On May 6, scouting on his own, he found Goering's Officer's Quarters and Club. In one room he found a dead German general, in full dress uniform, a bullet through his head, ear to ear, a pistol in his hand. He was a two-star general later identified as Kastner.

Winters wandered around, kicking open doors, when "Lord! I had never seen anything like this before." In a vaulted cellar, 15 meters by 10 meters, there were row after row of liquor racks stretching from floor to ceiling. The brand names covered the world. The later estimate was that the room held 10,000 bottles. Winters put a double guard on the officer's club entrance, and another on the cellar. And he issued an order: no more liquor, every man in the battalion was to go on the wagon for seven days.

Commenting in 1990 on this improbable order, Winters said, "Now, I am no fool. You don't expect an order like that to be carried out 100 percent, but the message was clear—keep this situation under control. I don't want a drunken brawl!"

That afternoon, Winters called Captain Nixon to him. "Nix," he said, "you sober up, and I'll show you something you have never seen before in your life."

The next morning, May 7, Nixon came to Winters, sober, and asked, "What was that you said yesterday that you were going to show me?" Winters got a jeep, and they drove to the officer's club. When Winters opened the door to the cellar, "Nixon thought that he had died and gone to heaven."

He was sure he had when Winters said, "Take what you want, then have each company and battalion HQ bring around a truck and take a truckload. You are in charge."

An alcoholic's dream come true, paradise beyond description. First choice of all that he could carry from one of the world's great collections, then a chance to let his friends have all they wanted, and the perfect excuse to celebrate, the end of the war had come, and he was still alive.

For the consequences, see the photograph of Nixon on the morning of May 8.

For the company as a whole, the celebration was grand and irresistible. Despite Winters's orders, and despite regular guard duty rotation, there was a party. There had to be: on May 7 the Germans surrendered in Reims to General Eisenhower, and word was flashed around Europe to cease fire, take away the blackout curtains, and let the light of peace shine out. News of the German surrender, Winston Churchill said, was "the signal for the greatest outburst of joy in the history of mankind." The men of Easy Company saw to it that Berchtesgaden participated in the party to the full.

Once the distribution of Goering's wine had taken place, Carson recalled that "you could hear the champagne corks going off all day long." As the celebration got noisier, Captain Speirs began to grow a bit worried that it would become excessive. Sergeant Mercier, remembered by Private O'Keefe as "our most professional soldier," got into the spirit of the day when he dressed in a full German officer's uniform, topped off with a monocle for his right eye. Someone got the bright idea to march him over to the company orderly room and turn him in at rifle point to Captain Speirs.

Someone got word to Speirs before Mercier showed up. When troopers brought Mercier up to Speirs's desk, prodding him with bayonets, Speirs did not look up.

One of the troopers snapped a salute and declared, "Sir, we have captured this German officer. What should we do with him?"

"Take him out and shoot him," Speirs replied, not looking up.

"Sir," Mercier called out, "sir, please, sir, it's me, Sergeant Mercier."

"Mercier, get out of that silly uniform," Speirs ordered.

Shortly thereafter, he called the company together. He said he noted that the men who were relatively new to the company were celebrating out of proportion to their contribution to the victory. He wanted it toned down. No more shooting off of weapons, for example, and especially not of German weapons, which made everyone jumpy when they went off.

But trying to stop the celebration was like trying to stop the tide. Not even Speirs could resist. Back in company HQ, he and Sergeant Carson sat in the orderly room, popping champagne bottles, throwing the empties out the French doors. Soon there was a pile of empties outside. Speirs and Carson went to the balcony for some fresh air. They looked at the bottles.

"Are you any good with that .45 pistol?" Speirs asked. Carson said he was.

"Let's see you take the neck off one of those bottles." Carson aimed, fired, and shattered a bottle. Speirs took his turn with the same results; soon they were banging away.

Sergeant Talbert came storming in, red-faced, ready to shoot the offenders of the company order. He saw Carson first. "Carson, I'll have your ass for this," he shouted. Just as he started explaining that Captain Speirs had ordered no shooting, Speirs stepped out from behind Carson, a smoking .45 in his hand.

After a few seconds of silence, Speirs spoke: "I'm sorry, Sergeant. I caused this. I forgot my own order."

Webster, Luz, and O'Keefe had meanwhile found their way to Goering's wine cellar. They were late; the other Easy men had already been there and Winters had withdrawn the guard, throwing the cellar open to anyone. As Webster, Luz, and O'Keefe drove to the site in Luz's Volkswagen, they saw a steady stream of German trucks, Volkswagens, even armored cars winding up the road to the officer's club.

The last contingent of E Company men had a wooden box with them, which they stuffed with bottles. "I was shocked to find that most of the champagne was new and mediocre," Webster remarked. "Here was no Napoleon brandy and the champagne had been bottled in the late 1930s. I was disappointed in Hitler."

What Webster failed to take into account was that Nixon had preceded him, and Nixon was a connoisseur of fine liquor, and he had picked out five truckloads for himself and the other officers long before Webster, also a self-styled connoisseur, arrived. "On this occasion," an amused Winters commented, "the Yale man [Nixon] pulled his rank on the Harvard boy."

Outside the club, Webster, Luz, and O'Keefe ran into a group of French soldiers, drinking, shouting *"La guerre est finis! La guerre est finis!"* shooting their machine-pistols into the sky, slapping the Americans on the back, asking for cigarettes, offering drinks.

The Americans gave away cigarettes, shook hands all around, and took off, driving back to their apartment as fast as possible. And there, Webster wrote, "began a party unequalled. Popping corks, spilling champagne, breaking bottles. Raucous laughter, ringing shouts, stuttering, lisping sentences. Have anusher glash. Here, goddammit, lemme pop that cork—ish my turn. Ishn thish wunnerful? Shugalug. Filler up. Where is Hitler? We gotta thank Hitler, the shun uvva bish. Bershteshgaden, I love you.

"And that was the end of the war."

• • •

Everyone in Europe was celebrating, victor and vanquished. First among the celebrants were the young men in uniform. They had survived, they would live, they had the best cause to celebrate.

On the morning of May 8, O'Keefe and Harry Lager went looking for eggs. They came to a farmhouse in a clearing, smoke curling up from the chimney. They kicked the door in, then ran inside with rifles ready to fire, and scared the hell out of two Italian deserters who jumped straight up and froze.

There was a bottle of champagne on a table. With one quick motion the Italian nearest it grabbed the neck of the bottle, stuck it out toward O'Keefe, whose rifle was pointed straight toward his stomach, and offered a drink, saying "Pax!"

The tension snapped. They drank to peace. The Americans left, to continue their egg hunt. They came to a lodge in the woods. "It was beautifully situated," O'Keefe wrote. "A man in his late twenties in civilian clothes was standing on a low porch at the front of the house. As we came to the steps leading up to the porch, he stepped down with a smile on his face and said, in English, 'The war is over. I have been listening to the wireless.'

"He was holding himself erect but it was noticeable

that he had a bad right leg. I glanced at it; he explained, 'I was with the Afrika Korps and was shot up badly and sent home. I was a soldier.'

"He asked us to come in and have a glass of wine. We said 'No' but he said 'Wait! I'll bring it out,' and he left, to reappear with three glasses of wine. We raised them in salute, as he said, 'To the end of the war.' We raised ours, and we all drank. There was something basically soldierly and right about it."

They found some eggs, returned to their apartment, and celebrated the end of the war with scrambled eggs and Hitler's champagne.

18

The Soldier's Dream Life

AUSTRIA

May 8–July 31, 1945

Late on the afternoon of May 8, Winters got orders to prepare 2d Battalion to move out that night for Zell am See, Austria, some 30 kilometers south of Berchtesgaden, where it would take up occupation duty. At 2200 hours the convoy began to roll, headlights on full beam. In the back of the trucks the men continued their party, drinking, singing, gambling. When the convoy arrived at Zell am See in the morning, the men were dirty, unshaven, wearing grimy Army fatigue pants and blouses.

German soldiers were everywhere. Zell am See was as far south as the Wehrmacht could retreat; beyond it were the peaks of the Alps, and beyond them Italy, and all the passes were still closed by snow. There were, it turned out, about 25,000 armed German soldiers in the area of responsibility of 2d Battalion, which numbered fewer than 600 men.

The contrast in appearance was almost as great as the contrast in numbers. The conquering army looked sloppy, unmilitary, ill-disciplined; the conquered army looked sharp, with an impressive military appearance and obvious discipline. Winters felt that the German soldiers and Austrian civilians must have wondered, as they gazed fascinated at the first American troops to arrive in the area, how on earth they could have lost to these guys.

Winters set up Battalion HQ in the village of Kaprun, 4 kilometers south of Zell am See. The valley was one of the most famous mountain resort areas in the world, especially popular with rich Germans. The accommodation, ranging from the zimmer frei at farmhouses to luxurious hotels, were stunning. All the rooms were occupied by wounded German soldiers. They had to move out, to be sent by truck or train to stockades in the Munich area. The Americans moved in.

Their job was to maintain order, to gather in all German soldiers, disarm them, and ship them off to P.O.W. camps. Winters got started the morning of May 9, immediately upon arrival. He had the senior German commander in the area brought to him. "I was twenty-seven years old," Winters recalls, "and like all the troops, I was wearing a dirty, well-worn combat fatigue jacket and pants, and had that bucket on my head for a helmet. I felt a little ridiculous giving orders to a professional German colonel about twenty years my senior, who was dressed in a clean field uniform with his medals all over his chest."

Winters gave his orders anyway. He directed the colonel to see to the collection of all weapons in the area and to stack them in the airport, at the school, and in the church yard. He gave officers permission to keep their side arms and allowed German military police to retain their weapons. And he said that the following day he would inspect the German camps, troops, and kitchens.

The next morning, May 10, Winters and Nixon drove by jeep to inspect the arms dumps. They were shocked by what they saw: in all three locations, a mountain of weapons. Winters realized he had made a mistake when he said "all weapons." He had meant military weapons, but the colonel had taken him too literally. There was a fantastic collection of hunting rifles, target rifles, hunting knives, antique firearms of all kinds, as well as a full division's stock of military weapons. It seemed enough to start World War III.

When he inspected the camps and kitchens, Winters found everything well organized. Troops were lined up for review, looking parade-ground sharp, clean, well-dressed, in good condition. The kitchens were in good order, the cooks were making large kettles of potato soup over fires.

Thereafter, Winters dealt with an English-speaking German staff officer, who came to his HQ each morning to report and receive orders. There was no trouble; in Winters's words, "We left them alone, they respected us." The German staff officer would tell stories about his tour of duty on the Eastern Front, and of fighting against the 101st in Bastogne. He told Winters, "Our armies should join hands and wipe out the Russian Army."

"No thanks," Winters replied. "All I want to do is get out of the Army and go home."

That was what nearly everyone wanted, none more

than the German troops. Before any could be released, however, all had to be screened. The German encampments were crawling with Nazis, many of whom had put on enlisted men's uniforms to escape detection. (The most notorious of these was Adolf Eichmann, wearing the uniform of a Luftwaffe corporal in a camp near Berchtesgaden. He managed to escape before he was detected, got to Argentina with his family and lived well until 1960 when Israeli agents discovered his whereabouts, captured him in a daring commando raid, brought him to Israel for trial, and hanged him.)

Lieutenant Lipton was serving as leader of the machine-gun platoon in HQ Company, 2d Battalion. Winters assigned him to oversee a lager of several hundred prisoners. One of them was Ferdinand Porsche, designer of the Volkswagen and the Panther and Tiger tanks. In mid-May, Lipton cleared about 150 of the prisoners for release. The senior German officer, a colonel, asked permission to talk to them before they were let go. Lipton agreed.

"His talk was long and was a good one," Lipton recalled. "He told them that Germany had lost the war, that they had been good soldiers and he was proud of them, and that they should go back to their homes and rebuild their lives. He said that all of them were needed for the reconstruction of Germany. When he finished, the men gave a loud cheer," and took off.

• • • •

Other high-ranking German officials, men who had good reason to fear that they would be charged with war crimes, were hiding in the mountains. Speirs was told by the D.P.s about a man who had been the Nazi head of the slave labor camps in the area and had committed a great many atrocities. He investigated, asked questions, and became convinced they were telling the truth. Further investigation revealed that this man was living on a small farm nearby.

Speirs called in 1st Sergeant Lynch. He explained the situation, then gave his order: "Take Moone, Liebgott, and Sisk, find him, and eliminate him."

Lynch gathered the men, explained the mission, got a weapons carrier, and took off up the mountain. During the trip, Moone thought about his predicament. He was sure that Captain Speirs did not have the authority to order an execution based on testimony from the D.P.s. But Speirs was the company C.O. and Moone was just an enlisted man carrying out an order. He decided, "I'm not complying with this bullshit. If someone has to do the shooting, it won't be me."

They got to the farm and without a struggle took the Nazi prisoner. Liebgott interrogated him for thirty minutes, then declared there could be no doubt, this was the man they wanted, and he was guilty as charged. The Americans pushed the man at gunpoint to the weapons carrier, then drove off. Lynch stopped beside a ravine. They prodded the man out of the vehicle. Liebgott drew his pistol and shot him twice.

The prisoner began screaming. He turned and ran up the hill. Lynch ordered Moone to shoot him.

"You shoot him," Moone replied. "The war is over."

Skinny Sisk stepped forward, leveled his M-1 at the fleeing man, and shot him dead.

• • •

After the P.O.W.s and D.P.s were sorted and shipped out of the area, the next job was to sort out and consolidate all the captured German equipment and the U.S. Army equipment no longer needed for combat. As the material was gathered and registered, convoys of trucks took it to depots in France.

Officers were ordered to turn in the silk escape map of France they had received before the jump into Normandy or be fined $75. As those maps were damn near sacred to the D-Day veterans, there was universal noncompliance. When told to pay the fine, Winters replied for the entire battalion, taking his line from General McAuliffe: "Nuts." The regimental supply officer, Capt. Herbert Sobel, backed down.

• • •

Given the absence of resistance, indeed the enthusiastic cooperation of the Germans and Austrians, by the end of the third week in May there was little real work left for the Americans. All KP, washing clothes, cleaning quarters, or construction tasks were done by local residents anxious to make some money or receive food or cigarettes. Time was hanging heavy on the heads of the young men lusting to go home.

Winters had a track built, a tennis court, and a baseball field, then a rifle range. Competitions were held, between companies, battalions, regiments, all the way up to ETO. He held daily close-order drills.

There were men who loved it. To the serious athletes, those with hopes of a future college or professional career, it was a marvelous opportunity to train. They were excused from all duties, lived in a separate athletic dorm, and got to practice or compete every day. To the few who planned to make a career of the

Army, it was a chance to practice their profession.

But to the majority, neither jocks nor career soldiers, it was a bore. They found their outlets in four other ways: as tourists in the Alps, hunting, drinking, and chasing women. The Zeller See, a lake some 4 kilometers in length and 2 in width, was a breathtaking bit of beauty, and a joy to swim in on the long, sunny days of late May and early June. "My bathing suit is getting quite a workout," Webster wrote his mother on May 20. "Will you please mail me another of very gaily colored trunks from Abercrombie and Fitch as quickly as possible? Waist 32, preferably shorts, not trunks."

On the mountain behind Kaprun there was a ski lodge. The chair lift to the lodge was kaput, but it could be reached by climbing the mountain trail. Winters set up a program to rotate one platoon every three days to the lodge for R and R. At the lodge there were Austrian servants and cooks, ski instructors, and hunting guides. The skiing was fabulous; so was the hunting for mountain goats.

There were deer at a lower level, hundreds of them, as this was a prime hunting area for the European aristocracy. The 101st was at the end of the pipeline in the distribution of food. Everyone from the ports of Cherbourg and Le Havre right on down the pipeline had a crack at the food first, and they all had civilian girlfriends to take care of and a flourishing black market to tempt them. So not enough food was getting to the Alps. The paratroopers went out in hunting parties for deer; venison became a staple in the diet. Private Freeman got a Browning shotgun and supplemented the venison with quail and other birds.

"Women, broads, dames, beetles, girls, skirts, frails, molls, babe, frauleins, Mademoiselles: That's what the boys wanted," Webster wrote. He went on to describe the results: "The cooks were keeping mistresses; the platoon lovers were patronizing the barn; McCreary had a married woman in town; Reese installed his in a private house; Carson fed an educated, beautiful, sophisticated Polish blond (whom he later married); the platoon staff visited a D.P. camp nightly; and in Zell am See, home of the most beautiful women in Europe, the lads with the sunburned blondes were fulfilling their dreams—after talking about women for three years, they now had all they could want. It was the complete failure of the non-fraternization policy."

For those who had wanted and could afford them, there had been women in London, Paris, along the Ruhr, but, Webster observed, "in Austria, where the women were cleaner, fairer, better built, and more willing than in any other part of Europe, the G.I.s had their field day."

The flow of booze was neverending. On May 28, Webster wrote his parents, "Since leaving Berchtesgaden, we've had a bun on every night. Two days ago we hijacked a German Wehrmacht warehouse to the tune of a couple of cases of gin—forty-eight bottles all told. Your package with the orange juice powder, therefore, came in very handy."

Captain Speirs had only one standing order about the drinking—no drunkenness outside. This was strictly enforced by the sergeants, who wanted no incidents with drunken soldier boys on guard duty, or just wandering the streets and mountain paths. In their quarters, however, the men were free to drink all they could hold. Most of them drank more than that.

Webster's squad kept a pitcher of iced tea and gin full and handy. Each night, he wrote, "by eight o'clock Matthews was lisping and stuttering; Marsh was bragging about his squad and how they obeyed him; Sholty was sitting quietly on a bed, grinning; Winn was laughing and shouting and talking about Bastogne; McCreary was boasting of his courage ('There ain't nobody in this platoon braver than I am, buddy') with immodesty but complete truth; Gilmore was pressing clothes furiously, a peculiar and most welcome manifestation of his high spirits; Hale slobbered and poured himself another drink; Chris, who never got rowdy, sat back in cold silence; Rader had passed out in the armchair; and I, who had passed out gracefully and without a struggle, was sound asleep."

The lads would work off their hangovers with an afternoon swim or game of softball. Winters was a nondrinker, who neither approved nor disapproved of drinking; his two best friends, Welsh and Nixon, were heavy drinkers. He never berated anyone for getting drunk on his own time. Had he ever been tempted to do so, he got a reminder each afternoon of why these excesses were taking place. The boys would wear shorts and nothing else in the warm sun while they played softball. Nearly every one of them had at least one scar. Some men had two, three, or even four scars on their chest, back, arms, or legs. "And keep in mind," he concluded, "that at Kaprun I was looking only at the men who were not seriously wounded."

There was another reminder of the price that E Company and the others had paid to get to where they were. On June 5, at 2200 hours, the men celebrated the first anniversary of their jump into Normandy. Webster was struck by the contrast. A year earlier, at 2200 hours, "My heart was beating like Gene Krupa's drum and my stomach was tied up and very empty. . . . Now I am sitting in a cosy house in the Austrian Alps. I have a tall glass of iced tea and gin in one hand, my pen in the other. A lot of boys who took off from that Devonshire airport are dead, buried in lovely cemeteries in Ste. Mère-Eglise, Son, and in Belgium, but I'm still here and very thankful for it and tonight we shall remember them in a way they would have thought most fitting—by having a wild, noisy party."

The officers too were having an ongoing party. Speirs had snatched a couple of cases of fine brandy, which he enjoyed in his living quarters with a beautiful Polish D.P. and her small child. Colonel Sink gave some memorable parties at his HQ, the Hotel Zell. One night he invited all 506th officers to meet General Taylor and his staff. It was a bash. Colonel Strayer, who according to Lieutenant Foley "could put away quite a bit of liquor, got a little rambunctious." He got into a fistfight with a general. Lieutenant Foley and a couple of others got a bright idea. They went to the parking lot and siphoned most of the gas from General Taylor's Mercedes (it had belonged to Hitler). They thought it would be very funny when he ran out of gas on his way back to Berchtesgaden in the middle of the night.

The next morning, Sunday, Colonel Sink ordered a special Officers Call. They assembled outside the hotel. Sink laid into them. He said their behavior was disgraceful. He touched especially on the brawling and on the practical joke. He had just gotten off the phone with General Taylor, whose car had run out of gas and who had sat there for hours while his driver searched for a jerrican. Foley, who did not confess, reported that "Sink didn't give a damn whether enlisted men stopped and listened, he was angry and he didn't care who heard him give everyone of us hell, spelled H-E-L-L."

Sink never stayed mad long. A week later he laid on a huge Fourth of July celebration. But on the Fourth it rained, and again on the fifth. Never mind: the sixth was a beautiful day and the celebration began. "Sink on the Sixth," the men called it.

There were athletic events of all kinds. Gliders and sail planes sailed across the lake, riding the mountain currents. Troop Carrier Command lent the regiment a C-47 for the afternoon, and there was a jump of twelve men into the lake. Food and drink was plentiful. In the park, local musicians dressed in lederhosen played all the *oomp-pa-pa* tunes. The G.I.s requested pop songs from America, but the Austrians needed practice. Everyone danced. All the girls wore D.P. armbands (nonfraternization applied only to Germans and Austrians; D.P.s were exempt; the armbands D.P.s wore to distinguish themselves were lavishly distributed to the local mountain girls) but, as Lieutenant Foley remembered it, "there wasn't one Displaced Person at the celebration."

Mountain weather, unlimited sports, women and booze, easy duty, good hunting, and a hard-assed colonel whom everyone loved. Zell am See provided, in Webster's view, "the soldier's dream life."

•   •   •

It should have been the most perfect summer ever for the men of E Company. In fact, after the first couple of weeks, most of them hated it. They were frustrated by the Army bureaucracy, they were bored, they were drinking far too much, and they wanted to go home.

Getting home depended on points, which became virtually the sole topic of conversation and led to much bad feeling. The point system set up by the Army gave a man points for each active-duty service month, points for campaigns, points for medals, points for being married. The magic number was eighty-five points. Those with that many or more were eligible for immediate shipment home and discharge. Those with fewer points were doomed to stay with the division, presumably right on through to the Big Jump in China or Japan.

So for the first time in their Army careers, the officers and men became seriously concerned with medals. A Bronze Star was worth five points. Inevitably the Army's hierarchical and bureaucratic systems played favorites. Lieutenant Foley recalled "the regimental adjutant who picked up a Bronze Star for—according to rumor—selecting the Hotel Zell for Sink's HQ."

The men of Easy felt cheated in another way: in the paratroopers it had been damn near impossible to win a medal other than the Purple Heart. "In the 101st, for example," Webster wrote, "only two men had been awarded the Medal of Honor—a private and a lieutenant colonel from the 502—and they had both been killed in action. Major Winters, who had acquired it legitimately in a fracas with a German battery in Normandy, wore the only Distinguished Service Cross in the 2d Battalion. In E Company, Captain Speirs and two or three others had 100-proof Silver Stars and about twelve men displayed Bronze Stars. Of Purple Hearts there were aplenty, but that was not a decoration but a badge of office: Infantry."

Most of the men in E Company had for decorations only the four battle stars on their ETO ribbon, no more than a personnel clerk who had never left base camp. "There was MacClung, for instance," Webster complained. "He was quiet, lanky, and unimpressive, and nobody noticed him. But his buddies in the third platoon swore that old One Lung had killed more Germans than any other man in the Battalion. MacClung could smell Kraut; he hunted them; he pursued them in dawn attacks and on night patrols; he went out of his way to kill them; he took more chances and volunteered for more dangerous jobs than any other man in E Company. MacClung had made every day of Normandy, Holland, and Bastogne, and what did he have to show for it? An ETO ribbon and four battle stars."

Sgt. Shifty Powers was in the same category. As good a soldier as there was in the 101st, he had no medals, no Purple Heart, so not enough points. But the grumbling had grown to such proportions that General Taylor decided to have a drawing in each company; the winner would be rotated home. Powers did not want to attend the drawing. "Hell, Paul," he told Sergeant Rogers, "I've never won anything in my life." But Rogers persuaded him to go, and he won.

Immediately, another soldier offered Powers $1,000 for that trip home. Powers recalled, "I thought about that for a while, $1,000 was a lot of money, but finally I said, 'No, I think I'll just go home.'"

Powers gathered up his loot, mainly pistols, got his paperwork done, drew his back pay, and joined the ten other lucky men for a ride to Munich. Going around a curve, a G.I. truck hit their truck head on. Powers flew out and over the top of the truck, hit the pavement, broke some bones, and got a bad concussion. Another one of the "lucky" soldiers was killed. Powers went to hospital, where he lost all his back pay and souvenirs to thieves. He eventually got home via a hospital ship, months after the comrades he had left behind.

• • •

Adding to the frustration of seeing cooks and clerks get the same points as front-line infantry was the haphazard record keeping. All the men spent hours totaling up their points, but the trick was to convince the regimental adjutant's office. Webster was sure he had eighty-seven points, but his records indicated he had fewer than eighty.

General Taylor tried to help his veterans. He decreed that every man who had taken part in Normandy, Holland, and Belgium, or who had made two of those campaigns and missed a third because of wounds, would receive a Bronze Star. This was widely appreciated, of course, but temporarily caused more frustration because it took weeks after Taylor's announcement before the medal and citation—and with them the all-important five points—actually came through.

All this chicken stuff created intense dissatisfaction with the Army and its ways. Recruiters were circulating among the officers and men, trying to persuade them to join the Regular Army. Almost none did. Webster articulated the feelings of most of his fellow soldiers: "I hate this army with a vehemence so deep and undying I'll never speak good of it as long as I live," he wrote his parents. "I consider my time spent in the army as 90% wasted." The only thing that he would concede was "I did learn how to get along with people." When Sink offered Winters a Regular commission, Winters thought about it for a moment or two, and then said he would rather not.

• • •

Adding to the problems of frustration and anger caused by the point system was the combination of too much liquor, too many pistols, and too many captured vehicles. Road accidents were almost as dangerous to the 101st in Austria as the German Army had been in Belgium. In the first three weeks in Austria, there were seventy wrecks, more in the six weeks of June and July. Twenty men were killed, nearly 100 injured.

One night Sgt. Robert Marsh was driving Pvt. John Janovec back from a roadblock by a side road. Janovec was leaning on the unreliable door of a German truck. They hit a log. He lost his balance, fell, and hit his head on the pavement. Marsh rushed him to the regimental aid station in Zell am See, but he died on the way of a fractured skull. Captain Speirs gathered up his few personal possessions, a watch, his wings, his wallet, and his parachute scarf, and mailed them to Janovec's parents. "He had come a long way," Webster wrote. "He had jumped in Holland and fought in Bastogne. He hated the army, and now, when the war is over and the golden prospect of home was in sight, he had died."

Marsh had not been drinking. Easy Company was proud of its record with regard to mounting guard duty or manning roadblocks with sober, responsible soldiers, and in not driving drunk. Others were not so careful. Private O'Keefe recalled the night he was at a roadblock with Pvt. Lloyd Guy halfway between Saalfelden and Zell am See. "An open German staff car came barreling down the road, not prepared to stop. Guy and I jumped out in front of it and made them stop. There were two men dressed in German uniforms, both drunk. 'What the hell you stopping us for? We're on your side.'

"They were a couple of our paratroopers, but from some other company. We told then, 'Damn it, you could have got your heads blown off!'

"They finally promised to slow down on the driving. We told them the next guard post was about ten miles up the road, to keep an eye out for it, and to slow down to a crawl. They promised to take it easy.

"But when we got back we learned that those two damn fools had barreled right through Welling's post with Welling out yelling, 'Halt! Halt!' After the third "Halt!' Welling took one shot and hit the driver." Later Welling visited the wounded man in the hospital; he said he had no hard feelings toward Welling, that he would have done the same thing.

Sgt. "Chuck" Grant, an original Toccoa man, was a smiling, athletic, fair-haired Californian who was universally respected—he had knocked out an 88 in Holland—and liked. One night he was driving a couple of privates to a roadblock for a changing of the guard. As they arrived, they saw a commotion.

A drunken G.I. was standing with a pistol in his

hand, two dead Germans at his feet. He had stopped them in their vehicle and demanded gasoline, as he was out. But he had no German, they had no English, he concluded they were resisting, and shot them.

A British major from military intelligence happened to have been driving by. He and his sergeant got out of their jeep to see what was going on. The drunken G.I. pointed his pistol at them and told them to back off.

At that moment, Grant came driving past. The drunk took a shot at him, but missed. The major made a move to disarm the man. The G.I. turned on him and shot him dead, then his sergeant. Grant came running over; the drunk shot him in the brain, then ran off.

Speirs thought the world of Grant. When he heard of the shooting, he and Lieutenant Foley jumped in a jeep, drove to the site, got Grant on a stretcher, and roared off for the regimental aid station. The doctor there was a disgrace, unshaven, unkempt, wearing a badly stained shirt. He took a quick look at Grant and said there was "no hope."

"Bull shit," said Speirs, who put Grant back on the stretcher and roared off again, this time for Saalfelden. Speirs had heard there were some German specialists there. One of them was a brain specialist from Berlin. He operated immediately and saved Grant's life.

Word of the shooting flashed through the billets. E Company went out en masse to find the culprit. He was found trying to rape an Austrian girl in Zell am See. He was a recent replacement in Company I. To the expressed disgust of many of the men, he was brought back to company HQ alive.

He almost wished he hadn't been. Half the company was milling around him, threatening, kicking, swearing vengeance. Before anything more serious happened, Captain Speirs came rushing in, straight from the hospital.

"Where's the weapon?" Speirs shouted at the prisoner.

"What weapon?"

Speirs pulled his pistol, reversed his grip to hold it by the barrel, and hit the man right in the temple with the butt. He started screaming. "When you talk to an officer, you say 'Sir,'" and hit him again.

The G.I. slumped into a chair, stunned. Pvt. Hack Hansen from Grant's 2d platoon, and close buddy, came running in. He whipped out his pistol. "You son of a bitch," he cursed. "I've killed better men than you." He put the pistol right in the man's face. Four men grabbed Hansen from behind and tried to pull him away, shouting that death was too good for such a coward, but he pulled the trigger. The pistol misfired.

"You ought to have seen the look of that guy," Gordon Carson remarked.

They beat him unconscious, then carried him to the regimental guardhouse and turned him over to the provost sergeant. When he revived, the provost sergeant beat him until the blood ran.

Sink came to company HQ. He strode in and asked Sergeant Carson, "Where's Speirs?"

"Up on the second floor, sir."

Sink went up and got the facts from Speirs. It took the better part of an hour. Sink left, and Speirs came down.

"How'd it go?" Carson asked.

"Pretty rough."

"Well, what did he say?"

"He said I should have shot the son of a bitch."

That he did not is remarkable. One explanation I got from a number of men was that Speirs must have had some doubt that the arrested man was the right man. When I asked Speirs about this, he replied, "As to the Sergeant Grant shooting you have it right. There must have been doubt in my mind, because summary action never troubled me."

But I wonder if there was not another factor at work. Speirs was not the only man who had a chance to shoot the coward. Grant had an opportunity in the initial encounter. The man who found the I Company drunk could have shot him on the spot, and nearly every man in the company interviewed by me said he wished it had been done. But many of them were at company HQ when he was brought in, wearing pistols, but only one of them actually tried to kill the man, and he was being held back by four others.

Almost every man in that room had killed. Their blood was up. Their anger was deep and cold. But what stands out in the incident is not the pistol whipping and beatings, but the restraint.

They had had enough of killing.

•   •   •

Shortly after the incident, Captain Speirs wrote a long letter to Sgt. Forrest Guth, who was in hospital in England and who had written Speirs expressing a fear that he would be transferred to another division. Speirs liked Guth, thought he was a good soldier, and was appreciative of his ability to keep all his weapons in prime condition. He especially appreciated the way

Guth could take a file and work on the tripper housing of an M-1 and make it fully automatic. (Winters got one of those Guth specials. He kept it and, when he set off for the Korean War, took it with him. Unfortunately, Guth cannot remember today how he did it.)

In his reply, Speirs expressed another side of himself. It was a long chatty letter about the doings of E Company since Guth went to the hospital, full of the kind of information Guth most wanted to hear: "Luz fell off a motorcycle and hurt his arm—not seriously, tho. Sgt. Talbert didn't like being 1st Sergeant so I gave him the 2nd Platoon and Sgt. Lynch (2nd Plat.) is 1st Sgt. now. Sgt. Alley got drunk again and we had to bust him. Lt. Lipton is on furlough in Scotland and is very happy. I'm sweating out a furlough to England to see my wife and baby. Sgt. Powers was on his way home and the truck overturned and he fractured his skull and he is hospitalized. Sgt. Strohl (3nd Plat.) is on his way home to the States. Chuck Grant got in the way of a bullet from a drunk American and his head is not too good—he is in a German hospital near here and is getting better. Sgt. Malarkey just came back from a long stretch in the hospital. Sgt. Rhinehard just came from the Riviera. McGrath won't take a furlough—he is saving his money."

Speirs gave Guth the details on the Bronze Star he was entitled to for participation in Normandy, Holland, and Belgium, and promised to inform him as soon as it came through. He added a postscript: "Clark is Armorer Artificer just now—sent Burlingame back to his platoon—he couldn't keep your Kraut generator going! We have regular electricity and hot water here in Austria.

"By the way, you can wear your 'Presidential Unit Citation' ribbon and an Oak Leaf Cluster on it no matter what outfit you are in—you earned it with the 101 A/B."

· · ·

The company was breaking up. General Taylor ordered all high-point men who had not yet been rotated home to be transferred to the 501st, stationed in Berchtesgaden. The 501st was being inactivated and was to serve as a vehicle to transport all high-point men from the division back to the United States for discharge. Others from the old company were in hospital or already discharged. Recruits who had joined up in Mourmelon or Haguenau were now regarded as veterans.

General Taylor made a trip to the States; when he returned toward the end of June, he announced that the 101st was to be redeployed to the Pacific, after a winter furlough in the States. Meanwhile the War Department insisted that the division undergo a full training regime, a critical process if it was to go into combat again, as more than three-quarters of the division was made up of recruits.

So close-order drill and calisthenics became the order of the day again, along with nomenclature of the M-1, nomenclature and functioning of the BAR, and nomenclature and functioning of the carbine. A road march. Arm and hand signals. Squad tactics. Barracks inspection. Mess kit inspection. Military courtesy and discipline. First aid and sanitation. Clothing check. Map reading. Dry run with the rifle. One solid week of triangulation. Firing on the range. "Thus it went," Webster wrote, "and I with it, in mounting disgust."

Lieutenant Peacock returned, more chickenshit than ever. "We suffered his excesses of training to such a degree," Webster wrote, "that the men who had known him in Holland and Bastogne hated even to look at him. I was so mad and exasperated that, if I had possessed fewer than 85 points, I would have volunteered to go straight to Japan and fight, rather than put up with another day's basic under Peacock."

• • •

By the middle of July every veteran of Normandy was gone, except the long-suffering Webster, who still could not get the adjutant to accept his point total. Colonel Sink had given the high-point men a farewell speech: "It is with mingled feelings that your regimental commander observes the departure of you fine officers and men. He is happy for each of you. You have worked and fought and won the right to return to your homes and to your friends.

"I am sorry to see you go because you are friends and comrades-at-arms.

"Most of you have caught hell at one time or another from me. I hope you considered it just hell and fair. It was never intended to be otherwise.

"I told you people to get those Presidential Citations and you did it. It will forever be to your credit and honor.

"Then God speed you on your way: May the same Fellow who led you by the hand in Normandy, Holland, Bastogne, and Germany look kindly upon you and guard you until the last great jump!"

At the end of July, the division was transferred by 40-and-8s to France. E Company went into barracks in Joigny, a small town south of Paris. Winters, Speirs,

Foley and others took furloughs in England. On August 6 the atomic bomb was dripped on Hiroshima, laying to rest the fears of another campaign in the Pacific. After that, everything in the airborne was in flux, with low-point men being transferred into the 17th Airborne, others into the 82d. The 101st magazine, the *Screaming Eagle*, complained, "The outfit seems more like a repple-depple than a combat division."[1]

On August 11, Colonel Sink was promoted to assistant division commander. On August 22, General Taylor left the 101st, or what was left of it, to become superintendent at West Point. Shortly thereafter, the 506th packed up and moved out, to join the 82d Airborne in Berlin. It was said that Colonel Sink cried when his boys marched to the Joigny depot for shipment to the 82d. Webster thought it fitting that he do so, as he was "the heart and soul of our regiment." Writing in 1946, Webster went on: "Our beautiful dark-blue silk regimental flag with Mount Curahee, the bolt of lightning, and the six parachutes embroidered on it is rolled in its case, gathering dust in the National Archives in Washington."

On November 30, 1945, the 101st was inactivated. Easy Company no longer existed.

•   •   •

The company had been born in July 1942 at Toccoa. Its existence essentially came to an end almost exactly three years later in Zell am See, Austria. In those three years the men had seen more, endured more, and contributed more than most men can see, endure, or contribute in a lifetime.

---

[1]Rapport and Northwood, *Rendezvous with Destiny*, 775.

They thought the Army was boring, unfeeling, and chicken, and hated it. They found combat to be ugliness, destruction, and death, and hated it. Anything was better than the blood and carnage, the grime and filth, the impossible demands made on the body—anything, that is, except letting down their buddies.

They also found in combat the closest brotherhood they ever knew. They found selflessness. They found they could love the other guy in their foxhole more than themselves. They found that in war, men who loved life would give their lives for them.

They had had three remarkable men as company commanders, Herbert Sobel, Richard Winters, and Ronald Speirs. Each had made his own impact but Winters, who had been associated with the company from Day 1 to Day 1,095, had made the deepest impression. In the view of those who served in Easy Company, it was Dick Winters's company.

The noncoms especially felt that way. The ones who served as corporals and sergeants in combat had been privates in Toccoa. They had spent their entire three years in E Company. Officers, except Winters, came and went. Many of the officers continued their association with E Company as members of the battalion or regimental staff, but only Winters and the noncoms were present and accounted for (or in hospital) every day of the company's existence. They held it together, most of all in those awful shellings in the woods of Bastogne and at that critical moment in the attack on Foy before Speirs replaced Dike. The acknowledged leaders of the noncoms, on paper and in fact, were the 1st sergeants, William Evans, James Diel, Carwood Lipton, and Floyd Talbert.

•　•　•

Sergeant Talbert was in the hospital at Fort Benjamin Harrison, Indiana, on September 30, 1945. He wrote a letter to Winters. He was no Webster as a writer, but he wrote from the heart and he spoke for every man who ever served in Easy Company.

He said he wished they could get together to talk, as there were a lot of things he wanted to tell Winters. "The first thing I will try to explain . . . Dick, you are loved and will never be forgotten by any soldier that ever served under you or I should say with you because that is the way you led. You are to me the greatest soldier I could ever hope to meet.

"A man can get something from war that is impossible to acquire anyplace else. I always seemed to strengthen my self-confidence or something. I don't know why I'm telling you this. You know all that.

"Well I will cut this off for now. You are the best friend I ever had and I only wish we could have been on a different basis. You were my ideal, and motor in combat. The little Major we both knew summed you up in two words, 'the most brave and courageous soldier he ever knew.' And I respected his judgment very much. He was a great soldier too, and I informed him you were the greatest. Well you know why I would follow you into hell. When I was with you I knew everything was absolutely under control."

• • •

Winters felt as strongly about the men as they did about him. In 1991 he summed up his company's history and its meaning: "The 101st Airborne was made up of hundreds of good, solid companies. However, E Co., 506 P.I.R. stand out among all of them through that very special bond that brings men together.

"That extra special, elite, close feeling started under the stress Capt. Sobel created at Camp Toccoa. Under that stress, the only way the men could survive was to bond together. Eventually, the noncoms had to bond together in a mutiny.

"The stress in training was followed by the stress in Normandy of drawing the key combat mission for gaining control of Utah Beach. In combat your reward for a good job done is that you get the next tough mission. E Company kept right on getting the job done through Holland—Bastogne—Germany.

"The result of sharing all that stress throughout training and combat has created a bond between the men of E Company that will last forever."

19

Postwar Careers

1945–1991

FORTY-EIGHT MEMBERS of Easy Company had given their lives for their country. More than 100 had been wounded, many of them severely, some twice, a few three times, one four times. Most had suffered stress, often severe. All had given what they regarded as the best years of their lives to the war. They were trained killers, accustomed to carnage and quick, violent reactions. Few of them had any college education before the war; the only skill most of them possessed was that of combat infantryman.

They came out determined to make up for the lost time. They rushed to college, using the G.I. Bill of Rights, universally praised by the veterans as the best piece of legislation the United States Government ever conceived. They got married and had kids as quickly as possible. Then they set out to build a life for themselves.

They were remarkably successful, primarily because of their own determination, ambition, and hard work, partly thanks to what they had taken from their Army experience that was positive. In the Army they had learned self-confidence, self-discipline, and obedience, that they could endure more than they had ever thought possible, that they could work with other people as part of a team. They had volunteered for the paratroopers because they had wanted to be with the best and to be the best that they could be. They had succeeded. They wanted nothing less from civilian life, and there too they succeeded.

They had a character like a rock, these members of the generation born between 1910 and 1928. They were the children of the Depression, fighters in the greatest war in history, builders of and participants in the postwar boom. They accepted a hand-up in the G.I. Bill, but they never took a handout. They made their own way. A few of them became rich, a few became powerful, almost all of them built their houses and did their jobs and raised their families and lived good lives, taking full advantage of the freedom they had helped to preserve.

• • •

It seems appropriate to start with the severely wounded. Cpl. Walter Gordon had been shot in the back at Bastogne and paralyzed. After six weeks in hospital in England, lying helplessly in his Crutchfield tongs, he began to have some feelings in his extremities. He had been helped by Dr. Stadium, who would stand at the foot of his bed and provoke him: "You're nothing but a damned goldbrick, Gordon." Gordon would stiffen, snap back, get angry. Because Stadium would not give up on him, Gordon says, "It never occurred to me that I could be a hopeless cripple."

When the tongs came off, Stadium got him to walking, or at least shuffling. In the spring of 1945, Gordon was listed as "walking wounded" and sent by hospital ship back to the States, where he slowly recuperated in Lawson General Hospital in Atlanta. He was there when the war in Europe ended. He walked with pain in the back, he sat with pain in the back, he slept with it. Any physical work was far beyond his capabilities; he was obviously of no further use to the Army. By the middle of June, his father was demanding to know when he would be discharged. "I don't know," was all Gordon could reply.

On June 16, Gordon had an examination. The young doctor then told him he was being transferred to Fort Benning, listed as fit for limited duty. So far as Gordon could make out, his reason was: "Nerve wounds are slow to heal, and to discharge a veteran with my degree of disability would justify a substantial award of compensation. By retaining me for additional months, my condition would no doubt improve."

Gordon called his father to give him the news. His father went into a tirade. "He pointed out to me that I had been wounded twice, and was now, in his words, a cripple. He felt that I had done my fair share and the time had come for me to return home." Then he gave his son an order to pass along a message to the Army doctor.

Gordon did as told, although with some embarrassment. He began by running on about how this was a message from his father and that he disavowed any connection with it.

"Get on with it!" the doctor barked, indicating how busy he was.

"My father says to tell you that if I am sent to any

location other than home, he will come fetch me and fly me to Washington, D.C., and, if necessary, strip me to the waist on the floor of the Senate."

The doc's face fell. Gordon thought it read, "Oh my God, that's all I need is a Mississippi Senator on my case. That's a ticket to the Pacific. Get him out of here."

Aloud he said, "O.K., immediate discharge with full disability." He saw to it that Gordon got a new uniform, took him to the dentist to have his teeth filled, and got him paid off.

Gordon went to law school at Cumberland University, Lebanon, Tennessee. With his 100 percent disability bringing in $200 a month, plus his G.I. Bill benefits, "I was a rich student." A good one, too. He passed the Mississippi Bar even before finishing his law degree, "so I was a licensed attorney still going to school." After graduation, he worked for several major companies in the oil business in south Louisiana. In 1951 he met Betty Ludeau in Acapulco, Mexico, on a vacation. They married a year later, moved to Lafayette, Louisiana, and began what became a family of five children, four of them girls. "I realized that I did not have sufficient salary to support Betty in the manner in which she required," Gordon relates, "so I became an independent."

He went into a high-risk business, buying and selling oil leases, speculating on futures. He was successful at it. The Gordons today have a home in Lafayette and apartments in Pass Christian, Mississippi, New Orleans, and Acapulco. He still has pain, walks with some difficulty, but the Gordons are blessed with wonderful children and grandchildren, they are still in love, they love to tell jokes on themselves. It's been a good life.

"And so what did the Army mean to you?" I asked at the end of our three days of interviewing.

"The most significant three years of my life," Gordon replied. "It had the most awesome effect. I developed friendships which to this day are the most significant that I have. I'm most incredibly lucky that I got through it and even more fortunate that I was with this group of outstanding men."

In December, 1991, Gordon saw a story in the Gulfport *Sun Herald*. It related that Mayor Jan Ritsema of Eindhoven, Holland, had refused to meet General H. Norman Schwarzkopf, because the commander of the UN forces in the Gulf War had "too much blood on his hands." Ritsema said of Schwarzkopf, "He is the person who devised the most efficient way possible to kill as many people as possible."

Gordon wrote to Mayor Ritsema: "On September 17, 1944 I participated in the large airborne operation which was conducted to liberate your country. As a member of company E, 506th PIR, I landed near the small town of Son. The following day we moved south and liberated Eindhoven. While carrying out our assignment, we suffered casualties. That is war talk for bleeding. We occupied various defense positions for over two months. Like animals, we lived in holes, barns, and as best we could. The weather was cold and wet. In spite of the adverse conditions, we held the ground we had fought so hard to capture.

"The citizens of Holland at that time did not share your aversion to bloodshed when the blood being shed was that of the German occupiers of your city. How soon we forget. History has proven more than once that Holland could again be conquered if your neighbor, the Germans, are having a dull weekend and the golf links are crowded.

"Please don't allow your country to be swallowed up by Liechtenstein or the Vatican as I don't plan to return. As of now, you are on your own."

•   •   •

Sgt. Joe Toye describes his experiences: "After being hit (my fourth Purple Heart) at Bastogne, I went through a series of operations. The main operation being the amputation of my right leg above the knee. Then, later, I had two more operations, these were to remove shrapnel from my upper chest cavity—to remove them the surgeon went in through my back.

"I was married Dec. 15, 1945, while still in the hospital at Atlantic City. I was discharged from the Army Feb. 8, 1946."

He was given an 80 percent disability. Before the war he had been a molder in a foundry, but with a wooden leg he couldn't do the work. He found employment in a textile mill in Reading, Pennsylvania, then worked twenty years for Bethlehem Steel as a bit grinder.

He has three sons and a daughter. "I used to take the boys hunting, fishing, but I never carried a gun—I was worried about tripping. This artificial leg, if something stops it, you're gone, you know. So I never carried a gun. But I took them out deer hunting and fishing. Every year I went camping in Canada with them."

There have been big improvements in artificial legs since 1946. Toye feels the doctors at the VA hospitals have treated him well and kept him up to date with the latest equipment. He does have one complaint. He wants two legs, one slightly larger where it joins the stump. But because the docs say one is enough, "I don't dare gain or lose any weight, else the darn thing won't fit."

• • •

Sgt. Bill Guarnere also lost his leg, above the knee, in Bastogne. After discharge in the summer of 1945, he was given an 80 percent disability. He married, had a child, and went to work as a printer, salesman, VA clerk, and carpenter, all with an artificial leg. There were some mix-ups in his records, which cost him money and led to much dispute with the VA. In 1967 he finally got full disability and was able to retire. He threw away his artificial leg, and for the past twenty-four years he has moved on crutches. He moves faster than most younger men with two good legs. He lives in South Philly, where he grew up, with his wife, Fran. They have five children; the oldest son was an Airborne trooper in Vietnam. He is very active in the 101st Association and in getting E Company men together.

• • •

Sgt. Chuck Grant, shot in the brain by the drunken G.I. in Austria after the war, had his life saved by a German doctor. He recovered, slowly, although he had some difficulty in speaking and was partly paralyzed in his left arm. After his medical discharge with full disability, he lived in San Francisco, where he ran a small cigar store. Over the years he regularly attended E Company reunions and was active in the 101st Association. Mike Ranney nominated him to be the 506th representative on the Board of the 101st Association; he was elected and served with great pride. He died in 1984.

• • •

Lt. Fred "Moose" Heyliger, shot twice by his own men in Holland, was flown to a hospital in Glasgow, then shipped on the *Queen Elizabeth* to New York. Over the next two-and-a-half years he was moved three more times. He underwent skin and nerve grafts before discharge in February 1947. Taking advantage of the G.I. Bill, he went to the University of Massachusetts, where he graduated in 1950 with a degree in ornamental horticulture. For the next forty years he worked for various landscape companies and on golf courses as a consultant and supplier. He has two sons and a daughter and continues his hobbies, arrowhead hunting, bird watching, and camping.

• • •

Sgt. Leo Boyle was discharged on June 22, 1945, after nine months in hospitals in Belgium, England, and the States. He was given a 30 percent disability. He got a job as a railroad brakeman, but his legs could not stand up to the strain. Then he worked in the post office, sorting mail, but again his legs gave out. "By that time I was so ill and confused that I checked into the VA hospital. After several days, a team of three medical doctors declared that I was 50 percent disabled and released me with no career guidance."

Boyle used his G.I. Bill benefits to go to the University of Oregon, where he majored in political science and earned an M.A. degree, with honors. He went into high school teaching and eventually into working with the educationally handicapped. "It was a career that was exceptionally rewarding. There is always a warm and good feeling between the handicapped and their teacher." When he retired in 1979, he was awarded the Phi Delta Kappa Service Key for Leadership and Research in Education for the Handicapped.

· · ·

Two other members of the company, the last 1st sergeant and the original company commander, were also victims of the war.

Sgt. Floyd Talbert had wounds and scars, which he handled without difficulty, and memories, which overwhelmed him. He became a drifter and a drinker. He made a living of sorts as a fisherman, hunter, trapper, and guide in northern California. He had a series of heart attacks.

Talbert was one of the few members of the company who just dropped out of sight. In 1980 Gordon enlisted the aid of his Congressman and of George Luz's son Steve, to locate Talbert. Sgt. Mike Ranney joined the search. Eventually they located him in Redding, California, and persuaded him to attend the 1981 company reunion in San Diego.

Ranney passed around his address. Winters and others wrote him. In his three-page handwritten reply to Winters, Talbert reminisced about their experiences. "Do you remember the time you were leading us into Carentan? Seeing you in the middle of that road wanting to move was too much! . . . Do you recall when we were pulling back in Holland? Lt. Peacock threw his carbine onto the road. He would not move. Honest to God I told him to retrieve the carbine and move or I would shoot him. He did as I directed. I liked him, he was a sincere and by the book officer, but not a soldier. As long as he let me handle the men he and I got along alright.

"Dick this can go on and on. I have never discussed these things with anyone on this earth. The things we had are damn near sacred to me." He signed off, "Your Devoted Soldier forever."

Talbert had enclosed a recent photograph. He looked like a mountain man. In his reply, Winters told him to shave off the beard and get his hair cut if he intended to come to San Diego. He did, but he still showed up wearing tattered hunting clothes. The first morning, Gordon and Don Moone took him to a men's store and bought him new clothes. Before the year was out, he died.

Gordon wrote his epitaph. "Almost all of the men of Company E suffered wounds of various severity. Some of us limp, some have impaired vision or hearing, but almost without exception we have modified our lives to accommodate the injury. Tab continued in daily conflict with a demon within his breast. He paid a dear price for his service to his country. He could not have given more without laying down his life."

Dick Winters paid him an ultimate tribute: "If I had to pick out just *one* man to be with me on a mission in combat, it would be Talbert."

•   •   •

Capt. Herbert Sobel had no physical wounds, but deep mental ones. He also disappeared from sight. He married, had two sons, got a divorce, and was estranged from his children. He worked as an accountant for an appliance company in Chicago. Maj. Clarence Hester was in Chicago on business one day in the early 1960s. He arranged for a lunch together. He found Sobel to be bitter toward E Company and life generally. Twenty years later Guarnere tried to locate Sobel. He finally found his sister, who told him Sobel was in bad mental condition and that he directed his rage at the men of E Company. Guarnere nevertheless paid Sobel's dues to the 101st Association, hoping to get him involved in that organization, but nothing happened. Shortly thereafter Captain Sobel shot himself. He botched it. Eventually he died in September 1988. His funeral was a sad affair. His ex-wife did not come to it, nor did his sons, nor did any member of E Company.

• • •

Sgt. Skinny Sisk also had a hard time shaking his war memories. In July 1991, he wrote Winters to explain. "My career after the war was trying to drink away the truckload of Krauts that I stopped in Holland and the die-hard Nazi that I went up into the Bavarian Alps and killed. Old Moe Alley made a statement that all the killings that I did was going to jump into the bed with me one of these days and they surely did. I had a lot of flash backs after the war and I started drinking. Ha! Ha!

"Then my sister's little daughter, four-years-old, came into my bedroom (I was too unbearable to the rest of the family, either hung over or drunk) and she told me that Jesus loved me and she loved me and if I would repent God would forgive me for all the men I kept trying to kill all over again.

"That little girl got to me. I put her out of my room, told her to go to her Mommy. There and then I bowed my head on my Mother's old feather bed and repented and God forgave me for the war and all the other bad things I had done down through the years. I was ordained in the latter part of 1949 into the ministry and believe me, Dick, I haven't whipped but one man since and he needed it. I have four children, nine grandchildren and two great-grandchildren.

"The Lord willing and Jesus tarrys I hope to see you all at the next reunion. If not I'll see you at the last jump. I know you won't freeze in the door."

•　•　•

Easy Company's contributions to the nation's defense did not end with the company's demise. A number stayed in the Army. Lt. S. H. Matheson, an original company officer who had quickly moved up to regimental staff, became a two-star general and commander of the 101st. Bob Brewer made colonel, spending much of his time working for the Central Intelligence Agency (CIA) in the Far East. Ed Shames made colonel in the Reserves.

Sgt. Clarence Lyall made a career out of the paratroopers. He made two combat jumps in Korea and in 1954 was assigned to the 29th French Parachute Regiment as an adviser. The 29th was at Dien Bien Phu. Lyall got out two weeks before the garrison surrendered. He is one of a small number who have made four combat jumps; surely he is unique in having been a participant in both the Battle of the Bulge and the Siege of Dien Bien Phu.

Sgt. Robert "Burr" Smith also stayed in the paratroopers, where he got a commission and eventually became a lieutenant colonel. He commanded a Special Forces Reserve unit in San Francisco. In December 1979, he wrote to Winters: "Eventually my reserve assignment led me to a new career with a government agency, which in turn led to eight years in Laos as a civilian advisor to a large irregular force. I continued to jump regularly until 1974, when lack of interest drove me to hang gliding, and that has been my consuming passion ever since. . . . For the present I am assigned as a special assistant to the Commander of Delta Force, the counter-terror force at Fort Bragg. My specialties are (surprise! surprise!): airborne operations, light weapons, and small unit operations.

"My office is on Buckner Road, right across the street from where we were just before leaving for England. The old buildings are exactly as you last saw them and are still in daily use. . . .

"Funny thing about 'The Modern Army,' Dick. I am assigned to what is reputed to be the best unit in the U.S. Army, the Delta Force, and I believe that it is. Still, on a man-for-man basis, I'd choose my wartime paratroop company *any time!* We had something there for three years that will never be equalled."

He was scheduled to go on the mission to Iran to rescue the hostages in 1980, but when the CIA learned this, it forbade him to go because he knew so many secrets. "So, I missed what certainly would have been the last adventure in my life," he wrote Winters. "I had lived, worked and trained with Delta every day for nearly two years, Dick, and I *Hated* to be left behind."

That got Smith going on leadership. He wrote of Winters, "You were blessed (some would say rewarded) with the uniform respect and admiration of 120 soldiers, essentially civilians in uniform, who would have followed you to certain death. I've been a soldier most of my adult life. In that time I've met only a handful of great soldiers, and of that handful only half or less come from my WWII experience, and two of them came from ol' Easy—you and Bill

Guarnere. The rest of us were O.K. . . . good soldiers by-and-large, and a few were better than average, but I know as much about 'Grace Under Pressure' as most men, and a lot more about it than some. You had it."

In 1980, riding an experimental hang-glider, Smith crashed and suffered severe injuries. In operating on his lungs, the doctors discovered a cancer. Rader, who had pulled Smith out of a flooded field on June 6, 1944, visited him in the hospital. They played a name game—one would call out the name of a Toccoa man, the other would supply a brief word portrait. Shortly thereafter, Smith died.

Sgt. Amos "Buck" Taylor spent a quarter-century with the CIA, working in the Far East Division of the Covert Operation Directorate, sometimes in Washington, often overseas. He won't say much about what he did, except that "the big threat to our country in that part of the world was Communist China and of course the USSR. That will give you some idea of the focus of my work. So much for that."

• • •

When Captain Speirs got back to England in the summer of 1945, he discovered that the English "widow" he had married, and who had borne his son, wasn't a widow at all. Her husband reappeared from a P.O.W. camp. She chose him over Speirs, and the couple kept all the loot Speirs had shipped back from Europe. He decided to stay in the Army. He made a combat jump in Korea and commanded a rifle company on the line in that war. In 1956 he attended a Russian language course in Monterey, California, and then was assigned to Potsdam, East Germany, as liaison officer with the Soviet Army. In 1958 he became the American governor of Spandau Prison, Berlin, where Rudolf Hess was serving his life term. In 1962 he went to Laos with the U.S. mission to the Royal Lao Army.

When old E Company men call him today and open the conversation by saying, "You won't remember me, but we were together during the war," Speirs replies, "Which war?" His son Robert, born in England during the war, is an infantry major in the King's Royal Rifle Corps, the "Green Jackets," and Speirs's "pride and joy."

* * *

David Webster could not understand how anyone could stay in the Army. He wanted to be a writer. He moved to California and paid his bills with a variety of odd jobs as he wrote and submitted articles and a book on his wartime experiences. He placed many of the articles, the top being in *The Saturday Evening Post*, but he could not find a publisher for his book. He became a reporter, first with the Los Angeles *Daily News*, then with the *Wall Street Journal*. In 1951 he married Barbara Stoessel, an artist and sister of Walter J. Stoessel, Jr., who became U.S. ambassador to Poland, the Soviet Union, and West Germany.

Webster had always been fascinated by sharks. Barbara writes, "The shark, for him, became a symbol of everything that is mysterious and fierce about the sea. He began gathering material for a book of his own. His research went on for years. He studied sharks first-hand, underwater, swimming among them; and caught many, fishing with a handline from his 11-foot sailing dinghy which he had named

Tusitala, which means 'Teller of Tales.'" He wrote the book and submitted it twenty-nine times, but could not convince a publisher that anyone wanted to read about sharks.

On September 9, 1961, Webster set sail from Santa Monica with squid bait, a heavy line, and hook for shark fishing. He never came back. A search the next day discovered the *Tusitala* awash 5 miles offshore. One oar and the tiller were missing. His body was never found.

Barbara was able to get his book on sharks published (*Myth and Maneater*, W. W. Norton & Co., 1963). There was a British edition and a paperback edition in Australia. When *Jaws* was released in 1975, Dell issued a mass-market paperback.

• • •

Three of the sergeants became rich men. John Martin attended Ohio State University on his G.I. Bill money, then returned to his railroad job. He became a supervisor, had a car, secretary, and pension building and was making money on the side by building houses on speculation. In 1961 he gave it all up and, over the intense protest of his wife and children, then in high school, moved to Phoenix, Arizona, and started building homes. He had $8,000 in total capital, and everyone thought he was crazy. At the end of the first year, he paid more in taxes than he had ever made working for the railroad. Soon he was building apartment complexes and nursing homes. He expanded his activities into Texas and Montana. In 1970 he bought a cattle ranch in the mountains of western Montana. Today he is a multimillionaire. He still likes to take risks, although he no longer jumps out of airplanes. He has resisted tempting offers to sell his business; the president of Martin Construction today is John Martin, while his wife Patricia is the vice president and treasurer. They are also the directors and sole stockholders.

Don Moone used his G.I. Bill benefits to attend Grinnell College, then went into advertising. He rose rapidly. In 1973 he became the president of Ketchum, MacLeod & Grove, Inc., a major New York City advertising firm. Four years later, at age fifty-one, he retired, built a home in Florida, and has lived there since in some splendor.

Carwood Lipton majored in engineering at Marshall College (now University), while his wife Jo Anne was bearing three sons. Lipton went to work for Owens-Illinois, Inc. He rose steadily in the firm; in 1971 he moved to London as director of manufacturing for eight glass factories in England and Scotland. In 1974 he went to Geneva, Switzerland, in charge of operations in Europe, the Middle East, and Africa. In 1975 Jo Anne died of a heart attack. The next year, Lipton married a widow, Marie Hope Mahoney, whose husband had been a close friend of Lipton's, just as Marie was a close friend of Jo Anne's. At the request of the CEO of United Glass, Ltd., he wrote a pamphlet, *Leading People.* It was a subject he knew well.

Lipton retired in 1983. He writes, "Currently living in comfortable retirement in Southern Pines, North Carolina, where I had decided when we were training in Camp Mackall that I would someday live. My hobbies are much travel throughout the world, golf, model engineering, woodworking, and reading."

Lewis Nixon had always been rich. He took over his father's far-flung industrial and agricultural empire and ran it while traveling around the world. His chief hobby today is reading.

•   •   •

Lt. Buck Compton stayed in public service jobs, so he became more famous than rich. He was a detective in the Los Angeles Police Department from 1947 to 1951, then spent twenty years as a prosecutor for the district attorney's office, eventually becoming chief deputy district attorney. In 1968 he directed the investigation of Sirhan Sirhan, then conducted the prosecution. In 1970 Gov. Ronald Reagan appointed him to the California Court of Appeals as an associate justice. He and his wife Donna have two daughters, one granddaughter. His reputation is that he remains the best athlete in the company; he is said to play a mean game of golf.

•   •   •

Sgt. Mike Ranney took a journalism degree at the University of North Dakota, then had a successful career as a reporter, newspaper editor, and public relations consultant. He and his wife Julia had five daughters, seven grandsons. In 1980 he began publishing what he called "The Spasmodic Newsletter of Easy Company." Some samples:

March 1982: "The Pennsylvania contingent got together at Dick Winters' place for a surprise party for Harry Welsh. Fenstermaker, Strohl, Guarnere, Guth had a great time."

1980. "The reunion this summer in Nashville is shaping up as one of the great turnouts in E Company history. A partial list of the attendees—Dick Winters, Harry Welsh, Moose Heyliger and Buck Compton from the officers; Chuck Grant, Paul Rogers, Walter Scott Gordon; Tipper, Guarnere, Rader, Heffron, Ranney, Johnny Martin, George Luz, Perconte, Jim Alley, and no less an personage than Burr Smith."

1983. "Don Moone retired from the advertising business and now lives it up down in Florida. He and Gordon and Carwood Lipton had a reunion in New Orleans."

With only a couple of exceptions, these men had no business or professional connections. None lived in the same town, few in the same state (except Pennsylvania). Yet they stayed in touch. In January 1981, Moone wrote Winters to thank him for a Christmas present and to fill him in: "It was great news that Talbert was finally located. I called him immediately and after an exchange of insults, we talked. I've always been fond of Tab. He took care of me in the old days. On New Year's Day at 6:00 A.M. my time, Tab called to wish me a good new year. He was bombed but coherent. He admits that he had a bottle problem, as we suspected, but was 'on the wagon' except for special occasions. Guess New Year's Eve was one of those 'specials.'

"Don Malarkey called me at 3:00 A.M. on New Years Eve morning and he too was well on his way."

Ranney retired to write poetry and his memoirs, but in September 1988 he died before he could get started.

• • •

Beyond Heyliger, Martin, Guarnere, and Toye, a number of men went into some form of building, construction, or making things. Capt. Clarence Hester became a roofing contractor in Sacramento, California. Sgt. Robert "Popeye" Wynn became a structural iron-worker on buildings and bridges. Pvt. John Plesha worked for the Washington State Highway Department. Sgt. Denver "Bull" Randleman was a superintendent for a heavy construction contractor in Louisiana. Sgt. Walter Hendrix spent forty-five years in the polishing trade, working with granite. Sgt. Burton "Pat" Christenson spent thirty-eight years with the Pacific Telephone and Telegraph Company, installing new lines, eventually becoming a supervisor and teacher. Sgt. Jim Alley was a carpenter, then worked on high-dam construction on the Washington State–Canada border. Eventually he had his own construction company in California.

Beyond Leo Boyle, a number of men went into teaching. After a twenty-year hitch in the Army, Sgt. Leo Hashey taught water safety for the Portland, Oregon, Red Cross. He became director of health and safety education. Sgt. Robert Rader taught the handicapped at Paso Robles High School in California for more than thirty years. Capt. Harry Welsh got married immediately upon his return to the States, with his bride Kitty Grogan wearing a dress made from the reserve chute he wore on D-Day and carried with him through the rest of the war. He went to college, taught, earned an M.A., and became a high school counselor, then administrator. Sgt. Forrest Guth taught printing, wood shop, electricity, electronics, and managed the sound and staging of school productions in Norfolk, Virginia, and Wilmington, Delaware, until his retirement. Pvt. Ralph Stafford writes: "Graduated in 1953 and started teaching the 6th grade in Fort Worth. Taught for three years and was elementary principal for 27 years, and dearly loved it. It was truly my calling. I was elected president of District V, Texas State Teachers Association (Dallas–Ft. Worth, 20,000 members).

"In 1950, I went bird hunting with some guys from the fire department. I shot a bird and was remorseful as I looked down at it, the bird had done me no harm and couldn't have. I went to the truck and stayed until the others returned, never to hunt again."

Sgt. Ed Tipper went to the University of Michigan for a B.A., then to Colorado State for an M.A. He taught high school in the Denver suburbs for almost thirty years. After retirement, he writes, "I went to Costa Rica to visit one of my former students. There I met Rosy, 34 years old. After an old-time courtship of about a year, we married in the face of great opposition from most everyone I knew, Dick Winters excluded. It was hard to disagree, especially with the argument that marriage to a 61-year-old man probably meant sacrificing any hope of having a family, a major consideration for Latin women. Our daughter Kerry was born almost ten months to the day after our wedding. Rosy went to medical school in Guadalajara and in 1989 got her M.D."

He has recently been operated on for cancer. "My wife, daughter and I have just moved into a new house. It may seem strange for a seventy-year-old to be buying a house, but our family motto is, 'It's never too late.'"

Sgt. Rod Bain graduated from Western Washington College (now University) in 1950, married that year, had four children, and spent twenty-five years as a teacher and administrator in Anchorage, Alaska. He spends his summers "as a drift gillnetter, chasing the elusive Sockeye Salmon."

Ed Tipper sums it up with a question: "Is it accidental that so many ex-paratroopers from E company became *teachers*? Perhaps for some men a period of violence and destruction at one time attracts them to look for something creative as a balance in another part of life. We seem also to have a disproportionate number of builders of houses and other things in the group we see at reunions."

• • •

Pvt. Bradford Freeman went back to the farm. In 1990 Winters wrote him, saying that he often came South to see Walter Gordon and would like to stop by sometime to see Freeman's farm. Freeman replied: "It would be a *great* honor for you to come to see us in Mississippi. We have a good shade to sit in in the Summer and have a good heater for Winter. About all that I do is garden and cut hay for cows in summer and feed in Winter. Fish and hunt the rest of the time. We have the Tombigbee water way close and I watch the barges go up and down the river. Sending you a picture of the house and cows. I have a good place on the front porch to sit. Here's hoping that you will come down sometime."

Winters did. They had a good visit. He asked Freeman to write an account of what he did after the war, for this book. Freeman concluded: "What I wrote don't look like much but I have had a real good time and wouldn't trade with no one."

• • •

Maj. Richard Winters also wrote an account of his life after the war: "On separation from the service on November 29, 1945, Lewis Nixon invited me to come to New York City and meet his parents. His father offered me a job and I became personnel manager for the Nixon Nitration Works, Nixon, New Jersey. While working, I took advantage of the G.I. Bill and took courses in business and personnel management at Rutgers University. In 1950 I was promoted to General Manager of Nixon Nitration Works.

"I married Ethel Estoppey in 1948. We have two children. Tim has an M.A. in English from Penn State and Jill a B.A. from Albright College.

"I was recalled to the army for the Korean War. At Fort Dix, New Jersey, I was put on the staff as regimental plans and training officer. After discharge, I returned to Pennsylvania, to farm and to sell animal health products and vitamin premixes to the feed companies. In 1951 I bought a farm along the foothills of the Blue Mountain—seven miles east of Indiantown Gap. That's where I find that peace and quiet that I promised myself on D-Day."

This is typical Winters understatement. He lives modestly, on his farm and in a small townhouse in Hershey, but he is a wealthy man who achieved success by creating and marketing a new, revolutionary cattle food and other animal food products.

He is also the gentlest of men. In July 1990, when he finished telling me about practically wiping out an entire German rifle company on the dike in Holland on October 5, 1944, we went for a walk down to his pond. A flock of perhaps thirty Canada geese took off; one goose stayed behind, honking plaintively at the others. Winters explained that the bird had a broken wing.

I remarked that he ought to get out a rifle and shoot the goose before a fox got her. "Freeze her up for Thanksgiving dinner."

He gave me an astonished glance. "I couldn't do that!" he said, horrified at the thought.

He is incapable of a violent action, he never raises his voice, he is contemptuous of exaggeration, self-puffery, or posturing. He has achieved exactly what he wanted in life, that peace and quiet he promised himself as he lay down to catch some sleep on the night of June 6–7, 1944, and the continuing love and respect of the men he commanded in Easy Company in World War II.

• • •

In one of his last newsletters, Mike Ranney wrote: "In thinking back on the days of Easy Company, I'm treasuring my remark to a grandson who asked, 'Grandpa, were you a hero in the war?'

"'No,' I answered, 'but I served in a company of heroes.'"

ACKNOWLEDGMENTS
AND SOURCES

IN THE FALL OF 1988, the veterans from Easy
Company, 506th Parachute Infantry Regiment, 101st
Airborne Division, held a reunion in New Orleans.
Along with my assistant director of the Eisenhower
Center at the University of New Orleans, Ron Drez, I
went to their hotel to tape-record a group interview
with them about their D-Day experience, as a part of
the Center's D-Day Project of collecting oral histories
from the men of D-Day. The interview with Easy
Company was especially good because the company
had carried out a daring and successful attack on a
German battery near Utah Beach.

When Maj. Richard Winters, an original member of
the company, later company C.O., finally C.O. of 2d
Battalion, read the transcript from the interview, he
was upset by some inaccurate and exaggerated state-
ments in it. He wanted to set the record straight. In
February 1990, Winters, Forrest Guth, and Carwood
Lipton came to Pass Christian, Mississippi, to visit

Walter Gordon. I live in the village of Bay St. Louis, across the bay from Pass Christian, so Gordon is my neighbor. He called to ask if the Easy Company veterans could do a follow-up interview. Of course, I said, and invited them to our home for a meeting and dinner. We spent the afternoon in my office, maps spread out, tape-recorder running. Later, at a roast beef feast prepared by my wife, Moira, the men sketched out for me their experiences after D-Day in Normandy, Holland, Belgium, Germany, and Austria.

They had all read my book *Pegasus Bridge*, which the Eisenhower Center gives to every veteran who does an interview for us. Winters suggested that a history of Easy Company might make a good subject for a book.

At that time I was working on the third and final volume of a biography of Richard Nixon. Winters's idea appealed to me for a number of reasons. When I finished Nixon, I wanted to go back to military history. I intended to do a book on D-Day, but did not want to begin the writing until 1992 with the intention of publishing it on the 50th anniversary, June 6, 1994. I have reached a point in my life where, if I am not doing some writing every day, I am not happy, so I was looking for a short book subject on World War II that would have a connection with D-Day.

A history of E Company fit perfectly. I knew the story of the British 6th Airborne Division on the far left flank on D-Day thanks to my research and interviewing for the *Pegasus Bridge* book. Getting to know the story of one company of the 101st on the far right flank was tempting.

There was an even more appealing factor. There was a closeness among the four veterans sitting at our dinner table that was, if not quite unique in my quarter-century experience of interviewing veterans, certainly unusual. As they talked about other members of the company, about various reunions over the decades, it became obvious that they continued to be a band of brothers. Although they were scattered all across the North American continent and overseas, they knew each other's wives, children, grandchildren, each other's problems and successes. They visited regularly, kept in close contact by mail and by phone. They helped each other in emergencies and times of trouble. And the only thing they had in common was their three-year experience in World War II, when they had been thrown together quite by chance by the U.S. Army.

I became intensely curious about how this remarkable closeness had been developed. It is something that all armies everywhere throughout history strive to create but seldom do, and never better than with Easy. The only way to satisfy my curiosity was to research and write the company history.

• • •

In May 1990, Drez attended the company's reunion in Orlando, Florida, where he video-recorded eight hours of group interview. That same month I did three days of interviewing with Gordon in my office. In July, I went to Winters's farm in Pennsylvania, where I did four days of interviewing. On the fourth day, a half-dozen men from the company living on the East Coast drove to the farm for a group interview. Later in 1990 I spent a weekend at Carwood Lipton's home in Southern Pines, where Bill Guarnere joined us. I flew to Oregon to spend another weekend with

Don Malarkey and a group of West Coast residents.

I interviewed a dozen other company members over the telephone and have had an extensive correspondence with nearly all living members of the company. At my urging ten of the men have written their wartime memoirs, ranging from ten to 200 pages. I have been given copies of wartime letters, diaries, and newspaper clippings.

In November 1990, Moira and I toured Easy's battle sites in Normandy and Belgium. I interviewed Frenchmen from the area the company fought over who had been living there at the time. In July 1991, we visited the scenes of Easy's battles throughout Europe with Winters, Lipton, and Malarkey. Winters, Moira, and I spent an afternoon with Baron Colonel Frederick von der Heydte at his home near Munich.

Mrs. Barbara Embree, widow of Pvt. David Webster, gave me copies of his letters to his parents and his book-length manuscript on his World War II memoirs. Webster was a keen observer and excellent writer. His contribution was invaluable.

Currahee!, the scrapbook written by Lt. James Morton and published by the 506th PIR in 1945, was also invaluable. Don Malarkey gave me a copy, most generous on his part as it is a rare book. *Rendezvous with Destiny*, the history of the 101st Airborne, written by Leonard Rapport and Arthur Northwood, provided the big picture plus facts, figures, details, atmosphere, and more. Other sources are noted in the text.

• • •

When I wrote *Pegasus Bridge*, I decided not to show the manuscript to Maj. John Howard, the C.O. of D

Company, Oxfordshire and Buckinghamshire Light Infantry, or any other of the thirty British gliderborne troops I had interviewed. I was working on a deadline that made it impossible to take up the months that would have been involved. The veterans had frequently contradicted each other on small points, and very occasionally on big ones. Not one of them would have accepted what I had written as entirely accurate, and I feared that, if they saw the manuscript, I'd be in for endless bickering over when this or that happened, or what happened, or why it happened.

I felt it was my task to make my best judgment on what was true, what had been misremembered, what had been exaggerated by the old soldiers telling their war stories, what acts of heroism had been played down by a man too modest to brag on himself.

In short, I felt that although it was their story, it was my book. John Howard was unhappy at being unable to suggest changes and corrections. Since the publication of *Pegasus Bridge*, he has convinced me that he was right, and I was wrong. Had I had time and allowed John and others to make corrections, criticisms, and suggestions, it would have been a more accurate and better book.

So I have circulated the manuscript of this book to the men of Easy Company. I have received a great deal of criticism, corrections, and suggestions in return. Winters and Lipton especially have gone through it line by line. This book is, then, very much a group effort. We do not pretend that this is the full history of the company, an impossibility given the vagaries of memory and the absence of testimony from men killed in the war or since deceased. But we do feel that, through our constant checking and rechecking, our phone calls and correspondence, our visits to the battle sites, we have come as close to the true story of Easy Company as possible.

• • •

It has been a memorable experience for me. I was ten years old when World War II ended. Like many other American men my age, I have always admired—nay, stood in awe of—the G.I.s. I thought that what they had done was beyond praise. I still do. To get to know so well a few of them from one of the most famous divisions of all, the Screaming Eagles, has been a privilege. It is my proud boast that they have made me an honorary member of the company. As I am also an honorary member of D Company of the Ox and Bucks, I've got both flanks covered. Truly my cup runs over.

STEPHEN E. AMBROSE

Eisenhowerplatz, Bay St. Louis
October 1990–May 1991

The Cabin, Dunbar, Wisconsin
May–September 1991

INDEX

ABOUT THE AUTHOR

STEPHEN AMBROSE was born in 1936 and grew up in Whitewater, Wisconsin. His father was the town doctor. Ambrose attended the University of Wisconsin, and was initially a pre-med major, with plans to take over his father's medical practice. But, inspired by a great professor, he changed his major to history, realizing then that writing and teaching would be his life's work. He went on to Louisiana State University to earn his master's degree and then returned to the University of Wisconsin to complete a Ph.D.

Ambrose's first book was his Louisiana State University master's thesis on Henry Halleck, and his second was his Ph.D. dissertation on Civil War general Emory Upton. In 1960, Ambrose began teaching at the University of New Orleans and working on a history of West Point called *Duty, Honor, Country*. He was twenty-eight years old when President Eisenhower, who had read Ambrose's book on Halleck, asked him to write his biography.

Ambrose's research into President Eisenhower's World War II career shifted the direction of his work from the Civil War to World War II. Later, his research into Eisenhower's political career led him to write political history.

Since then, Ambrose has written more than

twenty books. Among his *New York Times* best-sellers are *D-Day, June 6, 1944; Citizen Soldiers; Band of Brothers; Undaunted Courage; Nothing Like It in the World;* and *The Wild Blue.* He was the historical consultant for Steven Spielberg's movie *Saving Private Ryan,* and has also participated in numerous national television programs, including ones produced by the History Channel, National Geographic, and the upcoming HBO epic based on *Band of Brothers.*

Ambrose is a retired Boyd Professor of History. He is the Director Emeritus of the Eisenhower Center in New Orleans and is the founder of the National D-Day Museum. He is a contributing editor for the *Quarterly Journal of Military History,* a member of the board of directors for American Rivers, and a member of the Lewis and Clark Bicentennial Council board.